A CHILD'S FIRST BOOK OF

American History

BEAUTIFUL FEET BOOKS

SAN LUIS OBISPO CALIFORNIA

A CHILD'S FIRST BOOK OF

American History

BY

Earl Schneck Miers

ILLUSTRATED BY

James Daugherty

Library of Congress Catalog Card Number: 2012918351

Copyright © 1955 by The World Publishing Company.
Copyright © 2013 Beautiful Feet Books. All rights reserved. No part of this book may be reproduced in any form without written permission from the publisher, except for brief passages included in a review appearing in a newspaper or magazine. Manufactured in the United States of America. Design and typography by Jos. Trautwein
2012 Revisions by Rea C. Berg
If any person or persons has knowledge of the estate or heirs of Mr. Earl Schenck Miers it would be appreciated if they would contact the above publishers.
ISBN: 978-1-893103-41-2 Trade Paperback
ISBN: 978-1893103-42-9 Hardbound

CONTENTS

A Call to Adventure — PAGE 8

1. THEY NEVER TASTED DEW SO SWEET — 11
   Leif Ericson Finds Vineland, 1000 A.D.

2. THE LIGHT — 17
   Columbus Discovers America, 1492

3. THE TROUBLESOME CORPSE — 25
   The Quest for the Seven Cities, 1500-1542

4. CRADLE OF OUR LIBERTIES — 33
   The Founding of Jamestown, 1607

5. FREEDOM TO WORSHIP GOD — 41
   The Voyage of the Mayflower, 1620

6. BLACK ROBE — 45
   Marquette and Joliet, 1673

7. "A CLEAN-MADE PEOPLE" — 50
   How the Indians Lived, 1700

8. "SHOOT UM DOWN ALL ONE PIGEON" — 55
   The Delawares Capture James Smith, 1755

9. POOR RICHARD — 61
   Colonial America Produces a Genius, 1706-1790

10. SOLDIER WASHINGTON — 67
    The French and Indian War, 1754-1763

11. MOHAWK RAIDERS — 73
    The Boston Tea Party, 1773

12. YANKEE DOODLE — 79
    The Coming of the Revolution, 1775

13. "WE HOLD THESE TRUTHS" — 88
    Jefferson Writes the Declaration of Independence, 1776

14. THE WINTER OF DESPAIR — 93
    Valley Forge, 1777-1778

15. MARCH TO VINCENNES — 98
    The War in the West, 1779

16. "THE WORLD TURNED UPSIDE DOWN" — 103
    Victory at Yorktown, 1781

17	"WE, THE PEOPLE" *We Adopt a Constitution, 1787-1788*	108
18	IN PEACE AS IN WAR *Washington Is Inaugurated, 1789*	113
19	PIG IN A POKE *The Lewis and Clark Expedition, 1803-1806*	117
20	OLD HICKORY AND THE PIRATE *The Battle of New Orleans, 1815*	124
21	POISONED ARROWS AND GRIZZLY BEARS *Fur Trapping in the Old Southwest, 1820-1840*	130
22	DAME SCHOOLS AND BLAB SCHOOLS *American Education to the McGuffey Readers, 1836*	140
23	"REMEMBER THE ALAMO!" *Texas Fights for Independence, 1836*	144
24	MARK TWAIN'S MISSISSIPPI *The Boom Years of Steamboating, 1811-1873*	152
25	BY THE NORTH STAR *The Underground Railroad, 1804-1860*	159
26	"LOWER AWAY!" *The Golden Years of Whaling, 1840-1860*	165
27	CHRISTMAS AT DONNER LAKE *The Settlement of California, 1846*	172
28	A WORD THAT BURNS LIKE FEVER *Gold Is Discovered in California, 1848*	178
29	PROVING GROUND *The War with Mexico, 1846-1848*	183
30	"THE TALL SUCKER" *Lincoln Debates with Douglas, 1858*	188
31	HOW THE NEWS REACHED NEVADA *Riding the Pony Express, 1860*	195
32	JOHNNY REB *The South Fires on Sumter, 1861*	200
33	THE SECRET OF THE OLD DESK *From Bull Run to Gettysburg, 1861-1863*	205
34	WHEN THE WORLD ENDED *Sherman's March to the Sea and the Surrender at Appomattox, 1865*	211

35	"OU! BUM! HAUGH!" *The First Game of Intercollegiate Football, 1869*	220
36	"THE BONES OF MEN AND ANIMALS" *Life on a Cattle Drive, 1867-1884*	224
37	THE GOLDEN SPIKE *East Joins West at Promontory Point, 1869*	229
38	PRAIRIE TRAGEDY *The Great Chicago Fire, 1871*	234
39	ONLY COMANCHE SURVIVED *Custer's Last Stand, 1876*	240
40	SIX EGGS *Booker T. Washington Builds a School, 1881*	246
41	AMERICA ON WHEELS *The Automobile to the Model T, 1893-1908*	252
42	SMOKE IN THE HARBOR *The Spanish-American War, 1898*	258
43	"PLEASE DO NOT SHOOT THE UMPIRE" *Modern World Series Baseball Begins, 1903*	266
44	"WIZARD OF ELECTRICITY" *The Miracle Man of Menlo Park, 1847-1931*	271
45	"NAILS IN THE COFFIN OF THE KAISER" *The United States in World War I, 1917-1918*	277
46	TOMMY AND HIS CRYSTAL SET *America Discovers Radio, 1920-1930*	283
47	"WHICH WAY IS IRELAND?" *Lindbergh Flies to Paris, 1927*	287
48	"WAR IS A CONTAGION" *Japan Bombs Pearl Harbor, 1941*	292
49	OPERATION OVERLORD *We Land on Normandy Beach, 1944*	298
50	THE LONE PLANE *Birth of the Atomic Age, 1945*	304
	Postscript	310
	Index	313

A Call to Adventure

MARK TWAIN liked to tease boys and girls about the man in Nashville, Tennessee, who lived in a house that had been built in North Carolina.

"That's impossible!" the boys said, outshouting the girls as usual. "How could you move a house all the way from North Carolina to Tennessee?"

Mark's eyes twinkled. "Who said they moved it? Was a time, you know, when Tennessee used to be part of North Carolina. Now if you'd just studied up on your history a mite harder—"

In a way, Mark was telling his young friends a great deal about himself. No man ever enjoyed American history more. Along the Mississippi that he so dearly loved he could tell almost the spot where LaSalle had rested his paddle and where a catfish had jumped out of a wave to frighten poor Marquette and Joliet. With Mark, there was nothing dead about history. Wherever he went, whatever he did, history was all around him, a part of him as he became part of it. In thought, in humor, in feeling, Mark Twain was thoroughly and naturally all-American.

Often I've thought of those days in Hannibal, Missouri, when, stretched out on a river bank, wriggling a blade of grass between his teeth, the boy who would grow up to become Mark Twain looked up at the lazy clouds drifting overhead. It wasn't difficult for Mark to see in those clouds the ships of the Vikings who were the first white men to stumble on the land we now know as North America. As that blade of grass swished to and fro, and the clouds soared by, what wonderful stories there were to relive in imagination!

After the Vikings, came Columbus, heralding the great age of the Spanish explorers. Plunder filled their hearts, and the honored, ancient civilizations of Mexico and Peru were crushed under their merciless heels.

But at last the land was no longer just a mysterious place in a Norse legend. Next appeared the French and the English, bitter enemies in Europe who fought an old war in the New World. Soon the Swedes arrived, the Germans, the Irish. Slave ships brought captive Africans. The Dutch were as neat and industrious in New Amsterdam as they had been in old Amsterdam.

Together, first as colonists and then as Americans, they conquered the wilderness. Together, they grew to share common ideals.

They believed in freedom to worship God.

They believed that all men should be free and equal and that God had endowed them with inalienable rights to life, liberty, and the pursuit of happiness.

They believed that government should be a servant and not the master of a people.

Upon these ideals they founded a nation. They crossed the mountains, plains and deserts. What once had been 3,000 miles of wilderness they linked first by forest trail, then by wagon road, then by iron rail.

So the story unfolded—a story of war, of incredible bravery and courage, of hardship and endurance, of invention and industry and an unending struggle for social justice, until, on the new frontier of science, it now stands at its most challenging moment. *A Child's First Book of American History* relives great moments in this story.

This book is dedicated to David and William, my two sons, and to Meredith, my daughter; and it is dedicated also to all boys and girls who share with them the inheritance of an American belief in human justice, dignity, and equality.

I hope you will enjoy this book, and I know that the wonderful illustrations by James Daugherty will enchant you as they have me. As you begin this adventure, you are a Viking. The year is 1000 A.D. The winds are strong in the North Atlantic. A surprising voyage awaits you as you sail your ship with its stout, square sail. . . .

E. S. M.

1 . They Never Tasted Dew So Sweet

Leif Ericson
Finds Vineland, 1000 A.D.

ERIC THE RED felt sad. Never before had the wet north wind made his bones ache so badly. When he stood up, all his joints pulled stiffly, and going up a hill there was no longer any springiness in his step.

"Father," young Leif said, "you must come with us. The ship is all ready and a full crew has been engaged."

Eric thought of the vessel that Leif had bought from Biarni Heriulfson.

The craft's high prow gave promise of speed and power in the deep water of the ocean, its single square sail had been designed to race with the wind like a graceful gull, its carved heads fore and aft could frighten away any demon spirits that haunted the sea. The crew were strong and seasoned, the kind of crew Eric had sailed with many times when the name Eric the Red had designated the very greatest of Norse seamanship. He was especially glad that Tyrker, the German, was going, for Tyrker was like a foster father to Leif.

Nor did Eric wonder that his son

strained to be off. Talk of the discovery of new land was heard everywhere in this year of round figures, 1000 A.D. For a moment Eric was so strongly impelled by the old call to adventure that he almost said yes, he would go. Then the dogged honesty that a good sailor always must possess forced him to speak truthfully:

"Leif, you must see that I am too stricken in years to withstand now all the hardships of the sea."

Still, secretly, Eric hoped that he might go. Leif pleaded with him, for he loved his father and longed for his company on the perilous voyage across the cold, lonely ocean. Soon afterward, while Eric was riding on horseback, the animal stumbled, and the man bruised his foot in falling. Eric was too wise not to understand the meaning of such an omen.

"It is not ordained that I should discover more countries than that which we now inhabit," Eric said. In his voice was a note of finality, and Leif, respecting the strength of his father at such moments, argued no further.

Leif sailed away in the ship bought from Biarni Heriulfson. Thirty-five men pulled at the oars till the wind caught the sails. The strong voice of Tyrker, the German, could be heard, calling out the orders.

It was Biarni who had on a previous voyage discovered the new

country that we now know as Greenland, and which, geographically, is part of the continent of North America. As the boat tossed in the frigid seas and the winds off the glaciers howled around Leif and his rugged crew, the young Norseman wondered if the sight of land would justify their hard struggle.

Yet Leif was a true Norseman. His legs were firm when a sudden storm shook the craft. The wet cold of the North Atlantic could not strike through the woolen tunic covering his body, and since boyhood his bare arms and legs had been toughened like tree bark to such winds. Always his blood was warmed by the adventuresome spirit that already had carried Norsemen to many discoveries—to England three hundred years before, to Iceland and Ireland a century later, to Normandy and Greenland a hundred years after that.

At last Leif saw land and cast anchor. He put off in the small boats and went ashore. Everywhere the ground was flat.

"There is no grass," he said to Tyrker, and the German grunted, showing his own disappointment.

From the sea to the mountains they could see only a plain of flat stones, and beyond this rose the great icebergs. It was not Greenland that Leif touched upon, but probably one of the bleak stony tips of Labrador or northern Newfoundland.

"This land has no good qualities," Leif said. "Let us sail south."

Soon they found another land, one that heartened Leif a great deal more. Again the country was flat, but covered with a wood, and all around the low shore was a soft, white sand.

"This land we shall call Markland," Leif said, using the Norse word for woodland, and we do not know whether the soil where he stood was that of Cape Breton Island or Nova Scotia.

Once more Leif was dissatisfied, and his boat and crew sailed on. A northwest wind blew them to sea for two days before they again sighted land. They turned and came to an island that lay eastward to the land. Good weather swept the ruffled clouds from the sky. Here there was dew upon the grass, which they touched with their hands. Raising his fingers to his lips, Leif, who possessed the heart of a poet, said:

"I never before tasted anything so sweet."

Between the island and a promontory of the mainland was a sound, very shallow at ebb tide but extremely high when the tide was full. A lake lay beyond the sound, and it was here that they went ashore and decided to build houses to live in through the winter.

Many things amazed Leif and his men in this new country, but nothing so much as the salmon that abounded in the river and lake—the largest salmon any of them ever had seen.

"This is a good land," Leif said. "The cattle would not require house feeding here in winter, for the grass does not wither and therefore there can be no frost."

Day and night were more equal in length here than in Greenland or Iceland, for on the shortest day they noticed that the sun remained above the horizon from half past seven in the forenoon till half past four in the afternoon.

One evening a terrible tragedy overtook the party. Tyrker was missing! Remembering how much Eric loved the German, Leif grew very angry, and he spoke bitterly to everyone for allowing Tyrker to wander out of sight.

"We must find him," Leif cried, and he chose twelve men to go on the searching party.

A short way from the house, they found Tyrker, yet sadness soon overshadowed their joy, for it was plain that the German was no longer in his right senses. What had happened to him is simply a puzzling part of legend. Perhaps Tyrker had grown too old for the strain of the journey; it was fear of this that had kept Eric the Red at home.

"Where have you been?" Leif

demanded.

Tyrker rolled his eyes in an extremely unnatural manner and spoke for some time in German before he answered in the Norse that they could all understand:

"I have been not much farther off, but still I have something new to tell of. I found grapes and vines." To Leif, who appeared skeptical, Tryker added, "I was bred in a land where there is no want of either vines or grapes."

What Tyrker claimed, proved to be true. Leif ordered grapes gathered until a longboat was filled; then vines and trees were felled for loading the ship. When the next spring came, they had been almost two years in this land no one ever has been able to identify. They must sail away, Leif knew. Before a fair wind blew them out into the open sea, Leif turned for a final look at the country. The son of Eric the Red said:

"We will also give to this land the name of its qualities. This land we will call Vineland."

The following year, Thorvald, the brother of Leif, went on a voyage to the same land, or so it is related in the tales that Norse fathers told their sons. Thorvald spent a winter in the house Leif had built and also caught the great salmon. Upon returning home, Thorvald said that like Leif he had found neither man nor beast, but one day he had discovered a corn shed made of wood, so that there must have been men somewhere. But for almost five hundred years the mystery of Vineland slumbered until the eldest of five children of an Italian wool weaver solved it—quite by accident.

2 · The Light

Columbus Discovers America, 1492

Christopher Columbus was born in Genoa sometime during 1451. Papa Colombo (as the name was spelled in Italian) was a wool weaver, and, perhaps possessing prophetic insight, he named the lad after the patron saint of sailors and travelers.

Young Christopher helped his father at the loom, but his heart was never in the work. Whenever he could, he haunted the harbor of Genoa; he longed for adventure under the sails. Doggedly he studied Latin, the language in which all books of geography were written.

A Genoese galley chartered to fight the Barbary pirates carried Columbus, when he was nineteen or twenty, on his first voyage. Soon he found more adventure than he had sought, for pirates sank his ship off Lagos, Portugal. Columbus leaped into the sea. Wounded, and with only a long oar with which to keep afloat, he reached shore.

At about this time, the Portuguese had built the caravel, a ship that could make headway against the wind instead of

[17]

merely scudding before it. It was a high-sided boat, broad and deep, with a sturdy forecastle at the bow and a still sturdier sterncastle. Sometimes it carried four masts and sometimes only three. Square sails on the foremast gave power; triangular or lateen sails on the other masts made the caravel flexible to handle. This vessel fitted perfectly the dream that in time consumed Columbus. Books on geography had taught him that the world was round, and, he argued, to reach the gold, gems, and spices of the Orient he need only sail straight into the west. The distance from Lisbon, Portugal, to Japan he calculated at about three thousand nautical miles, but he underestimated the size of the earth and the width of the Atlantic. Thus he placed Japan in the approximate location of the Virgin Islands.

Columbus decided to appeal to King John II of Portugal to help him, but his journey to Lisbon ended unhappily. King John wondered what manner of rascal this upstart Columbus was and whether he was really in his right mind. The king's authorities on navigation told him that Columbus's plan was ridiculous. But even if the scheme had been pronounced sound, John II certainly had no wish ever to concede all that Columbus wanted from the expedition—a share of the profits, governorship of any lands he discovered, noble rank, and the title of admiral.

Undaunted, Columbus traveled to Spain to lay his plan before King Ferdinand and Queen Isabella. Again, the experts scoffed, and, a more discouraging circumstance, Spain was at that time engaged in the costly business of fighting the Moors. Still, the intelligent Isabella felt drawn to Columbus and his dream. Almost seven years passed, however, before the queen deter-

mined to give him his chance, even if she must pawn the crown jewels. The royal treasurer responded—a bit grudgingly—by finding the $14,000 necessary to outfit the expedition.

Ninety men were to sail with Columbus in three caravels, and to the first who should sight land the king and queen promised many princely rewards, among them 10,000 maravedis, a Spanish coin. From the port of Palos, before sunrise on August 3, 1492, the little fleet set sail. At the Canary Islands, the caravels were refitted and again took to sea on the 6th of September. The remaining distance to Japan Columbus estimated at 2,400 nautical miles.

A week passed, another. The three-masted caravels, each about 200 tons, rode the ocean well. Spirits ran high and tempers were even. But with the third week, some sight of land was expected. A kind of quiet settled over the crew. It seemed as though each pound of the waves shook the timbers more. The nights grew longer and lonelier; the strain of watching through the day frayed nerves and left a bite of acid on the tips of many tongues. Another whole week went by as the tension mounted. Now they had sailed a month and seen nothing but ocean and stars, ocean and stars. Was it mutiny to suggest that the admiral might well be crazy? Sailors

laughed with a sort of sneering defiance. Orders were answered surlily.

The mates sensed the danger. A mutiny was in the air. Worried, they faced the admiral with the stark, bitter truth. The day was Wednesday, the 10th of October. Columbus replied cheerily. His men despaired too soon. They must think of all the riches they would gain when they reached the Orient. They were sailing well, 59 leagues per day and night, which would be 177 miles on land.

At ten o'clock that night Columbus stood on the castle of the poop deck. Ocean and stars, God and faith were his companions. The frail caravels still bore west, with the *Pinta*, the best sailer, dipping first into the troughs of the waves and then bobbing up with her sides dripping in the moonlight.

Suddenly Columbus shouted, calling for Pedro Gutierrez, a gentleman of the king's bedchamber who had sailed with him, and for Rodrigo Sanchez of Segovia, inspector of the fleet.

"I think I saw a light," Columbus said. He asked them to look for a light like a wax candle burning—a light rising and falling. Gutierrez thought that he saw the light. Sanchez said that he did not.

The three men stood, uncertain. Behind them were thousands of miles of seemingly endless ocean. And ahead—land? In that moment all of eternity might well appear to stand still. The star-studded sky canopied them in awesome silence.

As men, they did the practical thing. The watch in the forecastles were cautioned to be extra sharp. Land could be near. To the treasures the king had promised the first to sight land, Columbus added a silk doublet.

With sunrise, on the 11th of

October, signs of land increased. The course now was west-southwest. To Columbus there seemed to be more sea around them than there had been during the whole voyage.

But they saw sandpipers and green reeds in the water. Those aboard the caravel *Pinta* spied a cane and a pole, then a second small pole which appeared to have been worked with iron, and later a bit of cane such as

comes from a land plant. The men on the *Nina* saw a small branch covered with berries.

The sunset streaked sky and water, lighting excited faces in its tints of color. Mutterings of mutiny disap-

peared. The men were almost bursting with song.

One sailor yelled aloud. He had seen land. To him belonged the prizes promised by the king, the silk doublet offered by Columbus. It

[22]

was there—the land, the land! The sailor's name was Rodrigo de Triana.

The vessels hove to, waiting for daylight. That Friday, the 12th of October, on a small island that the Indians called Guanahani (Watling Island in the Bahamas), Columbus stepped into the New World. He threw himself on his knees and kissed the earth. To God, he voiced his profound gratitude.

Around him stood the naked natives. Green trees, heavily laden with fruit, made a canopy along the shore.

Columbus drew his sword and seized the royal standard. Beside him walked two captains bearing the ban-

ners of the green cross, each with an "F" for Ferdinand and a "Y" for Ysabel (Isabel). The island the admiral renamed San Salvador. The men cheered and clutched his arm. Some kissed the hand that held the sword.

Childlike, the friendly natives approached the white men. Soon, in exchange for beads and small bells, they were bringing parrots, cotton threads, and darts. Some of the Indians were painted black, some white, some red, and almost all wore long hair that had never been cut. A few took the sword that Columbus carried and through ignorance wounded themselves. Otherwise, however, the Indians seemed intelligent. They easily would make good Christians, Columbus wrote in his journal.

So the epic story of discovery, begun in the year 1000 A.D. by the valiant Leif Ericson, ended that October 12th, 1492, on the sandy shores of the island the Indians called Guanahani and Columbus called San Salvador.

An even greater adventure would now unfold, for a new history had started—*our* history.

3 · The Troublesome Corpse

The Quest for the Seven Cities, 1500-1542

AFTER six hundred years of fighting the Moors, Spain faced bankruptcy. A miracle was needed to save the country from financial despair, but in Spain fantasy often passed for truth. One such fantasy was the island of Antillia. No two map-makers could agree where in the unexplored oceans this island could be found, but all believed that whoever reached Antillia would find the fabulous Seven Cities. Who had built these cities and paved their streets with gold? Spaniards smiled. One day, centuries ago, seven religious men had sailed beyond the horizon. They had discovered Antillia and built its cities. To scoff at the tale became virtually a heresy, and after hundreds of years of fighting the Moors, Spaniards had little sympathy for heretics.

Once Columbus had charted a sea lane to the New World, a steady stream of explorers followed the same general course, hoping to find the Seven Cities of Antillia. Within two short decades these seekers for fortune changed history. In 1513, Balboa crossed Panama and discovered the Pacific Ocean; by 1521, Mexico had been conquered; from 1519 to 1522, Magellan sailed around the world; and by 1533, the conquest of Peru had been achieved. Spaniards investigated the coast of North America from Newfoundland to Florida and learned the entire shore line of the Gulf of Mexico.

But there was a great deal that the Spaniards did not know. They believed that North America must be a peninsula of Asia, that somewhere existed an inland sea to the Orient, and all the unknown territory north of Mexico they called "Florida." The great Mississippi valley and the plains and mountains of the West had no meaning to them.

However, misfortune and a strange adventure greatly enlarged their knowledge. In 1528 another party of gold-seekers left Spain for "Florida."

The ship sailed over the horizon and vanished. Then one day, eight years later, a party of slave-hunters, striking into the mainland, stumbled upon an astonishing sight—three naked Spaniards and an African man accompanied by six hundred Indians who believed that they escorted four gods!

The leader of the naked Spaniards and the black man was Álvar Núñez Cabeza de Vaca, who told the slave-hunters a strange story. Cabeza de Vaca said he and his companions alone had survived when the ship in which they had sailed for "Florida" in 1528 had been wrecked on the coast of Texas. For six years, Cabeza de Vaca had lived in captivity, traveling wherever the bands of Indians wandered. Possibly he had journeyed as far north as Oklahoma, and he became the first white man to see a buffalo. In time, word of his remarkable power to heal spread among the Indians, and they accepted him as a god from the sun.

Now Cabeza de Vaca and his friends journeyed across Texas and through portions of New Mexico and Arizona. He told the slave-hunters of lands to the north that he believed might contain riches to surpass the riches of Peru. He described arrowheads he had seen and made them seem like emeralds. And he spoke of "populous towns" he had heard existed beyond the mountains.

Spanish ears pricked up at these words, and Spanish imaginations raced to romantic conclusions. These "populous towns" were obviously the Seven Cities! Then the cities with the streets of gold were real—perhaps not on Antillia, but somewhere here to the mysterious north!

The story Cabeza de Vaca told to slave-hunters spread across the ocean, and no one listened more attentively to it than Hernando de Soto, soon to sail for "Florida" on another expedition for the king. Excitedly, before leaving Spain, de Soto spoke with one of the four survivors of Cabeza de Vaca's expedition. Again an oath was given that every word about the Seven Cities was true. De Soto's heart leaped, his dark eyes flashed, his mind teemed with plans. Never once did it occur to him that when a Spaniard used the word "city" he thought of a place that had no meaning whatever to the Indians of North America.

Earlier de Soto had served with Pizarro in the conquest of Peru and the looting of the incredible riches of that country, so his gullibility was understandable. To a soldier of fortune who served his king well and who wanted to become a minor king in his own right in the wilderness, the quest of the Seven Cities promised to be an answer to a prayer. In recognition of de Soto's services with Pizarro, the king had appointed him Governor of Cuba with permission to conquer all of the unknown land north of the Gulf of Mexico. So history continued to play wry tricks upon the Spanish, and especially upon de Soto. There were no Seven Cities to find, which was a heartbreaking fact, but there was a great river to discover, which to de Soto was like finding the cage after the canary had escaped. He didn't need a river.

De Soto's hopes were not yet crushed nor his health broken when, at Havana in the spring of 1539, he collected nine ships and 570 men to follow the rainbow to the Seven Cities of gold. Instead, in Alabama, he spent several months matching his crossbows and guns against the arrows and tomahawks of the painted warriors of the Creek Confederacy. By December, 1541, de Soto's party had reached the banks of the

[29]

Yazoo, one of the tributaries of the Mississippi River. Exhausted, de Soto camped for the winter. With spring, he would start once more in search of his El Dorado.

Again the seasons changed. The maize in the Indian villages grew green and straight. The forests awakened to the trembling pulse beat of spring, and the dark bayous blossomed with pond lilies. De Soto's men took to their horses, fording the bayous where they could, swimming the lakes, and picking up a trail that brought them at last to the Indian village of Quizquiz.

A typical Spanish conquistador, de Soto played the tyrant and trickster. He ordered the startled Indians seized as they came out of their houses. Six Indian chiefs who arrived at his camp were cowed by threats of force and magic. He showed them a mirror he carried. He had only to look into its glass, and everything that they did, even everything they thought, would be revealed to him.

The Indians bowed in awe. An old legend foretold that one day white men would come and subdue them, and the arrogant de Soto looked the part of this conqueror! When de Soto demanded corn, the Indians said that they would lead him to a river where maize grew plentifully.

So at last the eyes of a white man gazed upon the broad, rolling expanse of the mighty Mississippi, but they were clouded, resentful eyes since the yellow ears of corn were scarcely the gold they sought. Moreover, they were feverish eyes, for illness burned in de Soto's body, and as he lay on the crude bed made for him, he knew that he would die. Still, he was a brave man; he faced the end calmly and named Luys Moscoso de Alvardo to succeed him as leader of the expedition. On the 21st of May, De Soto died.

Ironically, the man who had been a great leader in life made a troublesome corpse. De Soto had told the

[30]

Indians that he, like all Christians, was immortal, and now he was dead. The Spaniards feared the Indian reaction to this deception and hid de Soto's body in a house for three days before one night they crept out to one of the gates of the town and buried it. The Indians saw the loose soil over the grave and talked among themselves in a way that suggested that they hadn't been fooled.

The uneasiness of the Spaniards increased. On another night, they dug up de Soto's body, floated it in a canoe to the middle of the Mississippi where there was a good sandy bottom, and, in the river he had never wanted to discover, de Soto was laid in final rest. Later, under Luys de Moscoso, the expedition wandered as far northward as Missouri. Still they could find no trace of the Seven Cities. Discouraged, they turned south.

For Spain, still as desperately in need of gold as ever, other dangers were developing. In 1535 the Frenchman, Jacques Cartier, sailed up the St. Lawrence River, and about 1587 the Englishman, Sir Walter Raleigh, landed settlers on Roanoke Island. With reason, Spanish brows darkened suspiciously.

4 · Cradle of Our Liberties

The Founding of Jamestown, 1607

FOR A long time England had cast covetous eyes at North America. In 1497, King Henry VII sponsored the voyage of John and Sebastian Cabot to establish a claim in the new lands, but not until England defeated the Spanish Armada could serious attempts at colonization be tried.

Both failure and discouragement marked the first British efforts. Sir Humphrey Gilbert lost his life while returning in 1583 from an attempted colonization in Newfoundland. Two years later the second of two expeditions sent out by Sir Walter Raleigh landed on Roanoke Island off the coast of North Carolina. Here Virginia Dare became the first white child to be born on the soil of North

America, and then Virginia vanished—a part of the baffling mystery still surrounding the "Lost Colony" of Roanoke. Strange inscriptions found at the site of the Roanoke settlement suggest that the colonists went to live with the Croatan Indians. Did they go willingly? Did they wander off into the wilderness with the Indians or were they ambushed? No one ever has known.

After 1600, with the ascension of James I to the British throne, life in England changed. An uneasy peace was made with Spain, and restlessness affected numerous Englishmen. Some wanted more personal or religious freedom, some the chance to own land, some responded merely to the call of adventure. With money available for investing in expeditions, and with people eager to risk the long voyages, colonizing activities boomed.

Again, the British reaped nothing but failure. In 1602 Raleigh sent another ship to find the "Lost Colony," but the mystery of Roanoke remained as bewildering as before. That same year an English ship under Bartholomew Gosnold landed at the Elizabeth Islands, dots of land off Cape Cod seen today by ferry passengers to Martha's Vineyard and Nantucket. In 1603 Martin Pring sailed along the coast of northern Virginia, and two years later George Weymouth reached the Kennebec River and returned to England with a number of Indians.

These hit-and-run expeditions to North America were expensive, and Britishers wanted something more than tantalizing curiosities like Raleigh's tobacco or Weymouth's Indians. So, in 1606, colonizing was organized on a more businesslike basis. Investors in the city of Plymouth received a charter for settling the northern portion of the new continent, and investors in London were given a charter authorizing an expedition to south Virginia. The new arrangement made sense to everyone. With more careful planning, investors expected to secure larger profits. Churchmen, eager to have Christian religion carried to the Indians, supported these enterprises. The king wanted a firm hold on the territory against the day when he might wish to remove Spanish influence from the Western Hemisphere.

One of the Londoners who received the charter for the Virginia expedition was Richard Hakluyt. An authority on geography and colonization, Hakluyt also understood that if people were to succeed in settling a wilderness they must be granted personal liberties. In planning the colony, Hakluyt talked of more than ship tonnage and supplies; he was equally interested in the kind of lives the settlers should lead.

Principles that Englishmen cher-

ished were to be planted with the new colony. As a result, Jamestown is called the "cradle of our liberties." These principles included: 1) respect for church and God, 2) trial by jury, and, in time, 3) representative government.

Off the coast of Jamestown Island in Virginia on May 13, 1607, appeared three small ships. The *Susan Constant*, of one hundred tons under Captain Christopher Newport, brought seventy-one persons. Captain Bartholomew Gosnold commanded the *Godspeed*, of forty tons, carrying fifty-two persons. The little pinnace, *Discovery*, of twenty tons, under Captain John Ratcliffe, brought another twenty-one persons. That night the boats were moored to the trees on shore, and next morning the first permanent English settlers in America stepped upon the soil of their new homeland. They knew what their first job must be. They began to build a fort.

Yet the long voyage, which had begun when the three ships sailed down the Thames River the previous 20th of December, had created jealousies. A sound piece of advice, given on leaving, had been too quickly forgotten: "The way to prosper and achieve good success is to make yourselves all of one mind for the good of your country." On the voyage the leaders of the expedition frequently quarreled. Once, a mutiny seemed imminent; as a result of these dissensions, Captain John Smith was accused of being the troublemaker. The facts are not clear, but one result is certain—Captain Smith reached the New World a prisoner and was not released until June 10, when he took his seat on the governing council of the colony.

Despite occasional short tempers and harsh words, the settlers managed to pull together as they dug their first roots into North America. The Indians, the possible appearance of the Spanish, and the mosquitos were sufficient menaces without bickering among themselves. Enough work existed for six hands on the end of every arm.

Slowly, Jamestown began to take shape on the island which was not really an island, for an isthmus connected it with the mainland. With an area cleared of trees and the construction of the fort started, wheat was planted. A party of explorers under Captain Newport followed the James River as far as the falls near the present site of Richmond, looking for gold and silver. The Indians picked the time while Captain Newport and his party were away to attack the colonists. Cannon on the decks of the nearby ships drove off the Indians, but the prospect after the vessels had returned to England did not seem very encouraging.

By mid-June, when the wheat was through the ground and growing nicely, the triangular fort was completed. At each of the three corners stood a bulwark on which were mounted demiculverins, a type of early cannon that fired balls weighing about nine pounds. The walls of the fort enclosed an acre of land. with an entrance at each bulwark and the main gate opening on the river (or south) side of the settlement. The flimsily constructed church, storehouse, and living quarters stood within the fort.

A humid summer fell upon Jamestown. Food spoiled. Drinking water turned brackish and became infected. Sickness spread rapidly, especially during hot August, claiming among others the experienced Bartholomew Gosnold. Relations among the colonists worsened. Ailing from diseases that crept up from the marshes, the settlers grew at times almost to hate one another. At the end of the summer, only about fifty remained alive.

With the cool days of fall, conditions changed. Ducks flew across the marshes and other wild game became plentiful. As the heat lessened, so did disease. Even the Indians appeared less distrustful, and a lively trade developed between the colonists and the natives, that brought into the storehouse at Jamestown heartening supplies of Indian corn, peas, beans and pumpkins.

Still, not all of the troubles of Jamestown drifted away with the leaves falling from the trees. Neighbor scolded neighbor for whatever went wrong. Again John Smith became a source of contention. The captain had led a party to the Chickahominy

River, but had not discovered the head of that stream. Cutting and derisive remarks were made.

A headstrong man, who sometimes carried a chip on his shoulder the size of a log, Captain Smith stomped out of the fort one day in December to complete his exploration of the Chickahominy. Both history and legend are blended in the events that Smith said took place. Indians crept up on the party, killed at least three, and captured Smith after one arrow wounded his thigh and several others riddled his clothes.

An ivory compass saved Smith's life for a time. The Indians grew fascinated at the play of the needle, which they could not touch because of its glass covering. Holding the compass, Captain Smith explained to the Indians the roundness of the earth and skies, the spheres of the moon and the stars, and "how the sun did chase the night round about the world continually." He spoke of the greatness of the land and the seas, of the differences between nations, and the various colors of human skin.

All the Indians, Captain Smith said, stood "amazed with admiration." But Indian emotions were

difficult for the white man to read. Within an hour Captain Smith stood tied to a tree, as the Indians crowded around, elbowing each other for room to get a fair shot at Smith. An Indian leader, holding the ivory compass in his hand, stopped the proceedings. Instead, they all had a feast before carrying Smith to the Indian village of Werowocomoco where the noble emperor, Powhatan, sat upon "a seat like a bed-stead" covered with a robe of raccoon skins with "all the tails hanging by." A young girl sat on either side of the emperor,

and along each side of the room were two rows of men, and beyond them two rows of women, "with all their heads and shoulders painted red."

Each Indian, entering the room, gave a shout at the sight of the emperor. Water was brought to wash Powhatan's hands, and a bunch of feathers served as a towel for drying them. The monarch feasted before he called his councilors around him.

When the conference ended, two great stones were dragged before Powhatan. Warriors seized Captain Smith and forced him down on the stones. They held his head flat while others stood over him with raised clubs.

Into the group before the emperor rushed his daughter, Pocahontas. She was a maid of high spirit and intelligence who one day would marry another settler and return with him to London. Now Pocahontas clutched Captain Smith in her arms and laid her head upon his. If Powhatan would kill the white man, he must also kill his daughter.

Powhatan decreed that the prisoner should become a slave, but the tale had another ending. This final adventure Captain Smith related:

"Two days after, Powhatan having disguised himself in the most fearfulest manner he could, caused Captain Smith to be brought forth to a great house in the woods, and there upon a mat by the fire to be left alone. Not long after, from behind a mat that divided the house was made the most dolefulest noise he ever heard; then Powhatan, more like a devil than a man, with some 200 more as black as himself, came unto him and told him now they were friends, and presently he should go to Jamestown, to send him two great guns, and a grindstone, for which he would give him the county of Capahowosick, and for ever esteem him as his son Nantaquoud."

Life went a bit easier for John Smith when he returned to Jamestown, and in 1608 he served as the settlement's chief councilor. A second shipment of settlers arrived and raised the population to approximately 120. That fall, in the church at Jamestown, Ann Burras, a maidservant, wedded John Laydon, a carpenter, in the first recorded English marriage on the soil of North America; and the following year their baby, Virginia Laydon, was the first child born at Jamestown.

A third shipment of settlers, numbering about four hundred, arrived in 1609, but for this third "supply" the bottom of the London barrel must have been scraped, for they included ne'er-do-wells and renegades who brought, along with their lazy and bad habits, a variety of fevers and plagues. The winter of 1609-1610 became known as "the starving time." With disease, Indian uprisings, sickness, and little food, Jamestown's population of five hundred shrank to a dispirited sixty. Houses were falling apart, and the old distrust of neighbor for neighbor revived. There was a growing sentiment to abandon the colony when in May, 1610, Sir Thomas Gates arrived with two boats whose very names, *Patience* and *Deliverance*, seemed to spell a much needed moral.

Gradually, the settlement of Jamestown found fresh strength, and, with sounder government, the "cradle of our liberties" rocked more smoothly. Here in 1619 the first representative legislative assembly convened. Self-government in the New World had taken root.

5 · Freedom to Worship God

The Voyage of the Mayflower, 1620

"I WILL *make* them conform, or I will harry them out of the land!"

Stiff-backed and arrogant, King James I scowled at his court. He would have it known that he was the absolute ruler of England, with the power to enforce his demands even upon the church.

Defiantly, a little sect of worshipers, the Separatists, refused to be intimidated by the haughty James. Neither the king nor his bishops would dictate to them! Religion belonged to an individual's heart, an individual's conscience. Let James I "harry them out of the land" if he must. They still would organize their own congregations and choose their own ministers.

Yet the thought of leaving their homeland to go into a land they knew only by hearsay would be, one of their number said, "a misery worse than death." They were landed gentry, bound to their land for generations. But the angry James I was not a kindly ruler. If the Separatists remained and still insisted upon freedom to worship God, they understood what they must expect—persecution, imprisonment, exile.

In the winter and spring of 1607-1608 a band of Separatists found the heart to make the break with their beloved homeland. They determined to emigrate to Holland, where they could worship in freedom. In the beautiful Dutch city of Leyden, they struggled to build new lives for a decade. Much about Leyden they respected—its great university, its spirit of live-and-let-live that allowed them to worship as they chose. But in other ways Leyden and Holland were hard. The English children were losing their heritage, and a war between Holland and Spain threatened the peace.

With continual toil the Separatists made out, but their dissatisfactions

multiplied, and presently they talked of distant America. There they could build a state of their own, founded upon the principles for which they already had sacrificed one home. They would go as Pilgrims—as seekers of religious freedom.

In 1620 the first group of Separatists left Leyden for Southampton, where they had arranged to join a group of friends from London. Two boats, the *Speedwell* and the *Mayflower*, had been chartered to carry the Pilgrims to the New World, but the heavily overmasted *Speedwell* sprang a leak and had to be abandoned. Perhaps, as many grumbled, a plot existed to make the *Speedwell* seem unseaworthy, since the master and his company had grown to fear the long voyage and thought that they might starve in the wilderness. Alone, on September 16, 1620, the *Mayflower* sailed from Plymouth in Devon. On board were 102 passengers.

The little ship plunged in the great seas. One of the seamen, whom Governor Bradford described as "a proud and very profane young man,"

cursed the passengers who fell ill and swore that he would throw half of them overboard before the voyage ended. Governor Bradford, the spiritual leader of the Pilgrims, believed it a sign of providence that the seaman himself took sick, died, and was thrown into the waves.

Presently storms raged across the ocean. The upper works of the *Mayflower* began to leak, one of the main beams in the midships bowed and cracked, and there was serious discussion of turning back. Even the mariners differed as to the best course to take. But the *Mayflower* had now completed half her voyage—the way back was as far as the way forward. Moreover the underwater parts of the ship remained tight and sturdy. The beam could be repaired.

So the *Mayflower* sailed on. One gale died away and another swept in. Scurvy wracked the pinched bodies of the Separatists. They prayed and waited while the winds still howled, the waves rolled higher, the ship shivered and creaked.

Young John Howland was caught on deck when the boat made one of its frightening lurches. Screaming, Howland was swept overboard. His outflung hand snatched at the topsail halyards. Others rushed to the rail, pulled hard on the ropes, and saw Howland reappear. A boathook hauled him back on deck. Again the incident seemed a sign of providential care, but the greater miracle was the fact that only one Pilgrim, young William Butten, died at sea.

After sixty-five days, the highlands of Cape Cod were sighted. On November 21, 1620, the *Mayflower* anchored off present-day Provincetown, Massachusetts. Crew and passengers were assembled on deck for a meeting. Here the Mayflower Compact was read, the first written plan for self-government in America, founded upon a belief in "just and equal laws." Nearly all present signed the compact.

Several days then were spent cruising along the shore in search of a suitable harbor and a good place to settle. Finally, on December 21, the Pilgrims selected the spot they would name Plymouth and five days later sailed across the bay to begin their new life in America.

What the Pilgrims planted that winter on the coast of Massachusetts was more than another settlement that would endure. To Colonial America would come others of different faiths—the Quakers, the Catholics, the Huguenots, the Baptists, the Jews. And so the Pilgrims planted an ideal that was later to grow into the bedrock of a nation. Here men were free to worship God as they pleased; no matter what they believed, no ruler would "harry them out of the land."

6 · Black Robe

Marquette and Joliet, 1673

NINETY-FIVE YEARS after the death of de Soto, the first real explorer of the Mississippi, Jacques Marquette, was born in 1637 in an old chateau in Laon, a city north of Paris. The child's mother was an ardent Catholic, who wished that her son would become a Jesuit Father and carry the gospel of Jesus Christ to distant lands. Almost the only stories that little Jacques heard from his mother were about the fearless Jesuits. The boy was raised to love everyone, and one day in 1666 Madame Marquette saw her wish come true. Jacques Marquette, now a Jesuit missionary, sailed from France for the wilderness of Canada.

Father Marquette worked diligently, studying the languages of the several Indian tribes so that he might tell them the message of love that

Jesus Christ had brought to the world. The Indians were puzzled at a God, or Manitou, who loved everybody—even the war-hungry Sioux—but they soon adopted with affection the kind, unselfish priest who came to live among them. Their name for him was Black Robe.

In a little mission at Chequamegon Bay, on Lake Superior, Father Marquette dwelt with the Hurons and other peaceful tribes from 1669 to 1671. Then the war signals of the Sioux spread over the lake country. Black Robe gathered his faithful followers around him and led them to safety on Michilimackinac (now Mackinac Island). Here Black Robe listened to Indian stories of the *Missi Sepe*, words that meant "Father of Waters." The more Marquette heard of the river to the south, the more earnestly he wished to explore it.

At this time Louis Joliet, a young map-maker who had been educated in the Jesuit school at Quebec, also heard of the Mississippi and wondered if the fabled river might not provide the passage to China that both Columbus and Hendrik Hudson had been seeking. The governor at Quebec authorized Joliet to explore the river, and in time the map-maker arrived at Michilimackinac.

Louis Joliet liked Father Marquette immediately, and though Black Robe now was thirty-five, eight years Joliet's senior, his deeper wisdom strengthened their friendship. Joliet insisted that Father Marquette accompany him on the exploration of the Mississippi.

May, the month when de Soto's body had been thrown into the waters of the Mississippi, was again the month when, in 1673, the party of Marquette and Joliet set out in their canoes across Lake Michigan. At Green Bay, the Wild Rice Indians grew alarmed when Black Robe explained his mission, and they talked excitedly of bloodthirsty savages who lived along the banks of the Mississippi, of a vicious river demon, and of other monsters of the water that would devour them if the Indians and the demon did not. Black Robe listened with a smile. Manitou would protect him. The two white men paddled serenely up the Fox River.

At the head of the Fox, Marquette and Joliet carried their canoes across country to the Wisconsin, and a week later, on June 17, 1673, entered the Mississippi. The country was beautiful as a slow and gentle current carried them southward past high hills, rolling lands, and countless islands that divided the river.

Many of their experiences were frightening. Monstrous fish leaped from the water, and dashed against the canoes and threatened to stave in the sides. (Some Mississippi catfish have been known to grow to six feet and weigh 250 pounds). And Marquette and Joliet *did* encounter a sort of river demon that the Jesuit described as "a monster with the head of a tiger, a sharp nose like a wildcat, with whiskers and straight, erect ears: the head was gray and the neck quite black."

When the two men cast their nets, they caught a very extraordinary fish, resembling a trout but with a much larger mouth, and yet with a smaller nose and smaller eyes, and with a large bone that ended in a disc as wide as one's hands. They found turkeys, and saw herds of *pisikious* or wild cattle, as the buffalo was then known.

A sense of danger grew in the two explorers. Around each river bend they proceeded cautiously, and toward evening built only a small fire to cook their meals. Each night they anchored their canoes in the river and slept there so that it would be difficult for any*thing* or any*body* on shore to take them by surprise. Then, on the eighth day, they made their greatest discovery—tracks of men at the water's edge and a narrow, somewhat beaten path leading to a fine prairie!

The thrill that Daniel Defoe invented for Robinson Crusoe upon seeing a footprint in the sand now lay before Father Marquette and Louis Joliet. They remembered the terrible tales that the Wild Rice Indians had related of relentless savages, and yet the temptation to explore farther was irresistible. Leaving the canoes in charge of helpers with strict orders not to relax their guards for an instant, priest and fur trader pushed on.

Along the narrow path the two explorers moved in silence. At last they saw a village on the bank of the river, and, at a distance, two other villages on a hill. Father Marquette seized Joliet's hand and prayed. They stood so close to the village that they could hear the savages talking.

"Now we will reveal ourselves," Father Marquette said.

Together the men shouted.

Out of the houses tumbled the Indians. Four old men stepped forward, bearing tobacco pipes that were finely decorated and adorned with feathers. The Indians walked slowly, raised their pipes toward the sun, and spoke not a word.

Father Marquette watched solemnly the ceremonious approach of the four old men. But he saw that the Indians were clad in cloth and judged that they would be friends. He spoke first:

"Who are you?"

"Illinois."

Then the Indians extended their pipes in a token of peace and led Black Robe into the village.

In time Father Marquette and Louis Joliet continued their exploration of the Mississippi—into the hot, muggy climate of the lower river where the Indians slept on high scaffoldings and burnt smudge fires to drive off the mosquitos—until they

reached the mouth of the Arkansas. Here Joliet knew that they encroached upon the country claimed by Spain, so they turned back.

The return voyage brought them into the village of the Kaskaskia Indians, who begged Black Robe to remain with them. Weakened by the midsummer sun, Father Marquette had to go on, but he promised one day to return. In the spring of 1675, Black Robe fulfilled this vow, but again fell ill and returned to Michilimackinac, where, on May 18, he died.

America now was a little less unknown, and, in these years, had become a busy land, with the English and Dutch building settlements along the Atlantic Coast, and the Spanish pushing into Texas and California. Unhappily, the best lessons were not easily learned. The greed, the arrogance, the slashing sword of men like de Soto, made the triumph of the new country more difficult. With more of the patience and kindness and love of neighbor that Father Marquette possessed, there would have been less of the story to write in blood.

7 · "A Clean-Made People"

How the Indians Lived, 1700

ALMOST AS old as any Indian legend we know, was the belief of the red man that one day the white man would appear. Among ancient Mayans this legend became almost a religious doctrine—the white man would come as a son of God. When at last the Spaniards appeared, full of plunder, greed, and war, the Mayans saw their mistake. He was a god of evil, this white man.

Yet the Indian tried to make the best of the white man and taught him many arts: how to raise corn and tobacco, to snare fish and hunt game, to tap maple sugar and recognize herbs that were good for food and medicines. Sometimes the Indian must have wondered what drew the white man to the most unhealthful regions along the coast. Jamestown was little better than a mosquito-infested swamp, Massachusetts alive with typhus epidemics, Maryland so disease-ridden that Indians long ago had left the country.

But if the white man possessed manners that the Indian would never understand, with the passing years one fact about the settlers grew clear. With time to look around, white men seized the most tillable lands, the best streams for fishing, the best grounds for hunting.

Some white men made an honest effort to understand the Indian and to meet him on his own terms. During William Penn's lifetime, not one of his followers was killed by an Indian. In Rhode Island, Roger Williams lived peacefully with the Indians, treating them as fellow humans and, like Penn, paying them for the land he settled.

Still another who tried to make his fellow white men appreciate the Indian was James Lawson, an English traveler who in 1700 journeyed a thousand miles among the natives in the South and wrote a warmhearted book about what he observed and experienced.

Lawson saw the Indians as a "well-shaped, clean-made people," never bending forward or stooping at the shoulders, with flat bodies, black or dark hazel eyes, and legs and feet that were "generally the handsomest in the world." The tawny color of their skin—darker even than nature had intended—resulted from a practice, begun in childhood, of daubing themselves with bear oil and other substances that filled the pores of their bodies and thus enabled them better to withstand extremes of weather. The habit of greasing their hair with bear fat accounted for its fast growth.

The Indian was a person of the greatest steadiness who without fear could cross a deep brook on a small, bending pole. He could walk the ridge of a house or barn, looking down, and not feel the slightest dizziness. He could run and leap as gracefully as any animal. Not once, in one thousand miles of travel, did Lawson find a dwarf or humpback among the tribes he visited, and he found only one blind man. The other Indians, closing their lips over teeth yellow with tobacco, would furnish no information concerning the man's blindness.

Although intelligent and quick to learn, Indians were not industrious—tomorrow could take care of itself.

They disliked hard labor, but would dance all night, or for several nights, shouting and singing. Lawson described these occasions:

"Their dances are of different natures, and for every sort of dance they have a tune, which is allotted for that dance; as, if it be a war dance, they have a warlike song, wherein they express, with all the passion and vehemence imaginable, what they intend to do with their enemies; how they will kill, roast, scalp, beat, and make captive such and such numbers of them; and how many they have destroyed before. All these songs are made new for every feast; nor is one and the same song sung at two

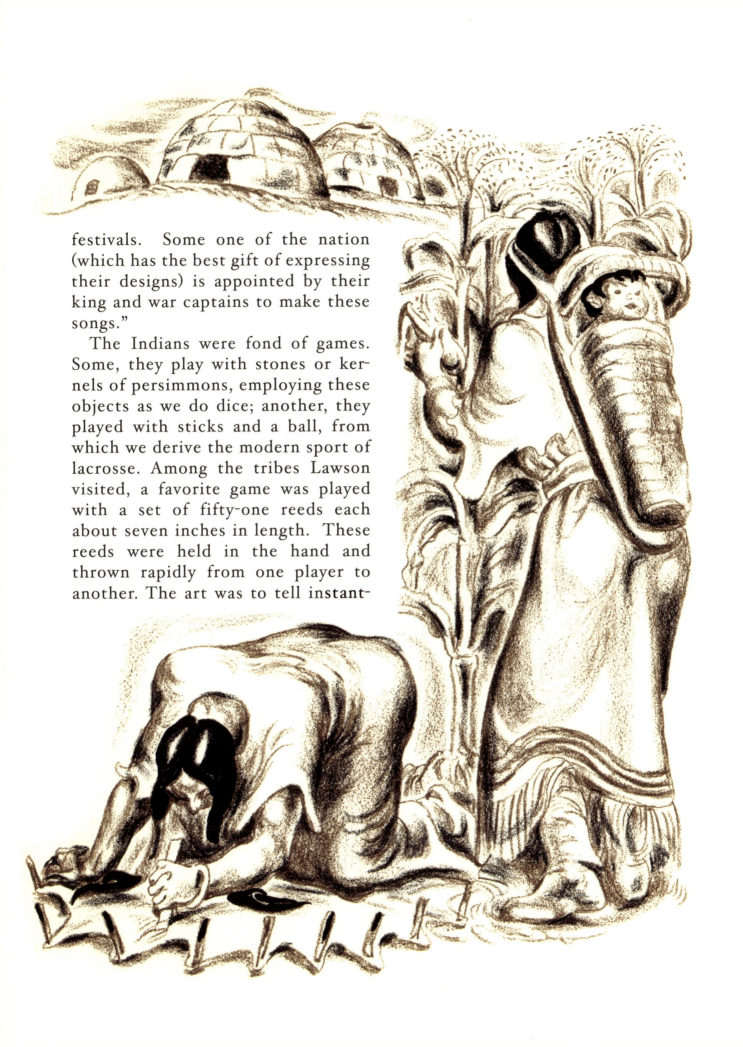

festivals. Some one of the nation (which has the best gift of expressing their designs) is appointed by their king and war captains to make these songs."

The Indians were fond of games. Some, they play with stones or kernels of persimmons, employing these objects as we do dice; another, they played with sticks and a ball, from which we derive the modern sport of lacrosse. Among the tribes Lawson visited, a favorite game was played with a set of fifty-one reeds each about seven inches in length. These reeds were held in the hand and thrown rapidly from one player to another. The art was to tell instantly how many you caught and some Indians were so skilled that after nine or ten lightning fast exchanges, they could calculate the exact number of reeds they held. Often great Indian estates were gambled on this shrill-voiced game. A good set of reeds sold for a dressed doeskin. The Indians lived in wigwams or bark cabins. In the center of the dwelling was the fire with a hole cut in the roof to let out the smoke. The houses, Lawson said, were "as hot as stoves, where the Indians sleep and sweat all night." Floors were never paved or swept, and multitudes of fleas infested them, especially near the places where the Indians dressed their deerskins. Again the English traveler marveled: "I never felt any ill, unsavory smell in their cabins, whereas, should we live in our houses as they do we should be poisoned with our own nastiness." To Lawson here was further proof that Indians were "some of the sweetest people in the world."

For his dwelling, the Indian chose cypress, or red or white cedar, and only when he could get neither of these woods would he be content with pine bark. The house builder began his structure with long poles of pine, cedar, hickory, or any wood that would bend. Generally as thick as the small of a man's leg, these poles were stripped of bark and warmed over a fire for greater toughness and elasticity. Set about two feet apart in a circle in the ground (or in an oval shape), the tops were bent together and tied either with elm bark or with the moss that grew on trees to a length of two yards and would not rot.

Other poles braced this basic frame; then the ribbing was completely covered with bark so that the dwelling would be warm and tight against any kind of weather. Some cabins were built without window openings and were used to store grains, skins, and other articles. A third type of building had a covered roof but open sides, and had reed tables on which the Indians could lie or sit in summer.

Inside the wigwam there were benches around the wall. Bearskins or mats, Lawson said, lay on these benches "whereon they sleep and loll." Indians commonly crowded several families into one cabin. Usually, however, these families were all related and constituted a kind of tribe within the tribe.

One important part of the unpredictable nature of the Indian Lawson failed to learn. In 1711 he returned to America for another journey among the Indians. But the red men had grown angry with their white neighbors. They seized Lawson and killed him. Elsewhere through the colonies, ears strained for the simulated call of the owl that meant that Indians had taken to the warpath.

8 · "Shoot Um Down All One Pigeon

The Delawares Capture James Smith, 1755

THE INDIAN was finding it harder to hunt and to fish. Women, children complained that hunger pinched their bellies. Through the forest stillness of North America sounded the ominous beat of war drums.

First to hear the rumble of the drums were the early settlers of the Connecticut Valley, where in 1637 the Pequot War was fought. In the great swamp at Mystic the colonists ended that struggle in a merciless massacre. The Indians did not forget. Yet the war drums remained silent until 1675, when New England was doused in the blood of the terrible King Philip's War.

King Philip, sachem of the Wampanoags, saw with narrowing eyes land being snatched from his people. Revenge burned in his throat. Out from Narragansett Bay, across the whole of Massachusetts, he led his warriors. Town after town was attacked until the number of colonists killed reached staggering numbers. Terror lurked behind every tree, every bush, every boulder where a painted warrior could wait with readied tomahawk or brand of fire. At last King Philip was shot, and though King Phillip's War came to an end, other conflicts awaited both Indians and colonists.

From 1689 to 1697 the King William's War left settlers in New Hampshire terrorized; from 1702 to 1713 the French joined with the Algonquins in the Queen Anne's War that resulted in the loss to the French of Acadia (Nova Scotia); and from 1744 to 1748 the King George's War wrought havoc around Cape Breton Island and settled nothing.

But these three wars—each named after the monarch ruling in England at the time they were fought and each nourished by the bad blood between the French and the English—were merely forerunners of a bitterer conflict. Control of the lands drained by the Ohio River finally provided in 1754 the excuse for the nine-year long French and Indian War. A principal figure in starting this struggle was a young planter-surveyor named George Washington who led an expedition of militia to force the French out of the Ohio valley. In 1755 an expeditionary force under General Edward Braddock reached the colonies to help the local militia crush the French and their allies.

Fighting the Indians involved terrors and techniques Londoners could never understand. Tomahawks and scalping knives were more than a match for muskets and red-coated soldiers in an almost trackless forest. Ambush was an Indian art. But the Indian evil most feared was capture.

When eighteen-year-old James Smith went with a group into the Allegheny Mountains to cut a wagon road for Braddock's army between Fort Loudon and Turkey Foot, he understood the risk. But Jim was a sturdy fellow, and a stubborn Ulster Scot. He did not scare easily.

The May weather was clear and warm when on a day in 1755 young Smith rode with his friend Arnold Vigoras along the road toward Bedford. Neither youth recognized the clump of bushes about fifteen feet from the road as a man-made blind. Suddenly three Indians sprang up. Their rifles blazed. Vigoras fell dead at the volley from the ambush. Smith felt his horse start, then hurtled through the air. Instantly the three Indians were astride him. One he recognized as a Canafatauga; the other two were Delawares.

Jim spent a miserable time guarded by the Delawares while the Canafatauga scalped Arnold. One of the Delawares, who spoke a kind of pidgin English, asked if any more white men were near. When Jim said no, the Indian shrugged. They had one scalp and one captive. They were satisfied.

That night Jim and his captors slept in the woods. They built no fire. Next morning all four breakfasted on moldy biscuit and a roasted young ground hog, then struck off on a fifty-mile journey to Fort Duquesne. Here Jim heard for the first time the "scalp haloo" that Indians gave whenever they returned from a raid—one long yell for each prisoner or scalp they brought back.

Yelling Indians raced from the French fort. Jim watched the joyous warriors—naked except for breechclouts—with bodies painted vermilion, black, brown, and blue. The Indians formed in two long rows two or three rods apart. Jim tells what happened next:

"I was told by an Indian that could speak English that I must run twixt these ranks, and that they would flog me all the way as I ran, and if I ran quick it would be so much the better, as they would quit when I got to the end of the ranks. There appeared to be a general rejoicing around me, yet I could find nothing like joy in my breast. I started to race with all the resolution and vigor I was capable of exerting. I was flogged the whole way.

"When I had got near the end of the lines, I was struck with something that appeared to me to be a stick or the handle of a tomahawk, which caused me to fall to the ground. On recovering my senses, I endeavored to renew my race, but as I arose, someone cast sand in my eyes, which blinded me so that I could not see where to run.

'They continued beating me most intolerably until I was at last insensible. But before I lost my senses, I remember wishing them to strike the fatal blow."

Half deliriously, Jim Smith lived through the next few days. A French doctor opened a vein in his left arm and bled him. His wounds were washed with French brandy. At times the pain seemed unendurable, but the French merely shrugged. He was alive, wasn't he? He was lucky.

One day the Delaware who could speak pidgin English visited Jim. He asked for news of Braddock's army. The Indian grinned. The white soldiers were being watched; soon Braddock's army would be surrounded.

"Shoot um down all one pigeon," the Delaware said good-humoredly.

Still ill and weak, the youth was led away a few days later. Sixty miles beyond Fort Duquesne, he arrived eventually at an Indian town on the west branch of the Muskingum called Tullihas. Delawares, Caughnewagas, and Mohicans dashed out to surround the captive. Again Jim tells the story:

"A number of Indians collected about me, and one of them began to pull the hair out of my head. He had some ashes on a piece of bark in which he frequently dipped his fingers in order to take the firmer hold, and so he went on, as if he had been plucking a turkey, until he had all the hair clean out of my head, except a small spot about three or four inches square on my crown. This they cut off with a pair of scissors, excepting three locks, which they dressed up in their own mode.

Two of these they wrapped round with a narrow beaded garter made by themselves for that purpose, and the other they plaited at full length and then stuck it full of silver brooches.

"After this they bored my nose and ears, and fixed me off with earrings and nose jewels; then they ordered me to strip off my clothes and put on a breechclout, which I did; then they painted my head, face, and body in various colors. They put a large belt of wampum on my neck, and silver bands on my hands and right arm; and so an old chief led me out in the street and gave the alarm hallo, *oo-wigh*, several times repeated quick, and all that were in the town came running and stood around the old chief, who held me by the hand in their midst."

The chief made a speech. His raspy voice droned on and on. Next three young squaws seized Jim. The youth felt himself propelled into the river until the water reached his middle. Jim guessed that it was no worse to drown than to burn at the stake, but one of the squaws, giggling, made a sign that meant "No hurt you."

The women plunged Jim under the water and scrubbed him as though he had never had a bath. Next they took him to the council house, and dressed him in a ruffled shirt, in leggings trimmed with ribbons, and in garters and moccasins decorated with beads, porcupine quills, and red hair. Again they painted his head and face and tied red feathers in his lock of hair.

Jim then was seated on a bearskin and given a pipe, a tomahawk, and tobacco in a pouch made from the skin of a polecat. Around him assembled the Indians, all grandly dressed. For a long time no one spoke as each puffed on his pipe. At last the old chief wished to make another speech.

"My son," he said, "you are now flesh of our flesh and bone of our bone."

The adopted James Smith lived among the Delawares, wandering with them through the Ohio territory and Canada, until 1759, when he succeeded in escaping to Montreal. He had survived the running of the gauntlet and was luckier than most Indian captives. Not many ever returned to their families and friends.

9 · Poor Richard

Colonial America Produces a Genius, 1706-1790

THE RAIN pounded against the roof of the old inn. Young Ben Franklin, soaked to the skin and shivering against the drafts of raw October wind that sifted through the walls, wished that he had never run away. No wonder people stared at him suspiciously—he cut a miserable figure with only his working clothes to wear; his trunk had been sent by sea. His entire wealth consisted of a Dutch dollar and a copper shilling.

Hungry and cold, Ben decided to keep to his room to avoid questions which his seventeen-year-old mind might find difficult to answer. Another day should bring him to Burlington, New Jersey, whence he could catch the boat to Philadelphia. Suddenly his sense of humor made him see the other side of the situation. If he felt distracted, imagine the bewilderment he must have left in Boston!

The boy flung himself on the bed, drawing up his knees and trying to absorb a little cheer from the warmth of his body. Events in an already busy life flashed across his mind, and from habit he sorted them into a logical order.

First he had been born—a hard fact to dispute insofar as there were fourteen brothers and sisters in the Franklin family to vouchsafe for his arrival in Boston on January 17, 1706. There had been talk of making a clergyman of him, but after one year of school Ben's father had abandoned that notion. Education was one extravagance Josiah Franklin couldn't afford. He now had two more children, making a total of seventeen!

Ben had not felt greatly dismayed at giving up his formal schooling. He could teach himself, and he believed he had been born with the ability to read, for he couldn't re-

[61]

member the time when the printed page had been any mystery to him. Bunyan's *Pilgrim's Progress*, the books of Daniel Defoe, Plutarch's *Lives*, Burton's *Historical Collections*, Cotton Mather's *Essay to do Good* were books over which he had pored till he knew large portions by memory.

Ben's real ambition had been to go to sea, but this scheme his father had sternly opposed. Instead, Ben found himself helping his father as a tallow-chandler and soap-boiler. Nothing in the trade of cutting wick for candles, filling the dipping molds, attending the shop or running errands had appealed to him. Even Josiah Franklin admitted that Ben was a poor hand at the craft, and so at the age of twelve the boy was apprenticed to his printer brother James.

James proved too strict the master, too ready to whip the rebellious spirit out of Ben. Of all the tricks Ben played, James resented most the articles Ben wrote under the assumed name of "Mrs. Silence Dogood." In James's newspaper, the *New England Courant*, these articles appeared until one day Ben inadvertently divulged his secret. For the next few moments the roof all but blew off the Boston print shop. Ben wasn't old enough to write anything worth space in the *Courant*! If ever the young whippersnapper deserved a caning, this deceit was the perfect example.

Ben's rebel heart had known then that his parting with James was only a question of time. He remained while James served a short prison term for printing satirical pieces in the *Courant* that offended the Crown's authorities, but soon afterward the breaking point came. So here he was, hearing the rain pound the roof, and wondering if he had jumped from the frying pan into the fire.

In another day Ben reached Burlington and the next morning Philadelphia. His wealth now was reduced to the single Dutch dollar, but his hunger had become so unbearable that he stopped at the baker's and parted with three pennies for three large rolls. With a roll under each arm, leaving him free to eat the third, he walked jauntily along Philadelphia's Market Street.

A young girl, standing at the door of one of the houses, turned and laughed at the ridiculous spectacle Ben made. Her name was Debby Read, and one day she would become Mrs. Benjamin Franklin, but at that moment nothing was further from Ben's mind than romance. Instead of letting the girl know that he noticed, he went on to a Quaker meeting, where, over-

come by the fatigues of the long journey, he promptly fell asleep.

Thus began the independent career of one of the most remarkable persons Colonial America would produce. With a great knowledge of books and an easy flow of conversation, Ben soon became the warm friend of Sir William Keith, governor of the colony, who offered to set him up in the printing business. Ben traveled to England to buy the equipment for his shop, but the money Sir William had promised to send never reached London. An undaunted Ben settled cheerfully into English life, supported himself as a printer, and after eighteen months financed his own voyage home to America. A year and a half after returning, he had established his own business and was busily publishing *The Pennsylvania Gazette*.

In 1732 there appeared in the book stalls a new publication—*Poor Richard's Almanack*. In a land where books were very scarce, almost every home in time seemed to contain two—the Bible and the latest *Poor Richard*. Franklin used the name of Richard Saunders to disguise his authorship, and the homely advice Poor Richard gave spoke the common sense people needed to conquer a wilderness. "A penny saved is a penny earned," wrote Franklin, who had turned vegetarian so that the money he saved on food could be used to buy books. "Like cats in air-pumps, to subsist we strive," wrote Franklin, now one of the busiest men in America.

Poor Richard caught the spirit of the struggle of the settler fishing the waters off the Maine coast, the farmer who left his plow to fight Indians, the planter of tobacco in Tidewater Virginia, and the planter of rice in the Carolinas. Poor Richard was quoted by father to son, and by son to his son. Even today it is a rare boy or girl who does not hear advice originally published in *Poor Richard's Almanack:*

God helps them to help themselves.

Little strokes fell great oaks.

Early to bed and early to rise, Makes a man healthy, wealthy, and wise.

For Franklin the days surely must have started early, and at times his neighbors must have wondered where next they would find him. One day he would be out in a thunderstorm, flying a kite to prove that lightning is electricity. Or he would be showing the lightning rod he had invented; or demonstrating the Franklin stove he had built, which began the stove industry in America; or the bifocal glasses he had designed; or the platform rocking chair that still can be found creaking in many American parlors.

"Debby," Franklin said to his wife, "I wish the good Lord had seen fit to make each day just twice as long as it is. Perhaps then I really could accomplish something."

So, handicapped by days that contained only twenty-four hours, Franklin organized the first fire de-

partment in Philadelphia, improved the city's police system, helped to organize the first hospital in America, reorganized the postal system in the colonies, founded an academy that became the University of Pennsylvania, started the first circulating library, and complained because he couldn't come back in a hundred years to see how things were working.

With the outbreak of the French and Indian War, Franklin felt strongly the danger in the conflict. Somehow the colonies should be united for mutual protection. The years had taught him great wisdom in getting along with people—a wisdom he would soon employ and which he summed up in his *Autobiography*:

"As the chief ends of conversation are to *inform* or to be *informed*, to *please* or to *persuade*, I wish well-meaning, sensible men would not lessen their power of doing good by a positive, assuming manner that seldom fails to disgust, tends to create opposition, and to defeat every one of these purposes for which speech was given to us, to wit, giving or receiving information or pleasure. For, if you would inform, a positive and dogmatical manner in advancing your sentiments may provoke contradiction and prevent a candid attention. If you wish information and improvement from the knowledge of others, and yet at the same time express yourself as firmly fixed in your present opinions, modest, sensible men, who do not love disputation, will probably leave you undisturbed in the possession of your error."

The ability to get along with others was one that Franklin would need many times before his life ended in 1790. One such occasion came during the French and Indian War. Braddock's forces arrived, and a crisis developed in Pennsylvania, where the Quaker and German farmers selfishly refused to aid Braddock. Franklin intervened, pledging his own resources to secure horses and wagons for the army.

In July, 1755, Franklin and Braddock met. The British general spoke boastfully. He would take Fort Duquesne, proceed to Niagara, then on to Frontenac in Canada—winning the war in his mind before fighting his first battle. Franklin tried to point out the danger of ambuscade in Indian fighting, but Braddock replied haughtily:

"These natives may, indeed, be a formidable enemy to your raw American militia, but upon the King's regular and disciplined troops, sir, it is impossible they should make any impression."

Franklin turned away. He feared for the future.

10 · Soldier Washington

The French and Indian War, 1754-1763

"I RECKON," the soldier said, "Washington never will enjoy smoking a peace pipe with them Indians, even if he gets the chance!"

"Why so?" a fellow militiaman asked.

"The tobacco," the soldier said. "A couple of puffs starts his head reeling!"

The pair leaned against their rifles and looked at the tall, powerful Virginian who was their leader. George Washington made sense. This expedition to Duquesne, the fort the French had built where the Monongahela joined the Allegheny to form the Ohio River, was dangerous enough without going at it pig-headed, like this English general, Braddock! Look at those red-coated, marching Britishers! Did they think this was a dress parade? What nice targets for tomahawks and bullets those fellows would make—spots of flaming red against the forest green!

Washington dressed his own men in buckskin and moccasins—neutral shades that blended with the trees. He stripped his boys of every ounce of superfluous weight, knowing that forest fighting called for moving quickly, like a cat.

Benjamin Franklin's fears after talking with Braddock were also felt by Washington. A man couldn't learn about a wilderness or Indian fighting from a book. Book-learning had its place, and at this thought Washington broke into a smile. He guessed he would never forget the 110 "Rules of Civility" his schoolmaster had made him memorize in that handbook by a chap named Hawkins. At least when he dined with Braddock he would know, thanks to Hawkins, not to pick his teeth with a fork or crack fleas before company.

Yet Washington wanted to be fair. Likely Edward Braddock was an extremely good general—in the right setting. But Washington had known the wilderness since, as a gangling boy, he had earned a doubloon a day (about $7.50) surveying for Lord Fairfax. The forest was a tough old schoolmaster and as full of rules as Hawkins. Its first lesson was vigilance. A forest could grow menacingly still with not a rabbit scurrying or a bluejay chattering. There was lurking danger then. And its second lesson was patience. Get headstrong and impulsive hunting a deer, and a man could be sure of one thing. When his temper subsided, the deer would be gone, and he'd still be hungry!

The French and Indian War was a full-scale affair now, instead of the local quarrel over control of the Ohio it had been a year ago when Washington had led his militia against the French and their Indian allies. He had made a stand at a place he had named Fort Necessity, since necessity was the mother of invention; he had been trapped, made to fight, been outnumbered and defeated, captured and pardoned with full military honors, a surprisingly sporting gesture for the French.

Obviously the French had thought they had ended their troubles, but George II of England had taken another view. He intended to broaden trade with the colonies, the king told Parliament, and to protect the possessions that constituted their sources of wealth. These words in a less pretty form meant that George II wanted the French kicked out of North America. So Braddock had come with his scarlet-clad regimentals.

Washington's militiamen, marching with the British regulars and sailors, gave Braddock a total force of about 2,200 men for the expedition against Fort Duquesne. The road they followed over the mountains of Virginia and Pennsylvania that hot June of 1755 was never wider than twelve feet. The local name for the surrounding pine forests Washington hoped would not be prophetic. They were called the Shades of Death.

The French were no fools. They knew the British and the Provincials advanced. Indian scouting parties watched, scalped the deserters and stragglers, then glided through the night to report to the French what they had seen. Indian raiders swept into the border settlements.

Washington chafed at the gathering dangers he sensed, and tried to confine his explosions of anger to the letters to his half-brother. So, at home in Mount Vernon the Washingtons heard that Braddock, when he was lucky, hacked his way forward three miles in a day. Morale ran low and nerves were tense. Instead of pushing on where he could, road or no road, meeting the wilderness with roughness and toughness, Braddock stopped to level every molehill and bridge every brook.

At length Braddock approached Fort Duquesne. For Washington and the Provincials, the big test for the general would come now. Without doubt, Braddock knew how to fight the French according to the rules of war. But could he fight Caughnawagas, Hurons, Abenakis, Pottawattamies, Mingos, and the painted warriors from a dozen other tribes who fought for their survival?

The month was July, the weather brittle-hot. Braddock advanced doggedly down the road, looking for his adversaries. Washington knew where the French, the Indians were. They were behind the trees and bushes. They were in the gullies and flattened against the rocks. They were under the ledges and just over the hills. They were all around him.

Then, like a cloudburst, the battle raged. If to east, west, north, south there had been simultaneously four claps of thunder and four bolts of lightning, the British could not have been more bewildered. Savage war cries shook every side of the forest. Arrows hummed through the air, French-made rifles cracked, scalping knives flashed in the glint of sun. Vainly the British strained to strike back. "Show me someone to fight with," an officer pleaded, voicing a common desperation.

The panic was more terrible, the rout more humiliating than Washington or anyone could have feared. The ground swelled with mounds of red-coated dead, the air quavered with moans of the wounded. Terrorized regimentals broke and fled—often to a lonelier death when Indian pursuers overtook them. Mortally wounded, an astonished Braddock gasped:

"Who could have thought it?"

Washington brought his own troops out of the disaster with credit. He knew the tricks of the forests—how to break a trail by wading streams, how to listen for the sounds that weren't made by beast or bird, how to fade among the trees. His retreat from Duquesne marked him a seasoned soldier.

Braddock's defeat was only the first for the British in 1755; other

crushing blows would be suffered at Crown Point and Fort Niagara. In retaliation, the British exiled a group of French colonists from Nova Scotia who had aided the enemy, but the chief result of this action would be to inspire Henry Wadsworth Longfellow to write "Evangeline," a romantic account of the later wanderings of these exiles.

In 1758 energetic William Pitt became Britain's Secretary of State,

[71]

and British strength in North America was revitalized. At last the English flag waved in victory at captured Louisburg, Fort Duquesne, Crown Point, and Niagara. The last battle of the French and Indian War came at Quebec, where the British army under General James Wolfe besieged 15,000 French soldiers under General Louis Joseph Montcalm.

General Wolfe was born in the same year that Montcalm received his first commission as an officer, so that youth was pitted against age on the Plains of Abraham, above Quebec. The fight was forced on Montcalm when Wolfe cut French lines of supply. Bravely the French general rode out on a dark bay horse, brandishing his sword. Wolfe led a charge of Highlanders, was shot three times, staggered and fell dead. The night before his death, Wolfe had perhaps had a grim premonition. As he led his men the evening before their early dawn attack, his men overheard him recite the following,

"The curfew tolls the knell of parting day,
The lowing herd winds slowly o'er the lea,
The ploughman homeward wends his weary way,
And leaves the world to darkness and to me."

"Gentlemen," said Wolfe very simply when he had finished. "I would rather have written that poem than take Quebec tomorrow."

Montcalm was borne with the tide of defeated French toward Quebec when, still mounted on the dark bay, the fatal shot passed through his body. Thus the war ended, but the treaty of peace was not signed until 1763. All that was left to France of her dreams of empire in the New World were the tiny islands of Saint Pierre and Miquelon, south of Newfoundland, which she was permitted to hold as unfortified fishing stations.

The year 1763 found Soldier Washington living at home in Mount Vernon as Planter Washington. He loved the old mansion house, the fields that he cultivated. Gunning and fox hunting were sports that he enjoyed, but his heart was in the land. He was a farmer. He had begun his own cider distillery, was experimenting with growing wheat and irrigation techniques, and derived great pleasure looking for ways to improve and expand his farms.

Yet Great Britain, having secured her colonial empire in North America, abused it. The life of quiet ease and comfort that Washington adored must end in time. Again he must be the soldier. Again he must use the lessons he had learned fighting in the wilderness.

II · Mohawk Raiders

The Boston Tea Party, 1773

IN THE flickering light from the candle, George Hewes stepped back and examined his reflection in the mirror. The Indian costume fitted snugly, though getting the headdress above his big ears had been a bother. The hatchet in his belt looked businesslike. When he stopped at the blacksmith shop for coal dust to paint his hands and face, his mother wouldn't be able to distinguish him from a genuine Mohawk.

George rehearsed his instructions: "Go to Griffin's Wharf. Tell no one your name. Your boat captain will tell you what to do next."

Later, warming his back against the glow of the forge, the smith watched George blackening his face.

"'Tis a veritable Injun you are for sure!" The brawny man broke into a chuckle, but quickly grew serious. "'Tis been brewing for a long time, this trouble. 'Tis what you can expect when you have a knucklehead for a king!"

George nodded. Ten years of a king's foolishness had rubbed tempers raw. Taxes and more taxes—on molasses, on cloth, on newspapers and books and pamphlets, on glass and paper. The people went hungry paying taxes, and when in 1770 a few snowballs were thrown in protest at a British sentry, shots had been fired. The Boston Massacre had seen three citizens killed, eight wounded. Sam Adams had emerged as the real leader then, organizing his Committee on Correspondence to write the letters that would tell the world the outrages that they suffered.

"All this hubbub over tea," the smith lamented.

"You know 'tis more than tea!"

"Aye, 'tis a principle."

George Hewes finished his disguise. Outside he heard a gust of wind. Before the night of December 16, 1773, ended, he was due for some cold, numbing work.

His mind put together the puzzle of events that had led to this newest crisis. The tax on tea had been the limit, but they didn't have to drink English tea. A belly felt just as warm drinking tea smuggled from Holland! Now George III had sent three ships loaded with tea and guarded by armed men-of-war. The price of the tea, even with the tax, had been made cheaper than smuggled tea, another demonstration of how George III thought he could buy a man's principles with pennies and bluster!

Under the leadership of testy Sam Adams, a meeting of aroused citizens had been held last night in one of the Boston churches to devise expedient means for preventing the landing of the English tea or for eliminating the collection of the tax. Since they were temperate men, they had decided to call today on Governor Hutchinson and seek his help. If they would come again

[74]

at five o'clock, that worthy had hedged, he would give his answer. They had followed his wishes, and what had been their reward? Governor Hutchinson had flown the coop to his house in Milton, six miles outside of Boston! George Hewes could still hear the cry that had gone up at the discovery of this deceit:

"Let every man do his duty, and be true to his country!"

Well, George thought, he couldn't stand here all night, as snug as a Charles River quahog, warming himself by the fire. He had work to do at Griffin's Wharf! He moved to the door and called back cheerily, "Till we meet again, if the Lord spares me."

"Good luck to you," the smith said earnestly.

Along the darkened streets George Hewes soon encountered other Bostonians, who, like himself, also were dressed as Mohawks. No one spoke, remembering the pledge that each would accept the consequences of his own actions.

At Griffin's Wharf the ships carrying the tea were clearly visible. Close by loomed the dark and menacing shapes of the men-of-war. The English already were calling Bostonians "rebels," and saying that if troublemakers prevented an orderly landing of the tea, it would be landed at cannon's mouth. George Hewes tightened his lips. Better the braggarts had made sure first that they had tea to land!

The "Mohawks" divided into three groups at the wharf, and each group was assigned to its boat to row out to the ships at anchor.

"Board them all at the same time,"

the order went round.

Hewes recognized only one person—Leonard Pitt, captain of George's boat. Pitt turned and spoke, "You act as boatswain. When we board the ship, go to the captain and demand the keys to the hatches and a dozen candles."

"I understand," George said.

The three boats bearing the "Mohawks" glided into Boston Harbor. The soft dip of the oars and the quick, tense breathing of the boat's painted occupants were the only noises that could be heard. Nearer drew the black hulks of the British ships. George could hear the groan of the anchor rope and see the flicker of candlelight in the captain's cabin. His hand slipped down to the hatchet in his belt. He patted the "tomahawk" for comfort. A hand reached up and seized the ship's ladder.

George bounded on board and went to the captain. A dark scowl—and yet was there the trace of a twinkle in the captain's eyes?—was the only answer when George stated his demands. Then the captain handed him the keys and the candles.

"See that you do no harm to the ship or the rigging," the old sea dog growled. It was difficult to tell whether the captain was a king's man or a rebel sympathizer.

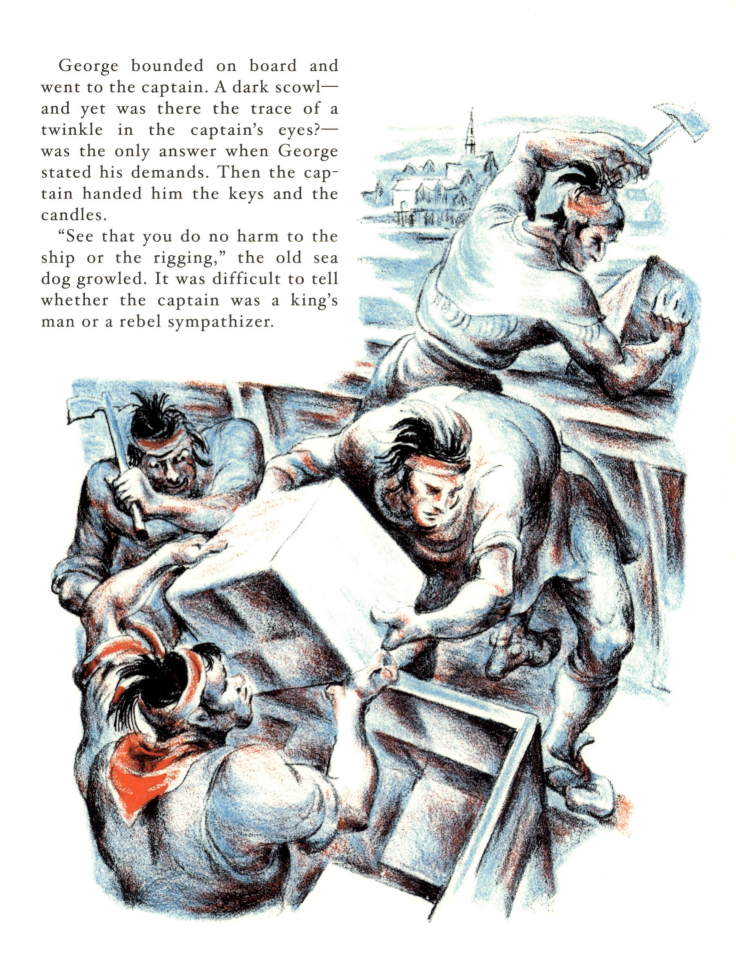

With the hatches unlocked, Leonard Pitt took command. Out with the chests of tea! Cut and split the cases! Over the rail with the contents! In the distance George Hewes heard parties similarly engaged on the other boats, but otherwise this was the "stillest night in Boston" he had ever known.

The chests kept coming out of the hatches, the hatchets continued smashing, the water echoed the splash of the tea striking its surface. The surrounding vessels of war showed almost no signs of life. An hour went by, then another, and the confidence of the rebels grew. George remembered again the cry that afternoon: "Let every man do his duty, and be true to his country!" Hot and sweaty, despite the December night, George thought that New Englanders did feel as though they belonged to a country of their own!

An agreement had been made that no tea was to be carried away, even for family use, since there was a difference between an act of rebellion and an act of theft. George watched suspiciously a tall old gentleman. Sure enough, the old fellow was slipping a little tea into his pocket.

Detected, the man made a break for freedom but was grabbed at the rail. His pockets were emptied, then his tall frame speeded along with a kick or two. Even so, because of his advanced years, he fared better than others who were caught. They were dumped overboard and made to run the gauntlet through the crowd at the wharf.

Next morning George served in the harbor patrol that rowed after any tea still afloat. With oars and paddles, they beat the tea until it was drenched and useless. George knew that some Bostonians were scandalized by the act.

"Ye'll pay for this," they moaned.

But Sam Adams strutted around like a peacock.

"'Tis all the doings of the Mohawks," he said, winking his fierce darks eyes.

12 · Yankee Doodle

The Coming of the Revolution, 1775

THE SPARK of freedom kindled by the "Mohawk" raiders in Boston Harbor lighted fires of rebellion elsewhere in America. Every colony except Georgia was represented when the First Continental Congress assembled in Philadelphia in September, 1774. The delegates drafted an appeal to the king to correct the wrongs causing dissension, then adopted an agreement: After December 1,

[79]

1774, unless colonial abuses ended, no merchandise would be imported from Great Britain or Ireland; after September 10, 1775, exports to these countries and the West Indies would cease.

In England, Edmund Burke arose to speak "On American Conciliation." Measures in the colonies should be restored to those used during the peaceful year of 1763, he urged. The aging Pitt asked Parliament to surrender its right to tax the colonies. Lord North, the Prime Minister, offered a plan to eliminate taxes if the colonies would raise their share of imperial expenses.

Other voices raised another chorus. Crack down on the colonies! Increase funds for military and naval forces to enforce the laws! A sharp answer was heard in Virginia. Offering a resolution for arming the militia, Patrick Henry asked:

"Why stand we here idle? What is it that the gentlemen wish? Is life so dear or peace so sweet as to be purchased at the price of chains and slavery? Forbid it, Almighty God! I know not what course others may take, but as for me, give me liberty or give me death!"

The English reaction to this impudence was reflected in Massachusetts, where British General Thomas Gage strutted around with square chin out-thrust. Boston he turned into an armed camp.

Brazenly, the spirit of rebellion among the colonists was expressed in a song:

Yankee Doodle keep it up,
Yankee Doodle dandy,
Mind the music and the step,
And with the girls be handy.

The tune was old. Probably the melody traced back to the Middle Ages in southern Europe; harvesters in Holland had sung it in the 1500's; and children in England had given it other words:

Lucy Locket lost her pocket,
Kitty Fisher found it;
Nothing in it, nothing in it,
Save the binding round it.

"Yankee Doodle" became a safety valve for the rising emotions of Colonial America. A revolutionary "underground" collected muskets, powder, and shot. Minutemen organized companies, and frequently at night hoofbeats were heard as couriers like the stanch rebel silversmith, Paul Revere, rode with news of British military movements.

February, 1775, threatened to bring war. Reports said that Gage had sent a force to Salem to search for stores of powder. The rumor proved false. An uneasy March passed, an uneasier April ended its second week. Out of Boston on April 17 Revere rode to Lexington to warn patriots that Gage seemed up to some devilment. Military supplies should be moved to Concord.

Gage decided to act. On the night

of April 18 a detachment under Major Pitcairn was dispatched to destroy the stores at Concord. That night a hand knocked on the door of Paul Revere's home.

"Dr. Warren wants to see you," an unidentified voice said.

Joseph Warren, a leader of the revolutionary underground, spoke briefly when Revere reached his house. A boat waited at the bank of the Charles River. A horse was ready on the opposite bank. When Gage started, a signal would flash—one light if the British troops moved by land, two if by water.

Across the river the signal flashed, the British were crossing in boats to Cambridge, and through the night—and into stirring lines of poetry by Henry Wadsworth Longfellow—rode the immortal horseman:

It was twelve by the village clock,
When he crossed the bridge into Medford town.
He heard the crowing of the cock,
And the barking of the farmer's dog,
And felt the damp of the river fog,
That rises after the sun goes down.

It was one by the village clock,
When he galloped into Lexington.
He saw the gilded weathercock
Swim in the moonlight as he passed.
And the meeting-house windows, blank and bare,
Gaze at him with a spectral glare,
As if they already stood aghast
At the bloody work they would look upon.

It was two by the village clock,
When he came to the bridge in Concord town.
He heard the bleating of the flock,
And the twitter of birds among the trees,
And felt the breath of the morning breeze
Blowing over the meadow brown....

So rode Paul Revere, carrying from village to village that night:

A cry of defiance and not of fear,
A voice in the darkness, a knock at the door,
And a word that shall echo for evermore!

That word was "liberty"!

The road entering Lexington was level for about a thousand yards. As the sun rose on the morning of April 19, 1775, marching British grenadiers awakened the dust. Behind hedges and trees, the minutemen stood. Spirits rode high. A sentry hid at the church; others across the road waited behind a stone fence. Now and then someone hummed "Yankee Doodle." Before the day ended, General Gage would cry:

"I hope I shall never hear that tune again!"

From the moment the British had crossed the river at Cambridge, their

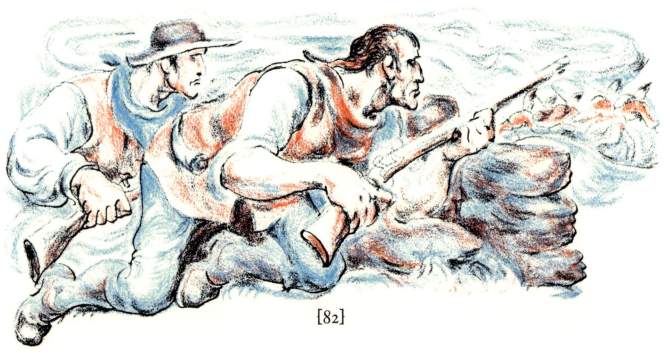

route had been known. Through the night at times it had seemed as though every road was filled with galloping horses.

Now the minutemen watched the scarlet-clad soldiers coming like rows of geraniums. In straight lines, stiff as pokers—hadn't they ever heard of trees or Injun fighting?

A British officer called out, "Throw down your arms, and you shall come to no harm."

Both sides claimed that the other fired first. A volley followed. Seven minutemen fell. Not until the British reached the bridge at Concord, however, did the minutemen fight back fiercely. Again Longfellow has told well

How the farmers gave them ball for ball,
From behind each fence and farmyard wall,
Chasing the red-coats down the lane,
Then crossing the fields to emerge again
Under the trees at the turn of the road,
And only pausing to fire and load.

In retreat, the British staggered out of Concord toward Boston. No fence, no tree seemed empty of hostility. Rifles snapped from front and right, left and rear. The British loss on the march was 273 men. Minutemen cheered. Yankee Doodle was doing dandy!

As news of the battles of Lexington and Concord spread throughout the colonies, everyone said: "This is war!" In June the Second Continental Congress, meeting in Philadelphia, summoned George Washington from his quiet life in Mount Vernon to command all troops "raised for the defense of American liberty!"

Meanwhile, in Boston, events moved swiftly. Before Washington could take command, the British determined to snuff out the rebellion in a stroke. Across the Charles

River stood two hills. One was called Bunker Hill, and for reasons no one can explain it gave its name to the battle soon to be fought; the other was Breed's Hill, where the fighting actually occurred.

Along darkened roads into nearby Cambridge, on the night of June 16, crept columns of minutemen. Silently, they encamped on Breed's Hill. All night leaders, like the stout old war horse Israel Putnam, drove their boys. Pile up the sod, earth and stone against those rail fences! Daylight edged the sky. Chin-high behind breastworks, Yankee Doodle commanded Boston!

British pride bridled. Breed's Hill had been stolen from under their noses! British men-of-war in Boston Harbor opened fire. For four hours the cannon raked the hill. The minutemen waited, snug behind their fortifications.

The British generals, Clinton and Howe, lost their military sense. Breed's Hill stood on a narrow neck of land approachable on all sides by water. A force landed behind the hill would trap the Americans on this peninsula, but British pride had been hurt. They would go straight up the hill and blast the Yankees!

Across the river, citizens in Boston saw the battle forming. Roof tops swarmed with women, children, men too old to shoulder a musket. The spirit of the scene was caught by Oliver Wendell Holmes when he told "Grandmother's Story of Bunker Hill":

*They were making for the steeple,—the
  old soldier and his people;
The pigeons circled round us as we climbed
  the creaking stair.
Just across the narrow river—O, so close it
  made me shiver!—
Stood a fortress on the hill-top that but yes-
  terday was bare.*

*How slow our eyes to find it; well we knew
  who stood behind it,
Though the earthworks hid them from us,
  and the stubborn walls were dumb:
Here were sister, wife, and mother, looking
  wild upon each other,
And their lips were white with terror as
  they said,* THE HOUR HAS COME!

With a roll of drums, scarlet regimentals marched up Breed's Hill. Across the grassy slope the red-coats spread in a thin, rigid line, bayonets fixed. Gaily, they sang their favorite song, "Hot Stuff." No shot fired down on them. As they had expected, the Americans had turned tail and run! Behind the parapet the steely voice of Israel Putnam spoke quietly:

"Hold fire! Wait until you can see the whites of their eyes! Then up and tear out their bellies!"

Stoically, the British marched on. In the steeple, Grandmother watched:

*Just a glimpse (the air is clearer), they are
  nearer,—nearer,—nearer—
When a flash—a curling smoke-wreath—
  then a crash—the steeple shakes—
The deadly truce is ended; the tempest's
  shroud is rended;
Like a morning mist it gathered, like a
  thundercloud it breaks!*

Oh, the sight our eyes discover as the blue-black smoke blows over!
The red-coats stretched in windrows as a mower rakes his hay;
Here a scarlet heap is lying, there a headlong crowd is flying
Like a billow that has broken and is shivered into spray.

The scattering regimentals were stopped at the foot of Breed's Hill and again whipped into line. Once more they started upward—more slowly, without singing. To the west, toward Charlestown, a fire had been started.

Silently, the minutemen waited. The British loaded and fired. An old apple tree behind the breastworks was stripped of its leaves. Then the Americans sprang up. Israel Putnam's order stood: "... tear out their bellies!" The regimentals scampered back down Breed's Hill—those who still lived.

The British had learned. Now they formed in columns. For the third time they advanced. The minutemen fixed bayonets. The wait was harder, for ammunition had dwindled to the point where only the American sharpshooters could load and fire.

Over the hill the British lunged.

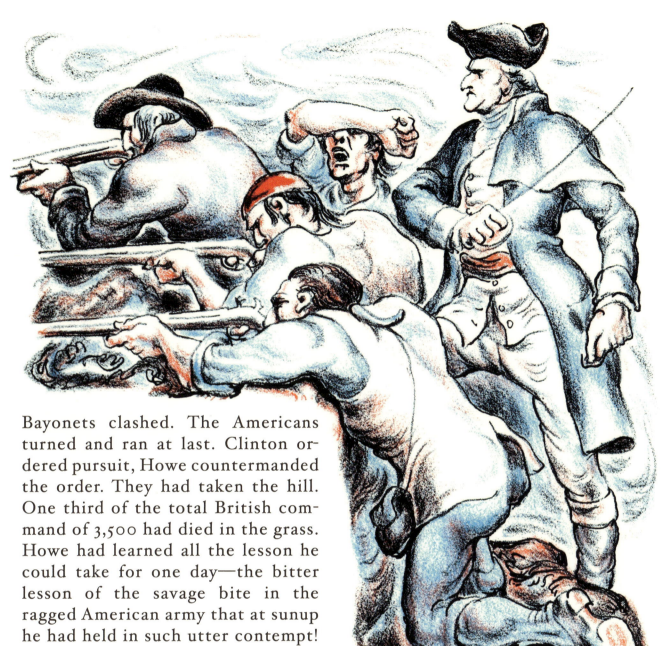

Bayonets clashed. The Americans turned and ran at last. Clinton ordered pursuit, Howe countermanded the order. They had taken the hill. One third of the total British command of 3,500 had died in the grass. Howe had learned all the lesson he could take for one day—the bitter lesson of the savage bite in the ragged American army that at sunup he had held in such utter contempt!

And how did the day end for Grandmother? There was a wounded soldier, whom she nursed:

—*"Why, grandma, how you're winking!"*
  —*Ah, my child, it sets me thinking*
Of a story not like this one. Well, he somehow lived along;
So we came to know each other, and I nursed him like a—mother,
Till at last he stood before me, tall, and rosy-cheeked, and strong.

And we sometimes walked together in the pleasant summer weather;
—*"Please to tell us what his name was?"*
  —*Just your own, my little dear,—*
There's his picture Copley painted: we became so well acquainted,
That—in short, that's why I'm grandma, and you children all are here!

13 · "We Hold These Truths"

Jefferson Writes the Declaration of Independence, 1776

WASHINGTON had assumed command of the Continental Army. The youth of the wilderness, the farmer of Mount Vernon, needed all the patience and self-discipline that experience had taught him, to organize high-spirited minutemen into seasoned soldiers. Meanwhile, Ethan Allen's Green Mountain Boys of Vermont struck a telling blow by seizing Crown Point and Ticonderoga, key fortresses to the control of northern New York. The jubilant Sam Adams asked, "Is not America already independent? Why not then declare it?"

In Philadelphia where the Continental Congress met on June 7, 1776, Henry Lee of Virginia offered a resolution:

"These United Colonies are, and of right ought to be, free and independent states."

The sons of Virginia were doing well. One commanded the armies in the field, another called for the birth of a new nation, and a third Virginian, Thomas Jefferson, was asked to draft the document justifying this fateful act.

Surely Jefferson had become a genius to compare with Franklin. At "Shadwell," in Virginia's Albemarle County, Jefferson's first lusty cries were heard on April 13, 1743. Tom grew up a thoroughly normal son of the frontier—a boy who liked to hunt and fish, who could handle a horse as well as anyone in Albemarle County, and whose quick, inquisitive mind frequently found him digging in nearby Indian mounds for relics.

At the age of nine, Tom Jefferson was studying Latin, Greek, and French; at seventeen, he had completed classical school and entered William and Mary College. When his studies ended there, he read law under George Wythe, one of the greatest jurists in America, and in 1767 was admitted to the Virginia bar.

The expanding brilliance of Jefferson's mind seemed to know no limit. Like Washington, he was the devoted farmer, but he was more the scientific farmer who added to the common knowledge of agriculture. Like Franklin, he was the imaginative inventor, and today we use a currency of dollars and cents based on the decimal system of coinage that he devised. Still other products of Jefferson's inventive mind were to be the weather vane, the first storm windows, a plow, a revolving writing chair, a dumbwaiter elevator, and a clock that told both the hour and day of the week.

Well may we ask when Jefferson found the time to do so much—to compile a dictionary of Indian dialects, to read the books in a personal library that one day would form the basis for the present Library of Congress, to learn architectural design so well that his magnificent home at Monticello, the State Capitol at Richmond, and the University of Virginia were each created by his restless imagination.

Such was the man and the mind that the Continental Congress selected to be its spokesman for liberty. For eighteen days Jefferson labored to draft the historic document. On long sheets of foolscap, the scratch of his quill pen worked out the case for the action Congress had taken. "The history of the present king of Great Britain," Jefferson wrote, "is a history of repeated injuries and usurpations, all having in direct object the establishment of an absolute tyranny over these states." Jefferson proposed that the "facts be submitted to a candid world."

Jefferson's probing, logical mind indicted the king for a conspiracy of enslavement. Among his accusations were refusing assent to laws that were wholesome and necessary for the public good and acts dissolving bodies of representative government. The king had obstructed justice and "kept among us, in times of peace, standing armies, without the consent of our legislatures," thus endeavoring "to render the military independent and superior to the civil power." For cutting off trade by sea, for imposing taxes without consent, for inciting Indians to insurrection, for turning a deaf ear to every reasonable plea for redress, Jefferson placed the king before the court of history.

The days went by. Jefferson dipped his quill pen and reflected. What did it all mean? The pen resumed scratching, slowly and thoughtfully, words destined to stand as a testament of faith for all willing to make the choice between liberty or death:

"We hold these truths to be self-evident: That all men are created equal; that they are endowed by their Creator with certain inalienable rights; that among these are life, liberty, and the pursuit of happiness. That, to secure these rights, governments are instituted among men, deriving their just powers from the consent of the governed; that, whenever any form of government becomes destructive of these ends, it is the right of the people to alter or to abolish it, and to institute a new government, having its foundations on such principles, and organizing its power in

such form, as to them shall seem most likely to effect their safety and happiness . . ."

The simple language and courageous spirit rather than the thought were new, for in the Declaration of Independence Jefferson used ideas by which, in 1686, Englishmen had justified revolt against King James II. At last the Virginian was ready to have his document read and criticized. Over the foolscap pages ran the eyes of two men whom all America respected—the eyes of Benjamin Franklin, all the sharper for the bifocal glasses he had invented; and the eyes of the distinguished John Adams, cousin of the firebrand Sam, and a fighter for freedom since that day in 1765 when he had written of the Stamp Act: "This tax [on newspapers and legal papers] was set on foot for my ruin as well as that of Americans in general."

Franklin occupied a unique position. Adams was destined to be the second President (1797-1801) of the country they were now declaring independent; Jefferson would be its third President (1801-1809). The three men discussed the document. Adams liked its "high tone" and "flights of oratory"; he would not have called the king a tyrant, but did not press the point. Franklin suggested only minor changes. Later all the members of Congress considered the declaration, cut here a line, added there another, but the basic thought and language remained Jefferson's.

The Congress met for the final reading. A hush fell over the crowded hall. A quiet voice spoke stirring words:

"When, in the course of human events, it becomes necessary for one people to dissolve the political bands which have connected them with another, and to assume among the powers of the earth the separate and equal station to which the laws of nature and of nature's God entitle them, a decent respect to the opinions of mankind requires that they should declare the causes which impel them to the

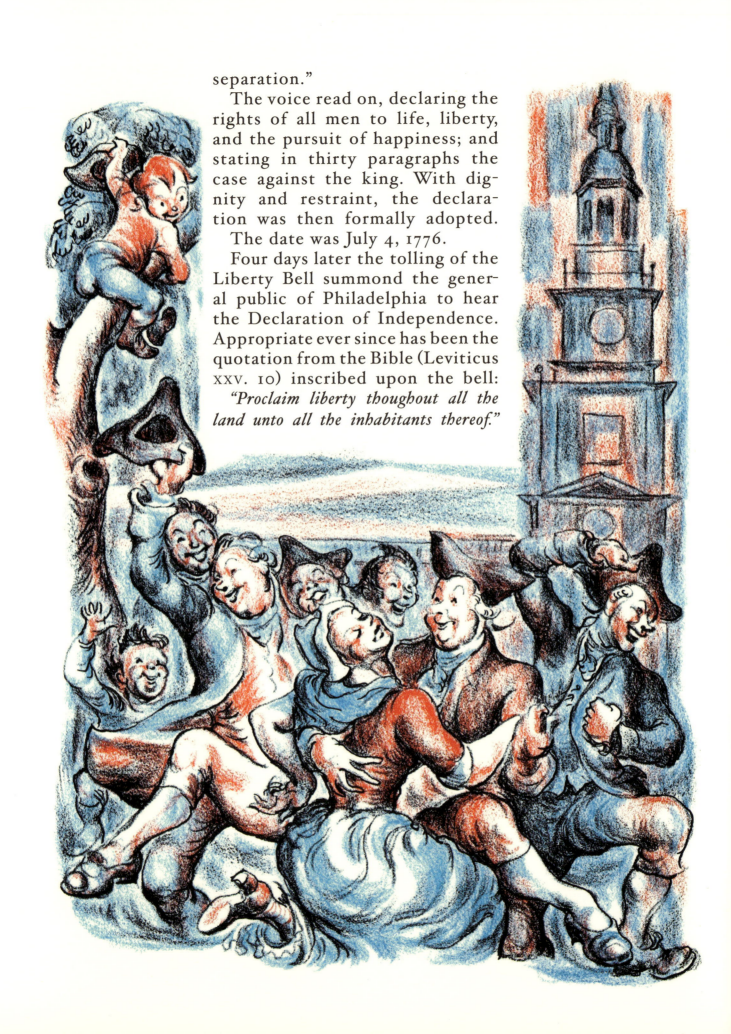

separation."

The voice read on, declaring the rights of all men to life, liberty, and the pursuit of happiness; and stating in thirty paragraphs the case against the king. With dignity and restraint, the declaration was then formally adopted.

The date was July 4, 1776.

Four days later the tolling of the Liberty Bell summond the general public of Philadelphia to hear the Declaration of Independence. Appropriate ever since has been the quotation from the Bible (Leviticus XXV. 10) inscribed upon the bell:

"Proclaim liberty thoughout all the land unto all the inhabitants thereof."

14 · The Winter of Despair

Valley Forge, 1777-1778

WHILE THE Liberty Bell tolled in Philadelphia to celebrate the Declaration of Independence, on Staten Island 30,000 British troops under General William Howe tensed for a crushing blow against Washington's army. About 17,000 Americans were camped on Manhattan and Long Island. Howe, a good general, prepared a careful attack, cleverly maneuvering his troops so that he could strike both Washington's front and flank. On August 27, 1776, Howe closed his pincers.

Disaster threatened Washington. Small boats ferried his frightened soldiers across the Hudson. Not only had he lost New York; he had come within a hair's breadth of losing the war. Across New Jersey the determined British and the retreating Americans played a grim game of cat and mouse. Washington had one hope—to cross the Delaware before the British trapped him—and he succeeded, with the enemy's hot breath on his neck. At Trenton, New Jersey, three regiments of hired German Hessians under Lord Charles Cornwallis waited for the Delaware to freeze. Once they could move, they would finish Washington.

American spirits sank. Soldiers refused to re-enlist. Many deserted. Washington moved boldly, crossing the river on Christmas night, and surprised the festive Hessians. For ten days Washington taunted Cornwallis in a hit-and-run campaign across New Jersey called "the most brilliant in the world's history." A grumpy Cornwallis returned to New York while Washington quartered his troops in Morristown, and like a vigilant, panting watchdog looked over a New Jersey saved to the patriot cause.

From Canada 7,000 troops under General John Burgoyne reenforced the wily Howe. Spring came. Washington was frankly puzzled. Where would the British strike next—at Philadelphia, Virginia, or the Carolinas? Then Howe's forces sailed into Chesapeake Bay and revealed his objective as Philadelphia. Washington, following with his army, tried to throw back the British only to suffer two humiliating defeats—at Chad's Ferry on the Brandywine River on September 11, 1777, and at Germantown on October 4. Reeling under these bitter blows, Washington fell back to Valley Forge.

In France, where Benjamin Franklin had gone to represent the young nation, it seemed the fall of Philadelphia almost ended American

[93]

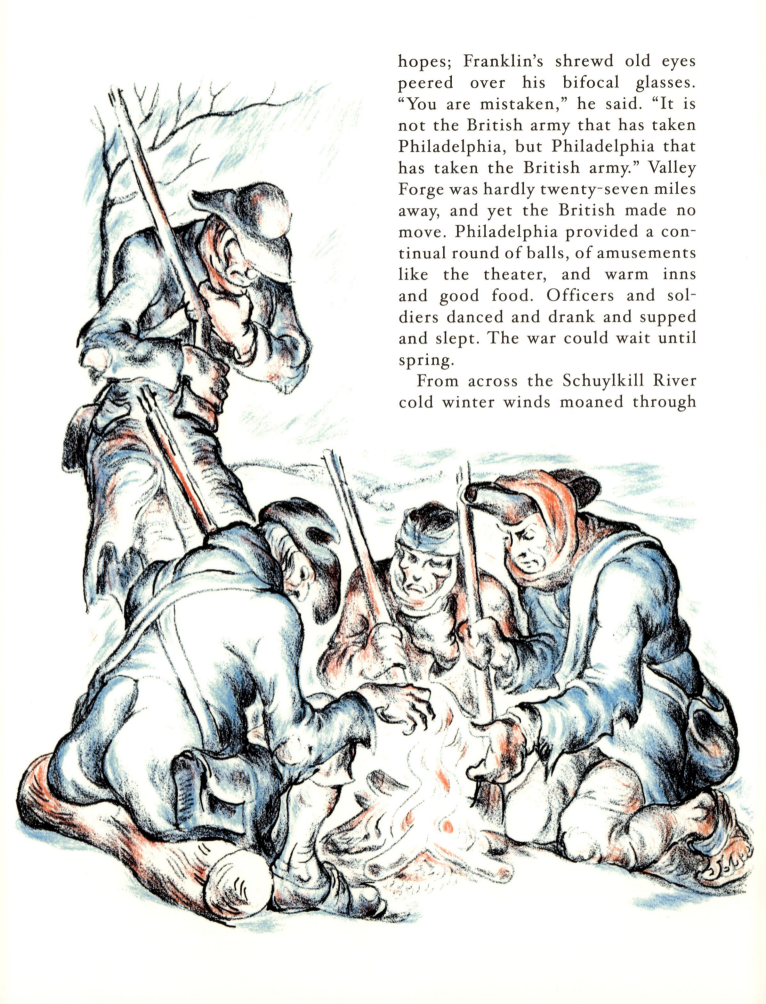

hopes; Franklin's shrewd old eyes peered over his bifocal glasses. "You are mistaken," he said. "It is not the British army that has taken Philadelphia, but Philadelphia that has taken the British army." Valley Forge was hardly twenty-seven miles away, and yet the British made no move. Philadelphia provided a continual round of balls, of amusements like the theater, and warm inns and good food. Officers and soldiers danced and drank and supped and slept. The war could wait until spring.

From across the Schuylkill River cold winter winds moaned through the stark, bare trees. Washington must have thought often of comfortable Mount Vernon as he walked among the crude, drafty huts at Valley Forge where his army, now dwindled in numbers to about 10,000, shivered and groaned.

Skies darkened with gathering clouds. Snow was whipped by the wind. At first a thin carpet on the ground, the drifts soon piled waist-deep. One storm ended and another began. In the intervals black crows cawed in the ice-encased trees, singing a dirge for the misery and sickness that afflicted Valley Forge. In despair, on December 23, 1777, Washington wrote:

"We have this day no less than 2,873 men in camp unfit for duty because they are barefooted and otherwise naked."

Harsh and bitter grew the grumbling now heard everywhere in the colonies. Why not admit the war was lost? Why not give up this silly talk of liberty that had produced hardships never imagined? The army would never win under Washington—why didn't Congress replace him?

Washington walked across the snows at Valley Forge. His dark eyes looked hard, his big hands closed tightly. Faith and loyalty, patience and self-control—these were the qualities that shaped his character and gave sinew to his spirit. They were qualities he never had needed more desperately.

Inside the flimsy huts at Valley Forge ragged soldiers huddled on the dirt floors, trying to coax a bit of warmth from mean, smoky fires. Roof tops sagged under the snow; howling winds raced through the wall chinks, sputtering the fires, blackening the walls with smoke, freezing water in the buckets. The sick coughed with long, hacking gasps that seemed to pull a man apart. Food was scant, medicine almost nonexistent. Yankee Doodle in tatters, his belly empty, his chest raw, his heart heavy—this was the tune to sing at Valley Forge, if anyone was fool enough to want to!

The hopeful said bravely, "Wait till spring!" Men who were waiting for the weather to break for just one thing—to sneak out some night and head hard for home—listened with curled lips. Or asked when Congress intended to pay them. Or sneered at officers who "resigned," a fancy word for deserting.

In France, the cunning old diplomat, Benjamin Franklin, had played his hand well. Perhaps France was not yet ready to come into the war on the American side, but French pride still burned at the losses suffered after Montcalm's defeat by the British at Quebec in the French and Indian War. So, sent by the French, Prussian-born Baron von Steuben arrived at Valley Forge. An officer who had served with Frederick the Great, von Steuben's mission was to train the American army into a fighting force that could cut off the tail and pluck out the claws of Britannia's lion!

American officers watched aghast as the bustling German seized a musket from a soldier and demonstrated how to use it. "Like *dot*, no?" No, said the American officers—such fraternizing with ordinary soldiers was bad form. "*Ja?*" asked von Steuben, flicking up his harsh, black brows. You could explain how a musket worked without touching it? Or that a bayonet could be used for something besides an ice pick? Bah!

Von Steuben swore at officers and soldiers in German and French and employed an interpreter to swear for him in English. He wanted results. That was why he had come—as good a drillmaster as could be found in Europe. No one could fight the British with a mob of raw recruits who marched as though they were following a lazy mule behind a plow!

"Dunderheads, *dunderheads*" . . . in three languages von Steuben bawled and bullied. Militiamen, wearing cotton nightcaps beneath their hats for warmth, scowled at their German drillmaster, mocked him in private, but they obeyed. Spring, at last creeping into the valley of the Schuylkill, brought to many a strange new sense. Von Steuben's dunderheads had begun to feel like soldiers.

The army that finally stirred to leave Valley Forge for another thrust at the British was not quite the disorganized, dispirited throng that had run pell-mell from defeat at Germantown. June brought more than temperatures in the near nineties to mark the difference between winter and summer at Valley Forge. When von Steuben smiled, he spoke the now universal language of growing confidence.

15 · March to Vincennes

The War in the West, 1779

"Those British rascals have come back," the ranger said.

"Where?" his comrade asked.

"At Vincennes. About eighty of 'em, from what I hear."

"That's enough to stir up Indian raids against every settlement in the Northwest. Where'd they come from?"

"Detroit."

"We going after them?"

"You know the colonel. Any Britisher in this country is like a flea in his whiskers—no sleep till he scratches it out."

From the outbreak of war, Colonel George Rogers Clark had been alert to the menace represented by the British forts on the Wabash and Mississippi. Not the number of English agents, but their strategic position in inciting the Indians to massacre, determined the course history could take here. Fortunately Governor Patrick Henry of Virginia had agreed with Clark and outfitted his small band of rangers. Already these frontier fighters had captured the Illinois settlements of Kaskaskia and Cahokia, but if the British now held Vincennes on the Wabash, there was still work to do.

February, 1779, had started as a mean, wet month—cold and raw, with flood water everywhere. Colonel Clark's rangers numbered about 170, enough to clean out the British if they could make the march.

"Think you better wait?" the priest at Kaskaskia asked.

"The boys will want absolution before they start," Clark said.

The priest understood. When the major's eyes grew steely there was only one way to deal with him—wish him luck and speed him on his way. It would take luck to reach Vincennes this time of year.

The rangers came to the Little Wabash River on February 13, eight days out of Kaskaskia. Clark knew he was in trouble. The river divided into two streams with perhaps five miles of ground between—and every inch of it under three feet of water! The rangers pitched camp on a bit of high land and waited. But for what? For spring to come and the Indians to start butchering and burning? For their leader's cold feet to thaw out?

Clark now was twenty-six—scarcely a boy any longer. He admitted his own irresolution and tried to disguise it by keeping his boys occupied building a pirogue. They had waded through water before. Why did he hesitate? Then, unexpectedly, February turned springlike, and the warm, moist day gave Clark the prod he needed. March on to Vincennes, he ordered.

The colonel's outward bravado was bluff. Scouts were ordered to bring back word of good camping sites ahead, even if none existed. On February 15 the rangers crossed the Little Wabash and sloshed onward. In water to their hips, they pawed with their feet in the slime. Funny, the tricks leg muscles played in water, producing knots that felt as though the devil had tied them. Funny, how a rifle could feel like the weight of a cannon, a powder horn like a millstone around the neck. Those who took sick were loaded into the canoes. The others simply thought how better off they would be if they had been born beavers.

Clark had hoped that the mouth of the Embarrass River would permit him to get to the Wabash, but high water stopped him flat-footed. Luckily there was again a spot of high ground for a camp. Exhausted men could sleep almost anywhere.

With the rising sun, the colonel sat up suddenly and listened. There was no mistake—that echoing sound was the morning gun of the British garrison at Vincennes! They had to push on.

About two o'clock in the afternoon of the 18th, the rangers gained the banks of the Wabash and camped again. They were three leagues from the town, and it seemed a million. Two days later the rangers were still camped when a boat appeared.

Clark ordered the capture of the five Frenchmen it carried. *Non*, the boatmen told Clark, they were not spies but on their way downstream to join a hunting party. *Oui*, the presence of the rangers was known. In Vincennes everyone except the British was happy they were coming.

Clark quizzed the Frenchmen sharply. *Non*, the rangers could not make Vincennes that night. The colonel disagreed. With the hunters in tow, the march resumed.

"Now, this is real pretty," one ranger told another. The water was up to their armpits.

At night they had reached a place called the Upper Mamel—a league short of a sugar camp that promised good camping, but how far short of the town was a guess. Two leagues? Spirits seemed high, considering everything. The boys wanted to get on and finish the job. Rations were growing short. A man could march just so far on a half-starved belly.

Clark went to inspect the sugar camp. Approaching the camp, he waded neck-deep in water, and he was a tall man. He returned to the Upper Mamel with more than hunger giving his stomach a sharp pinch. Sober eyes fixed steadily on him. Could they make Vincennes?

Inadvertently, by a slip of tongue, Clark revealed his own concern. The spirit of the rangers broke, crisply, as a twig snaps.

Clark whispered to his officers, "Do what I do." Scooping water into his hand, he mixed in gunpowder and blackened his face. Then, with a war whoop, he plunged through the water, remembering later:

"The party gazed at me for an instant and then like a flock of sheep fell in, one behind the other, without saying a word. I ordered the men who were near me to strike up one of their favorite songs. It soon passed down the line, and all went on cheerfully."

The sugar camp stood on half an acre of dry ground, and here, while his boys rested, the colonel made a speech. They knew that he loved them. How far off was the fort—a few hours? Vincennes meant the end of all their sufferings. The rangers cheered.

The marchers went forward single file. Slowly, in torment, tired legs moved, numb feet prodded for a hold. Eyes blurred with reddened veins told their own story. Clark sent his strongest men ahead to cry "Land!" and thus encourage the weaker ones. The water deepened. Those who faltered were supported by the more able-bodied.

Ahead was a wood, where shallower water was expected. Shoulder deep, the men staggered on. The woods were better only because weak and shorter men could cling to trees or float on logs. They slogged on, gasping, reeling, sometimes seeing images that didn't exist—until they reached Vincennes!

The battle with the British was not dramatic, for the real fight had been the march. How much they had won would be revealed afterward at the peace table, when, with claims established by Clark's men to boundaries as far west as the Mississippi and as far north as the Great Lakes, the United States added to its territories the first part of the vast domain of the Northwest. Later in the war, George Rogers Clark served with Baron von Steuben in the defense of Virginia, and in time a grateful Virginia legislature gave him an estate in present-day Indiana, where Vincennes is now a city of 18,000.

16 · "The World Turned Upside Down"

Victory at Yorktown, 1781

THE American Revolution was like a three-legged stool.

The first leg was the period from the battles at Lexington and Concord to the Declaration of Independence. The period that constituted the second leg had for its low point the winter at Valley Forge and for its high point the victory at Saratoga. At last France agreed with suave old Ben Franklin and on February 6, 1778, signed a formal alliance with the struggling young nation across the seas.

The third leg took much more labor to build, for to this point the war had been largely confined to the northern colonies. Now George Rogers Clark carried the conflict up the banks of the Mississippi and the Wabash. A young navy of five ships under John Paul Jones pursued British merchantmen across the seas and once even shelled the coast of England. Next the vessels of France, and of Spain, which declared war a year later, harried the British navy and made the land war truly a sea war also.

Actually, by 1780, the American Revolution had become part of a world war. Holland came in. Russia,

Denmark, Sweden, Prussia, and Austria banded into the League of Armed Neutrality, posing another serious threat to the British. Still, for all the strange bedfellows the war made for America, the ordeal at home grew no less painful.

Through 1780 into early 1781 the war in the colonies represented a gigantic seesaw, more often tipping toward disaster than triumph. The nation's shocks were many. One was the plot by which Benedict Arnold maneuvered to surrender West Point to the British, and for complicity in this treason Major John André, who had danced so prettily during the winter when the British held Philadelphia, now dangled his legs from a scaffold. Prices soared, paper money became next to worthless. For all the fine lessons of military discipline Baron von Steuben had taught, state militia quarreled with state militia until Washington said grimly, "I see one head gradually changing into thirteen—one army branching into thirteen."

Were there no bright clouds? Cornwallis and his army seemed to tramp the South at will until suddenly, on October 7, 1780, a patriot army at King's Mountain, South Carolina, spanked the British in a battle as vicious as that of Breed's Hill. Cornwallis faltered in his strut across North Carolina. Then, equally important, the South heard the name of another American gen-

eral—Nathanael Greene.

At the outbreak of war, Greene, a Rhode Island Quaker, had traveled to Boston to buy a musket and some military books. The most useful volume he could find was a dog-eared copy of Caesar's *Gallic Wars*. Greene set to teaching himself the un-Quakerish art of war with more perseverance than any American schoolboy has ever given to Caesar. How much he learned from studying the military exploits of the mighty Roman became apparent when in December, 1780, he assumed command of American forces in the South.

Quickly Greene's eye spotted the talents of such typical North Carolinians as Francis Marion, the Swamp Fox, and wily Dan Morgan, who at Cowpens on January 17, 1781, wiped out almost an entire British force by quick wit and inspiring pluck. Greene didn't mind losing an occasional battle if he won the ultimate campaign—reading Caesar had taught him that war was won by gaining the commanding position. Caesar also had taught him that a general needed good lieutenants—like the Swamp Fox and Dan Morgan.

The approaching spring found Greene chafing. The little Rhode Island Quaker wanted to quit North Carolina for Virginia; he wanted a chance at the main British army under Cornwallis. His troops were fewer than he wished, but they had style—another compliment to Greene, who possessed gifts as a drillmaster that would have brightened the eye of Baron von Steuben.

Two sharp, hard battles, first at Guilford Court House and then at Eutaw Springs, set the stage precisely as Greene wanted. Cornwallis retreated into Virginia.

Washington, watching the British in New York from a base on the upper Hudson, jumped at the chance to gain by what had happened in Virginia. Cornwallis, doubtless counting on reinforcements or escape by sea, had concentrated his troops, no more than 7,000 strong, on the Yorktown peninsula. A small army, under France's gallant Lafayette, pressed forward. If the French fleet now would stand off the capes of Chesapeake Bay, isolating Cornwallis from any communication by water, the British were in a trap!

Couriers sped from Washington to the French admiral, to Lafayette, to Greene. Then along the upper Hudson, roads echoed to the noises of an army moving on the double-quick—the tramp of feet, the creak of rolling cannon, the rumble of supply wagons, the neigh of horses nicked by spurs. After six weary years, Washington saw the end if he could force a march overland.

Rarely has any military movement worked so well. At almost the time the French fleet anchored off the capes of Chesapeake Bay, Washington's army advanced down the road on Yorktown. Twenty-four hours earlier Cornwallis could have escaped with his forces across the river; he had waited as one hypnotized, or perhaps more like a runner who at last realizes he is winded. All of South Carolina could have become his battleground; he saw his risk and his chance, and yet couldn't move.

American spirits bubbled over. The French soldiers under Lafayette, neat as a pin, were a cheerful group, fond of song, and the Americans got along with them very well. The siege at

[105]

Yorktown found Americans cheering each blast of the mighty French guns at the British fortification, and the French cheering when the Americans gained the forts at Yorktown and turned British guns on the dispirited soldiers under Cornwallis. In the bay the French admiral waited and smiled. He could hear the guns roar. He could picture the walls of Yorktown crumbling to dust. This was the end for the British. This was the time when "the world turned upside down."

In October, 1781, General Henry Clinton sailed from New York for Yorktown with 7,000 British reinforcements. That same day Cornwallis surrendered. Then, on October 19, the French and Americans lined up in two trim columns. Washington, mounted on an elegant horse, waited for the captive British to march between the columns and ground arms.

For this dark hour, the proud Cornwallis issued new uniforms to his men, yet he himself could not appear, and, pleading illness, sent another to lead his forces in formal surrender.

The bands stopped playing. On a field swarming with spectators, the last moment had come. Washington's head lifted, and with determined chin emphasizing his strong character, he watched. The British marched poorly, unable to conceal their strain. A cracked shrillness rose in the voices of red-coated platoon officers. "Ground arms!" they cried. The surrendering soldiers could not hide their sullenness beneath new uniforms. Their guns were flung viciously on the pile, as though to knock them to pieces, until Washington's friend, General Benjamin Lincoln, spoke sharply, and the display of bad temper ceased. The British marched back; then the allied army turned to leave the field. The timbrel, an instrument peculiar to the French military band, struck up its cheerful music.

When the sun set that evening at Yorktown, and General Washington was alone, his thoughts turned to Mount Vernon. Soon now he would be able to return to the rolling fields he loved so dearly. Yet another duty was to call him once the nation had beaten its swords into ploughshares. So often great men are lonely men, divided by duty from places and persons where their hearts would lead them.

17 · "We, the People"

We Adopt a Constitution, 1787-1788

WHEN TOUGH old Daniel Shays spoke to war veterans who had suffered through the winter at Valley Forge and had not yet collected their back pay of twenty-two cents a day, his words of rebellion fell on receptive ears. A captain in the Revolution, Shays returned to his farm in Massachusetts to find conditions a scandal. Because of high and unfair taxes, farms, homes, and small businesses were being auctioned at public sales. War veterans were being thrown in jail for their debts. Daily, the poor grew poorer, paper money more worthless, the spirit of despair more acute. Daily, Daniel Shays grew madder.

Not without purpose had the war taught Shays how to handle a musket or organize a regiment. Massachusetts required property ownership to vote, depriving the poor of redress for their troubles through the ballot box; but Shays saw

another way. On a brittle September day in 1786, a mob of six hundred citizens who had acquired Shays' fighting mood appeared before the courthouse in Springfield. The Supreme Court, then in session, received an ultimatum. If it continued to foreclose mortgages and to imprison helpless debtors, it was asking for war!

A series of skirmishes between the state militia and Shays' ragtag rebels, in succeeding months, brought a sense of shock to the colonies not felt since the Boston Tea Party. At last Washington's old friend, General Benjamin Lincoln, managed to

smash Shays' Rebellion and send its leader high-tailing into Vermont with a price on his head. Underneath, however, Shays seemed more hero than scoundrel. Single-handedly, he had dramatized the need for some better system of government, if only to suppress uprisings.

Actually at the root of many troubles that followed the end of the Revolution were the Articles of Confederation by which the colonies governed themselves. We were not one well-run family, but rather thirteen jealous, bickering brothers and sisters who threatened to tear asunder the house we inhabited. Under the Articles of Confederation, a Congress deprived of the power to tax could never pay off its debts. Insofar as all states must agree on any amendment to the Articles, it became virtually impossible to correct even glaring grievances. There was no central authority for settling border disputes, no strong executive head to lead the country, no system of court rulings guaranteeing equal justice.

So Shays' Rebellion—shocking thoughtful minds in America into acknowledging injustices that should be eliminated and the state of anarchy that could exist—served a good purpose. In its wake began the movement that produced a new constitution, but this movement claimed none of the clear-cut singleness of purpose that led to the writing of the Declaration of Independence. Rather the necessity of ironing out regulations between Maryland and Virginia for the navigation of the Potomac River and Chesapeake Bay provided the excuse by which Alexander Hamilton maneuvered Congress into calling a constitutional convention. Delegates from every state except Rhode Island came to Philadelphia when the convention opened on May 25, 1787.

Early to arrive in Philadelphia was Washington, dusty after the hard journey from Mount Vernon, but warmly greeted by Philadelphia's own first citizen, Benjamin Franklin. Another prominent Pennsylvanian was the brilliant, witty merchant-statesman, Governor Morris, who had aided in the financial affairs of the colonies during the Revolution; and also from Virginia came the frail and quiet-spoken James Madison, an extremely modest and sweet-tempered man, whose knowledge of public affairs would win him the title of "Father of the Constitution" and make him the country's fourth President (1809-1817). From New York came the strong-minded, rather stiff-necked Alexander Hamilton, a small, lean, vain man of undeniable brilliance, who would become the nation's first Secretary of the Treasury; and from South Carolina came the statesman-soldier, Charles Cotesworth Pinckney, who had served as aide-de-camp on Washington's staff and whose legal knowledge was the match of any in America. Such was a cross section of the fifty-five delegates who attended when the gavel fell that opened the convention.

The election of Washington as president of the convention was universally approved, but little else about the deliberations of the delegates aroused public enthusiasm. Sentries stood guard at the doors to insure the secrecy of the meetings, and this undemocratic atmosphere sharpened deep-seated suspicions. Even though the Constitution would open with the words, "We, the people," the delegates were of the wealthier class. To many the very word, "democracy," was distastefully suggestive of an uneducated rabble; others openly preferred some aristocratic system of government, perhaps a limited monarchy. Hard-fought were the sessions of the convention, and each sentence that went into the document represented a compromise between sharply contending points of view. Behind the closed doors, James Madison took the lead. Not by nature an orator, he rose to eloquence through his sheer clarity of thought and the unreserved charm of his personal manner.

At last the country had a look at this document which, once ratified, would become the supreme law of the land. The framers of the Constitution advanced the belief that the people were sovereign and created their own government. The people could both give and reserve rights, in the case of the central government or the individual states. These powers were limited—a state could not usurp the authority of the central government nor the central government usurp the powers of a state—and where laws were passed that created conflicts, the courts were empowered to decide where the proper authority belonged.

At the time the states deliberated whether to ratify the new Constitution, attacks upon the document reached extremes of acid bitterness. In Massachusetts, Sam Adams raised his voice in rasping opposition, and, at the state's ratifying convention, a veteran of Shays' Rebellion, comparing the Congress to the Spanish Inquisition, roared at the delegates: "Racks and gibbets may be amongst the most mild instruments of their discipline!" In Virginia, the voice of Patrick Henry was no less scornful in denouncing the Constitution as a product of watered-down democracy. How did it protect the *people* against possible oppressions of the national government? Where was its bill of rights?

These debates reflected a struggle that was centuries old. The same determination that the rights of the individual must be protected had forced from King John, in the meadow in Runnymede in 1215, assent to the Magna Carta. Justice must not be sold, proclaimed the

Magna Carta; persons must not be imprisoned, or deprived of their property, without due process of law; taxes must be collected by legal means rather than by force. The constitutions of seven colonies—Virginia, Pennsylvania, Maryland, Vermont, New Hampshire, North Carolina and Massachusetts—contained a bill of rights, and the constitutions of the others at least carried some form of guarantee to protect civil liberties. In 1690, when the great English philosopher, John Locke, published his *Second Treatise on Government*, he had clearly enunciated the principle that whereas the people could give some rights to the government, out of a decent respect to their children and the descendants of their children other rights must never be surrendered. These rights Locke had called *inalienable*, and in writing the Declaration of Independence that word had been used by Thomas Jefferson: Men and women were "endowed by their Creator with certain *inalienable* rights"—among them, "life, liberty, and the pursuit of happiness."

Foremost among those who defended the Constitution were Hamilton, Madison, and John Jay, a lawyer and statesman from New York who would become Washington's choice for the first Chief Justice of the United States. These three learned men wrote a series of informative essays, since known as *The Federalist Papers*, that supported the Constitution as the only basis of government all the people could accept. On June 21, 1788, New Hampshire became the ninth state to ratify the Constitution, making it the law of the land.

Yet the opponents of the Constitution had not lost their struggle. Within a year, ten amendments were added that constituted a bill of rights.

Freedom of religion, of speech and press, of assembly, and the right to petition the government were guaranteed.

Fair arrest and fair trial were assured to even the most hardened criminal, and courts were forbidden to impose cruel or unusual punishments.

The right of citizens to bear arms was asserted; and other rights and powers not specified in the Constitution were reserved to the people and the states.

An atmosphere of suspicion and uneasiness still remained. North Carolina had refused to ratify the Constitution until the Bill of Rights was written, and Rhode Island for a time would not even call a ratifying convention. (The last state to accept the Constitution, Rhode Island, signed on May 29, 1790.) Jefferson once said that the prime requirement of freedom was eternal vigilance. The citizens of the new government agreed. They knew the rights that they would never surrender!

18 · In Peace As in War

Washington Is Inaugurated, 1789

IN MORE than a century and a half of history, the city of New York never had known so glorious a day. Packets and sloops rode gracefully at anchor in the great harbor that was probably first seen by the Italian navigator, Giovanni da Verrazano, and through which in 1609 the Dutch explorer, Henry Hudson, sailed the brightly painted *Half Moon* and discovered the river that still bears his name. Remnants of the Dutch settlement of New Amsterdam, established in 1625, remained—nowhere more unmistakably than in the neat clapboard houses with their leaded windows, their upper stories that jutted out to protect doors and windows from unpleasant weather, and their front porches where on summer evenings many a Dutchman once had been seen smoking his pipe and patting his portly mid-region. The Dutch had been traders rather than builders of colonial empire; they had not possessed the genius for granting even elementary self-government, on the limited, grudging basis the British often manifested; and so in 1664 the control of New York had passed to the English and had remained with them to the close of the Revolution.

In excitement, in the number of notables who jammed the streets and taverns of the city, April 30, 1789, surpassed any day that New Yorkers could remember. This day, on the balcony of the Federal Building on Broad Street, George Washington was to become the first President of the United States.

Now fifty-seven, Washington had hoped that he would not be called to this duty. "I have no wish now," he had said, "but that of living and dying an honest man on my own farm."

But the public had insisted; in peace as in war, Washington must lead his country. Few realized the personal hardship imposed, for Washington actually had borrowed money to defray his traveling expenses from Mount Vernon to New York. The public saw only the national hero, the undisputed first citizen of America. Even the neat brown suit he wore encouraged the country's young textile industry, for every thread of the cloth had been woven in America.

The barge that carried Washington across the bay was surrounded by boats and sloops that had come out to greet him. In one sloop, with its full sail spanking, a chorus of some twenty ladies and gentlemen sang new words to "God Save the King." Hats were thrown in the air, and mighty cheers rolled across the harbor. Even a school of porpoises appeared, adding their touch of frisky playfulness to the occasion. A Spanish packet decked its rigging with the flags of nearly thirty countries; from her decks boomed a thirteen-gun salute to which the eighteen-pounders at the Battery responded.

To Elias Boudinot of New Jersey, sailing with the boats that surrounded the official barge, the shore was lined with "heads standing as thick as ears of corn before the harvest." At the ferry landing, crimson carpeting covered the stairs and railings. The governor and his welcoming committee

came forward to greet the President-elect, but in the shouting voices of others was a welcome that contained, perhaps, a more personal meaning.

The grave face of Washington softened into a smile. These voices he loved—these voices of officers and soldiers who had fought with him in skirmishes and battles along the long, hard road from the first crushing defeat on Long Island to the victory at Yorktown. He saw toughened faces now red with the exertion of their booming hurrahs, and he remembered the leathery lines that had seamed those faces at Valley Forge and crossing the ice-packed Delaware one Christmas night.

These voices, these faces were everywhere as the procession wound through the streets of New York. The windows of every house front seemed jammed to overflowing—the women waving, the men cheering, the youngsters defying gravity as they squeezed as far out as a tight grasp on their trouser-seats would allow. When evening approached, lamplighters scurried from corner to corner. This was to be both a day and night of celebration!

Washington reached the balcony of the Federal Building ill with fatigue. Heavily he sank into a chair. But the general was a fighter, and, as the moment for which the crowd waited now came, the proud head of Washington lifted.

A Bible was extended. Standing, Washington rested his right hand upon the Scriptures and his left upon his heart. Then for the first time in America a President-elect was asked to affirm these sober words:

"I do solemnly swear that I will faithfully execute the Office of the President of the United States, and will to the best of my ability preserve, protect and defend the Constitution of the United States."

In ringing tones, Washington said: "I swear—so help me God!"

19 · Pig in a Poke

The Lewis and Clark Expedition, 1803-1806

WASHINGTON died in 1799, ending an age. Now the country began a new century and had to be willing to take new risks.

So President Thomas Jefferson bought "a pig in a poke." Circumstances, Jefferson argued reasonably, forced his action. Surely for pioneers in Kentucky, Tennessee, and Ohio, who must ship their crops along the Mississippi, control of the mouth of the river was of paramount importance. With a nation as weak as Spain holding this control no one worried, but in 1803 the United States learned that by secret treaty Napoleon had forced Spain to cede its Louisiana territory to France. Napoleon was ambitious and France strong. Pioneer settlements depending on the Mississippi might find that to survive they must secede from the United States and join with France.

Jefferson discovered himself juggling two propositions. If possible, he wanted to buy New Orleans and the north coast of the Gulf of Mexico; if necessary, the United States might join with Great Britain in war against France. American diplomacy

in Paris was being asked to dance around the edge of a volcano, and, to make certain the volcano didn't erupt, Jefferson chose as his personal representative in these negotiations a gifted fellow Virginian, James Monroe, who later would be our fifth President (1817-1825).

Monroe found Napoleon not only worried over an impending war with England, but also badly in need of money. Presently Jefferson received astonishing news—the United States was buying the 827,000 square miles of France's entire Louisiana territory for the sum of about fifteen million dollars. A treaty, signed April 30, 1803, consummated the Louisiana

Purchase, while Jefferson wondered if he had achieved anything quite so certain as his own political ruin.

Frankly, Jefferson didn't know what he had bought, but he intended to find out. Congress granted $2,500 for an expedition into the unexplored country. The President selected Virginians as the leaders of the party that would map the new territory, report on its resources, negotiate treaties with its inhabitants, and chart the course of future settlement.

Captain Meriwether Lewis, an experienced Indian fighter who once had served as Jefferson's private secretary, was a moody man who often lapsed into spells of melancholy, but he liked the solitude of the wilderness and exhibited great resourcefulness when pitted against the hazards of nature. William Clark, a younger brother of George Rogers Clark, had been born in the wilderness and possessed the easy-going, reliable disposition that an expedition like this required. Clark was the natural, good-humored frontiersman whom even Indians admired. They named him "the Red Headed Chief."

In late 1803 Lewis and Clark assembled their party in St. Louis— four sergeants, twenty-three privates of the United States Army, two interpreters, Clark's Negro servants, and sixteen other men who would travel part way with the group. With spring, the explorers started up the Missouri in flatboats, and by the end of the summer of 1804 had journeyed 1,600 miles into the lands of the Mandan Indians, where they camped at the approximate site of present Bismarck, North Dakota.

When, from this point, messengers brought Jefferson news of the territory he had bought, they also brought, alive in three cases, a burrowing squirrel, a prairie hen, and four magpies. Still other presents included a stuffed male and female antelope, with their skeletons; also the horns of a mountain ram, or Bighorn; also a buffalo robe depicting a battle fought about eight years

before between the Sioux and the Arikaras against the Mandans and Minnetarees, in which the combatants were mounted on horseback.

Not without reason did these presents whet the interest of Jefferson and the public. Lewis and Clark were engaged in enchanting discoveries. In April, 1805, they pressed on to the source of the Missouri; by September they had crossed the Rocky Mountains and after two more months sighted the Pacific Ocean. Here they camped until March, 1806; then, re-crossing the Rocky Mountains, they divided into separate parties and came down

both the Missouri and Yellowstone rivers. When on September 23, 1806, they returned to St. Louis, they had covered 9,000 miles of wilderness.

In time the published journals of Lewis and Clark became a monumental work among explorers, telling a succession of almost unbelievable tales and containing enormous resources of information about geography, plants, and flowers, the animals of interior America, mineral deposits, and similar data. In these pages also were found the vivid personalities of explorers who possessed "that gallant spirit": the fine plainsman-riverman-trapper Drewyer, who could hold his own against any master of the sign language; the big, rollicking Newfoundland dog Scammon, who was a resourceful companion except when temperatures in the high 90's stretched him limp on the ground with panting tongue out-thrust; the uncomplaining Pierre Cruzatte, blind in one eye, poorly sighted in the other, who could teach the unhandicapped the skills of the frontier.

Adventures were virtually unending. If there was a trick about ticks, snakes, and mosquitoes that Lewis and Clark didn't learn, it was of minor annoyance. They could tell the Kansas by its willow-choked bottoms, the Platte by its muddy channels, the Missouri by the tenacious currents that swept under its sluggish surface. Sometimes they were led

on fool's errands (once, in quest of the fabled dwarfs of Missouri with 18-inch-high heads, who were supposed to enjoy killing Indians). And they were not long among the docile, dispirited Otos before they understood what a terrible scourge smallpox could bring to the wilderness.

With the Indians, Lewis and Clark were firm and determined. They represented the President, the new "Great Father" of the country, and his will must be obeyed. This message they carried into the wilderness—enforced by firearms, it was true, but supported more by their own pluck in refusing to be bluffed

or intimidated, especially by the Sioux. Indian grumblings that they were stingy with the presents they brought—though they were not accused of being as mean as the Spanish—they threw off with shrugs. Perhaps they fared well with the Indians because they understood his shrewdness, his native intelligence, his habit of giving up sulking when he could see he was only losing face. They learned something of the vastly complicated relationships among tribes. The Crows and Minnetarees were cousins, regularly the Cheyennes visited with the Arikaras.

As the Lewis and Clark party approached the Rocky Mountains, one of the most unusual figures in American history came to help them. Her name was Sacagawea, meaning "Bird Woman." Born in what is now Idaho, among the Shoshones or Snake

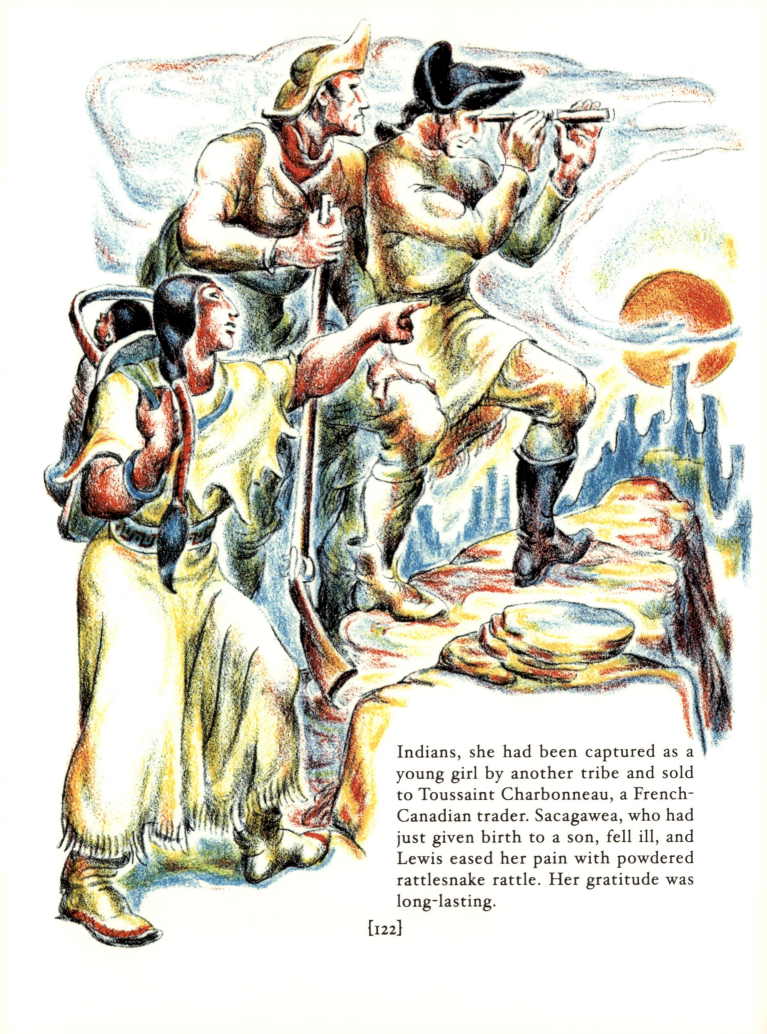

Indians, she had been captured as a young girl by another tribe and sold to Toussaint Charbonneau, a French-Canadian trader. Sacagawea, who had just given birth to a son, fell ill, and Lewis eased her pain with powdered rattlesnake rattle. Her gratitude was long-lasting.

Few white men knew the language of the Shoshones, so that as a guide across the Rockies and to the coast of Oregon, Sacagawea became an invaluable ally. So much about Sacagawea today is myth that it is difficult to judge her true historical place, but certain it is that she and her infant son, Pomp, were popular with all in the Lewis and Clark party, that she worked unceasingly for their comfort, that she found edible roots where their presence was unsuspected, and that, by recognizing landmarks from her travels among the Indians, she guided the white men over trails they might never have found.

The Lewis and Clark expedition proved Jefferson's "pig in a poke" to be a sound investment and provided the States a claim to the Oregon territory against the rival claim of England. The more immediate result, however, was the roll of settlers' wagons into lands that later would make the states of Louisiana, Arkansas, and Missouri.

20 · Old Hickory and the Pirate

The Battle of New Orleans, 1815

WEST OF the Mississippi Delta, sixty miles below New Orleans, Jean Lafitte and his pirates hid in isolated Barataria Bay. The arrogant Lafitte, born in France, had sailed the seas almost from as far back as he could remember, and the troubles that had befallen him he blamed on the "vices of the law." To clear the bayous of this lean-faced, mustachioed smuggler-privateer, Louisiana's Governor Claiborne offered a reward of $500. Lafitte roared with laughter. He, too, would offer a reward—$30,000 for the capture of the governor!

That a quirk of history would change Jean Lafitte from a hunted criminal into a patriot and hero was one more absurdity in the War of 1812. Two days before the "shooting war" began, the British Foreign Minister announced that the King's Council would repeal the laws which had brought his country and the United States to the point of hostilities. Unhappily, in 1812 news traveled slowly.

For the causes involved, the wrong people wanted war. English policies, growing out of the bitter struggle with Napoleon, had disrupted the freedom of the seas, crippled American shipping, and produced such outrages as the search of our vessels and the impressment of our sailors. To these early provocations of war, America retaliated with the Embargo of 1807, whereby Congress closed its ports to all foreign ships. Neither Britain nor France lost much by the Embargo, whereas shipping in New England was virtually ruined and Southern planters asked bitterly what they should do with the rice, cotton, and tobacco normally sold to England. Opponents of the Embargo made the act ridiculous by spelling the word backward: "O-Grab-Me!"

After fifteen months, the Embargo was repealed, but now Napoleon pretended to lift decrees that had hurt American shipping and cunningly drew the United States one step closer to war with Britain. New Englanders, whose shipping stood to gain or lose the most from war, strongly opposed being tricked by Napoleon. The "Warhawks" in Congress were represented by Henry Clay of Kentucky and John C. Calhoun of South Carolina, young legislators seeking cause for pushing the British forever out of the Northwest and Britain's ally, Spain, out of Florida. So the war that need not have been fought was declared by Congress, at the request of President Madison, on June 18, 1812.

Vicious fighting followed, both on land and sea. The fall of Detroit—the garrison at Chicago massacred—New England invaded and Maine subjugated—Washington burned and the President and Congress in flight—Baltimore attacked by land and sea . . . in grim events such as these the War of 1812 spelled out its costly story for America.

The morning of September 13, 1814 found British men-of-war anchored off Fort McHenry with Baltimore at the mercy of their guns. Through that day and night a garrison of about 1,000 Americans suffered a punishing bombardment, for the guns of McHenry could not reach the British vessels.

A captured Washington lawyer aboard a British vessel watched the brutal battle develop. With nightfall he could tell that the warship edged forward, intending to sneak by McHenry and reach Baltimore through the mouth of the Patapsco River. As the men-of-war drew within range, the cannon of McHenry

blazed defiance. The Washington lawyer waited prayerfully. If at dawn the flag still waved over McHenry, Baltimore could be saved! The tune of an old English song, "Anacreon in Heaven," thrummed through the lawyer's head, but the words were new:

And the rockets red glare, bombs bursting in air,
Gave proof through the night that our flag was still there!

With morning the joyful eyes of Francis Scott Key glimpsed the flag spanking bravely from the staff of Fort McHenry. By the time the British were driven out of Chesapeake Bay and Baltimore was liberated, America had taken to its heart the rousing words of "The Star-Spangled Banner."

With 8,000 troops under General Sir Edward Pakenham, the brother-in-law of England's warrior Iron Duke of Wellington, the British

[126]

struck at the South. In Barataria Bay the pirate Lafitte received an offer of $30,000 if his band would aid the British in capturing New Orleans. Within the old city, sometimes called "Paris in America" and "the City that Care Forgot," the pirate's brother, Pierre Lafitte, sat in jail. The pirate saw a chance to free his brother and lift the price on his own head. Accordingly he betrayed British plans to the Americans.

Andrew Jackson, the defender of New Orleans, showed no alarm at the British threat. Square-jawed, leathery-skinned—he was "Tough as Hickory," Tennesseans said—Jackson wasn't afraid to fight the devil. He had been eight when the Revolution started and twelve when, refusing to black the boots of an officer in a British raiding party, he had been struck by a sword that cut his arm to the bone. But Andrew was never afraid to pay the price of spunkiness; by 1812 and the outbreak of war, that trait had carried him to success as a lawyer, senator, and judge—and into any number of duels, for his temper, like the sword of Damocles, seemed suspended by a hair.

Against the British military traditions of the Wellingtons, with the glory of European battlefields to support them, Jackson proposed to throw buckskin-clad militiamen from Kentucky and Tennessee, and the finest shooting gun in the world—the Kentucky rifle. This gun, imported into the wilderness from Germany by way of the gun foundries of Lancaster, Pennsylvania, was as deadly at 150 yards as anything the mind of man had conceived. Moreover Jackson knew how to fight with a "Kaintuck"—in groups of threes, one firing, another standing ready, a third loading. So, warned by Lafitte, confident that he could meet the emergency, Old Hickory took a post on the third floor of a plantation house, and, telescope to eye, watched the British advance.

Cold, rainy, with temperatures sometimes falling below freezing, the closing days of December, 1814, saw the British coming through the bayous until they were within a day from launching an attack. Jackson, who had declared martial law, had executed six mutineers, and had been throwing up entrenchments in a frenzy of unceasing toil, spoke with the impulsive resolution that was always his principal trait:

"Gentlemen, the British are below; we must fight them tonight!"

Thus began the four battles that comprised Jackson's defense of New Orleans. The brother-in-law of the Iron Duke was to have many complaints over the military traditions that Old Hickory ignored. Jackson's raiders were constantly prodding at the British encampments, giving the enemy scant chance to sleep! Lafitte and his Baratarians blasted the neat scarlet-clad columns with a twenty-

[127]

four pounder that seemed especially suited to pirate's play. Tennesseans and Kentuckians fought loosely, slipping out of line, liking darkness, using rifle, knife, and tomahawk. This style of fighting they called "going hunting."

Pakenham planned a final, all-out British assault on January 8, employing a dangerous military scheme that often misfired—simultaneous attack by two widely separated forces.

Jackson's backwoodsmen received but one order—hold fire until the British were within effective range of a "Kaintuck," then let 'em have it just above the breastplate! The battle was like a squirrel-shooting bee—700 British killed, 1,400 wounded, 500 captured, against American losses of 8 killed and 13 wounded. Aghast, the British quit New Orleans.

Like so many other ridiculous features of the War of 1812, the battle of New Orleans was fought fifteen days after the peace treaty had been signed in Ghent. Slowness of communications, however, failed to let either Jackson or Pakenham know that the two nations had ended the war of which both Britain and America were heartily sick and which both vainly claimed as a victory. Not a single concrete gain could either side show, though America profited from two important indirect results: the rise of domestic manufactures when imports from Britain were cut off and a strengthening of national patriotism.

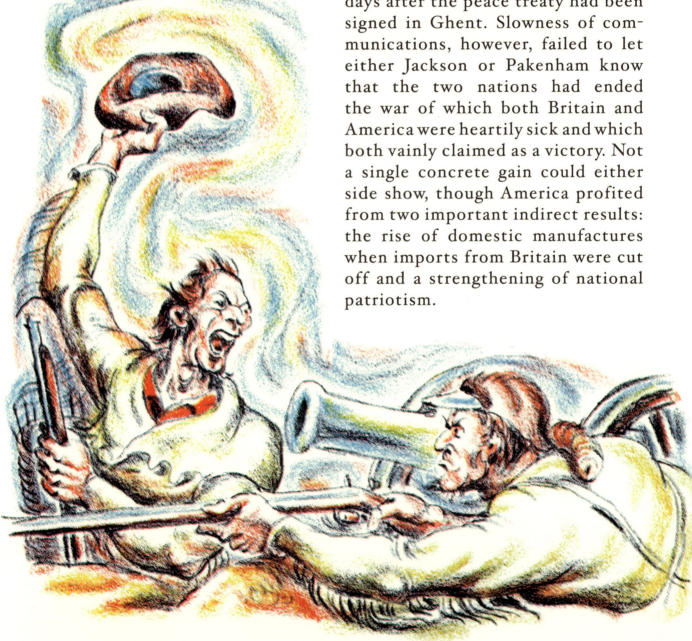

Lafitte, receiving a Presidential pardon for past crimes, could not resist old habits; soon he had established new privateering headquarters on Galveston Island, whence the United States Navy routed him out. About 1826, Jean Lafitte died in exile on an island off the coast of Yucatan. Three years later Andrew Jackson became the seventh President of the United States (1829-1837).

Definitely, with the end of the War of 1812, America entered a new age, and the young nation acquired a character that was entirely its own. Sometimes the forces that motivated great changes were difficult to recognize. A craze in hats, for example, had a far-reaching effect on the nation's future; patterns of education changed and moved westward with the course of settlement; a speech by a Mexican priest in an obscure village altered the history of the South; Fulton's Folly revolutionized river transportation and Eli Whitney's genius resulted in organized lawlessness.

21 · Poisoned Arrows and Grizzly Bears

Fur Trapping in the Old Southwest, 1820-1840

> TO ENTERPRISING YOUNG MEN: The subscriber wishes to engage one hundred young men to ascend the Missouri River to its source, there to be employed for one, two or three years.

Readers of the *Missouri Republican* for March 22, 1822, who answered this advertisement became part of the most significant group of explorers in our nation's history. They were "the Mountain Men" who followed the streams of the Southwest and Far West in search of the beaver. They were the trail blazers of a new empire—the first to know where mountains started and ended, how far the sandy areas of desert reached, and where crossed the boundaries of a hundred unsuspected Indian territories. Into the Mexican-held lands from Santa Fe to California they were an advance guard of Americans who came to know this country so well that they thought of it as their own. Typical of the group was Joseph Reddeford Walker who wished inscribed on his tombstone the single fact that he had been the first white man to behold the beauty of the valley of the Yosemite. These men dwelt among the wonders of the world.

The date 1778 brought changes in the fur trade. That year Britain's Captain Cook sailed into the Pacific Northwest and anchored in Nootka Sound. For bits of iron, the Indians loaded his decks with furs of the wolf and bear, sea otter and marten, fox and beaver. When these furs were brought to the ports of China, even defective skins sold at princely prices. The British did not know their granite-faced Yankee kinsmen if they thought the boat masters of Salem and New Bedford could be elbowed out of this China trade. Even before the Revolution fur trading in the Northwest promised to become a lively enterprise.

The boom years of fur trapping, however, grew out of a strictly domestic circumstance. In the early part of the 19th century, beaver hats for men became a national rage, and a prime beaver skin brought from four to six dollars a pound. A party of fur trappers, finding an untouched beaver colony, could take two hundred furs in a day. Then history played an ironic trick. The China trade that started the flurry in fur ended it sometime around 1840. Now from China came silk and other materials that hat manufacturers fancied more. The beaver craze had died, but the feats of the mountain men lived on as a chapter in American history without parallel.

America always had known such men. The first among these pioneer heroes likely was born in a suit of buckskin and a coonskin cap. Fighting in the French and Indian War against Fort Duquesne, Daniel Boone

struck up a friendship with John Finley, a hunter who told him about the beautiful country west of the Alleghenies. Boone blazed the trail of the "Wilderness Road," built the first fort (Boonesboro) on the Kentucky River, pushed on into Spanish territory beyond St. Louis, mapped wilderness routes through North Carolina, Tennessee, and Virginia, and at the age of eighty-two was seen hunting alone in Nebraska. In 1820, when the golden years of the mountain men were just beginning, Boone died.

Mountain men followed a pattern. Perhaps a few were roustabouts and renegades, but the larger number were sober, serious, God-fearing men who handled an axe, a knife, and a rifle as naturally as they flexed the fingers on their hands. Rivers no one dreamed existed became familiar haunts to them—the Gila that flowed through portions of Arizona; the mighty Colorado with its treacherous and dazzling canyons; the Virgin, the Sevier, the Green, and the San Juan in Utah; the Humboldt in Nevada, and the Snake and the Bear in Wyoming.

Prodigious stamina was their chief characteristic. The achievement of Jedediah Strong Smith is as astonishing today as it was in 1827 when he and two companions crossed the seventy-five miles of waterless, plantless wastes called the Great Salt Desert. The ordeal might well have killed an ordinary man, or driven him crazy, for neither Smith nor his comrades knew where they wandered or when, if ever, they might see grass and water again. Mirages fooled them, hunger constricted their stomachs, wind tortured their throats, but they reached safety. It was their code to keep going!

One mountain man looked like another, for all affected the same attire: buckskin clothes fringed at the seams, deer or buffalo moccasins, leather belt for pistols and butcher knife, bullet pouch hung from the belt and powder horn slung under the right arm, crowned homemade wool hat on bushy hair that curled over the shoulders. In the Indian country, they added a deerskin overshirt that covered the body from chin to thigh. Soaked in water and wrung dry, this garment was the next best thing to medieval armor for deflecting arrows.

Knowing the traits and tricks of the Indians was essential to a mountain man's survival. Once each year when the trappers met for a "Rendezvous" in the Rockies, new wrinkles in Indian tactics were discussed and stored away for future use. These annual meetings had a fiesta quality and some of the young men lost their heads, drinking and gambling too much. The level-headed trapper traded in his furs, laid by supplies for the coming year, and planned carefully where he would strike for furs next.

The trail from St. Louis to Santa Fe was traveled constantly. The route carried the trapper through the territories of the Osages, the Kiowas, the Pawnees, the Comanches, and the Apaches, so that when at last he arrived at the Mexican post he could feel he had experienced a good sampling of Indians. Of these five tribes, the Comanches required the closest watching. Proud and strong-willed, the most daring horsemen on the plains, Comanches neither asked, nor ever gave, a truce. Tribes that tolerated the mountain men the Comanches ridiculed as "slaves of the Europeans."

An Apache, on the other hand, could be persuaded now and then to dig a hole in the ground, spit in it, fill it with earth, dance around it, stick an arrow in the mound, pile stones on top, and then paint himself red—signs that he had spat out his spite, buried his anger, and was now at peace. But no mountain man really trusted any tribe of Indians an inch further than the range of his gun except the Flatheads in western Montana, who, unlike neighboring tribes, even looked upon stealing as a disgrace.

In time, when the movement west

drew greater numbers of settlers, officials in Washington courted the lore of the Indians that the mountain men could teach them. Up on the Humboldt lived a tribe of Shoshones with digestive tracts that would consume anything from seeds and insects to birds and reptiles. The strength of an Apache's bow was such that he could drive an arrow through a man's body at a hundred yards. The arrowheads of the Snakes and Mojaves were the most poisonous because they mixed antelope or deer liver with rattlesnake venom in dipping them.

Next to Indians, the mountain men knew and feared the grizzly, who had turned large parts of the West into his private domain. One of the immortal figures among the fur trappers, James Ohio Pattie, sighted as many as two hundred grizzlies in a single day. The bear—gray, white or grizzly—had a mean temper to go with his enormous strength. Pattie told of an experience in the Mexican country. The powder in his gun was damp and fired slowly— "made long fire," the mountain men said. Hit in the belly instead of the head, the grizzly charged with open mouth. Pattie didn't wait to argue—he dove headlong over a precipice and cracked his jawbone. Later, when a companion had "bled him"—the mountain remedy for all complaints—Pattie tracked down the wounded bear and settled the score.

Buffalo hunting also was part of the trapper's day. Mountain man, Rudolph Friederich Kurz carried his reader into the midst of a herd:

"The hunter chases buffaloes at full gallop, discharges his gun, and reloads without slackening speed. He holds the weapon close within the bend of his left arm, and, taking the powder horn in his right hand, draws out with his teeth the stopper, which is fastened to the horn to prevent its being lost, shakes the requisite amount of powder into his left palm, and again closes the powder horn. Then he grasps the gun with his right hand, holding it in a vertical position, pours the powder down the barrel, and gives the gun a sidelong thrust with the left hand, in order to shake the powder well through

the priming hole into the touchpan (hunters at this place discard percussion caps as not practical).

"Now he takes a bullet from his mouth and with his left hand puts it into the barrel, where, having been moistened by spittle, it adheres to the powder. Hunters approach the buffaloes so closely that they do not take aim but, lifting the gun lightly with both hands, point in the direction of the animal's heart and fire."

The continual reappearance of bands of American trappers in Mexican territory was not a source of joy to the officials there. No American was supposed to trap the streams of this territory without a permit from the Mexican Government, but many a mountain man ignored this diplomatic formality. True, a governor possessed full police authority and a few hot rancid jails in which to incarcerate those he apprehended, but there was a lot of wilderness to patrol and no record of a governor who claimed more than two eyes.

Government officials in California, like their colleagues in Santa Fe and Taos, came to possess tempers that often grew hostile. The Americans shrugged, managed to get along with the local inhabitants, and felt at home beneath the cane-grass roof of a mission. With elk, deer, and wild horses plentiful, the call of California sounded especially irresistible to the trapper. If desert and mountains could not keep him out, governmental regulations written somewhere south of the Rio Grande stood less chance of curbing his independence.

Except for poisoned arrows and grizzlies, little worried or frightened the mountain man. On the night of November 12-13, 1833, a great shower of meteors filled the skies over North America, and in the cities terrorized persons thought the world was ending. In the San Joaquin Valley, where Joseph Reddeford Walker and his party watched the meteors exploding in air or splitting to pieces against the ground, the awesomeness of the heavenly display simply added to the wonder of all nature.

A fur trapper who deserves to be remembered was a youth of nineteen, with soft flaxen hair and a rather girlish voice, who ran off to the Southwest in 1826 because he couldn't stand the drudgery of a Missouri saddle and harness business.

The reward that the employer offered for the return of this apprentice tempted few sleuths. The amount was one cent. Meanwhile the youth reached Taos, New Mexico, and joined a trapping party under Joaquin Young. Soon the most blasé wagon men were saying that this lad had the makings of a real mountain man.

Shortly Young's party encountered

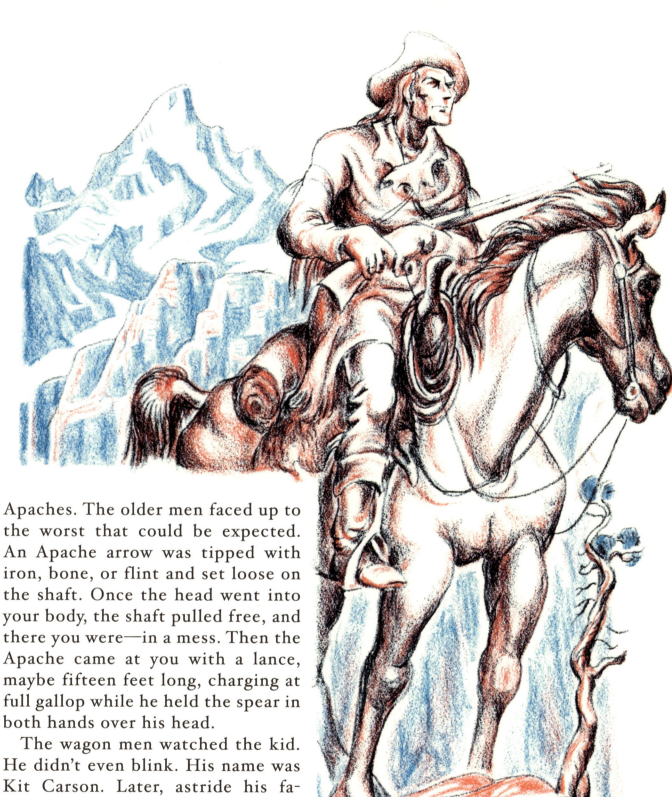

Apaches. The older men faced up to the worst that could be expected. An Apache arrow was tipped with iron, bone, or flint and set loose on the shaft. Once the head went into your body, the shaft pulled free, and there you were—in a mess. Then the Apache came at you with a lance, maybe fifteen feet long, charging at full gallop while he held the spear in both hands over his head.

The wagon men watched the kid. He didn't even blink. His name was Kit Carson. Later, astride his favorite horse, Apache, young Carson guided the military explorer, John C. Frémont, across the Rockies as the movement westward to California gathered momentum.

22 · Dame Schools and Blab Schools

American Education to the McGuffey Readers, 1836

"IN THE Presence of Others Sing not to yourself with humming Noises, nor Drum with your Fingers or Feet."

"Gaze not on the marks or blemishes of Others and ask not how they came."

"It's unbecoming to Stoop much to ones Meat."

In the Library of Congress, boys and girls may see the exercise book into which, at the age of fifteen, George Washington diligently copied these admonitions. Early education in America placed first emphasis on proper moral conduct. Since books were scarce, they were often self-made. Migrating from Indiana to Illinois—and crossing the Wabash at almost the spot where George Rogers Clark had routed the British from Vincennes—in 1830 a lanky, dark-eyed youth carried his homemade arithmetic. On the title page, in his own handwriting, would be preserved his earliest composition:

*Abraham Lincoln
his hand and pen
he will be good but
god knows When*

Among the colonies, Massachusetts took the lead in education, passing a law in 1647 that required every town of fifty homeowners to establish a primary school and every town of one hundred homes to provide, in addition, a secondary or grammar school. The following year, Dedham, Massachusetts, became the first community in America to tax property owners in order to support a local public school. Boston already claimed the first Latin, or high school, established in 1635, where, by the age of fifteen, students were supposed to be ready for college after intensive instruction in Latin and less vigorous preparation in composition, literature, mathematics, modern languages, philosophy, and science.

Types of early schools in America could be distinguished by the names attached to them. The private "dame school," presided over by a maiden or widowed lady, taught boys and girls reading and writing. Higher forms of learning usually must be gained elsewhere—almost all local ministers conducted schools—and so to sterner disciplinarians was left the teaching of "cyphering," algebra, geometry, geography, navigation, surveying, and astronomy.

The "prevocation school," such as the academy established in Philadelphia by Benjamin Franklin, was found only in the larger towns and concentrated on training pupils for "real life." Another standard form of education in early America was "apprenticeship training," illustrated by Franklin's service to his father as a candlemaker and to his brother James as a printer's devil. Before leaving Indiana, young Abe Lincoln experienced a short period of education in a "blab school," where the proof of a student's attention to study was the sounds he made and those who remained silent invariably drew a sharp snap of the switch from the suspicious, prowling schoolmaster.

Before the Revolution, nine colleges had been established in America. Harvard College was being organized as early as 1636, and to train clergymen the Congregationalists subsequently founded two other colleges—Yale (1701) and Dartmouth (1769). Other denominations started colleges with equal zeal. The Episcopalians sponsored both William and Mary (1693) and King's College, now Columbia (1754). The Presbyterians founded the College of New Jersey, now Princeton (1746); the Baptists established Rhode Island College, now Brown (1764); and the Dutch Reformed started Queen's College, now Rutgers (1766). Only one colonial college, the University of Pennsylvania, which grew out of Franklin's academy (1751), claimed nonsectarian origins. Dartmouth was unique in its purpose—to educate Indian youth.

Early schoolbooks were often "hornbooks"—that is, thin, flat pieces of wood, five inches by two, on which paper was placed and the day's lesson copied. A thin sheet of horn, covering the paper, protected it from wear. For over a century the first real "study book" American youngsters toiled over was the *New England Primer*—sometimes called the "Little Bible"—with its rhymed alphabet and numerous moral fables based on Biblical teachings. Noah Webster's "Blue-Backed Speller" and Nicholas Pike's *Arithmetic* were other early

textbooks that found son following father, and his son following him in dogged perusal of thumb-marked pages.

William Holmes McGuffey was a clergyman, lecturer, and college president who gave American children a long-enduring companion when in 1836 he published the first of the *McGuffey Eclectic Readers*. Over a hundred million copies of McGuffey's books, passing from one generation to the next of school-goers, introduced young Americans to "selections" from the classics and provided instruction in such fascinating subjects as "How a Fly Walks on the Ceiling."

Discipline was strict in early American schools, and the cone-shaped dunce cap, the cane, or the "whispering stick," (which was placed in the mouth of an over-talkative student, making him look like a horse with a bit), were no inventions of grandfather's imagination. With good reason America learned to "the tune of a hick'ry stick."

Still, the rough, free life of the frontier in America often required a firm hand to hold in line lads who had been in Indian fights or killed their first grizzly. As the settlements grew in the wilderness, so did the schools and, in time, the colleges. It took brain as well as brawn to beat back the forests and build fort into town, town into city.

23 · "Remember the Alamo!"

Texas Fights for Independence, 1836

EVER SINCE there had been people in the green valley, there had been trouble.

The first settlers were the Coahuiltecan Indians, who gave to the Alamo River winding through the valley a name that meant "drunken-old-man-going-home-at-night." The houses they built of brush and dried grass seemed to doze peacefully under the hot Texas sun. The name for the country was taken from another tribe, the Tejas, and the word was believed to mean "friends."

With deer to hunt, with the red fruit of the cactus, wild grapes and pecans to harvest in season, the Coahuiltecans were content to live in the fertile valley without hindering anyone. But other tribes moved restlessly along the river to disturb the peace. Out of the west, migrating from the Pecos in New Mexico to the coast of Texas, came the Lipan Apaches, the ferocious Tonkawas, and finally the Comanches, who had learned to ride the horses left behind by Coronado.

Who was the first white man to enter the valley where the Coahuiltecans lived is not known for certain. Perhaps he was Cabeza de Vaca, shipwrecked with a party of Spanish explorers near the present site of Galveston. In any case, a half century after the Pilgrims had landed at Plymouth, white men in Texas pursued their ancient pastime of sending soldiers with swords to stand beside ministers with Bibles as they claimed new territories for their king.

Don Domingo Terán de los Rios led the first party of Spanish settlers known to have reached the green valley. Don Domingo arrived on June 13, 1691, the feast day of the beloved Franciscan preacher, St. Anthony of Padua, and to honor the sacred memory of this great Italian holy man, Don Domingo renamed the village San Antonio.

More than twenty years passed before another group of settlers came. Among these Spaniards was an old man wearing the simple brown cloak of a Franciscan monk and who had walked the hot, weary miles across the Texas prairie in bare feet. Soon even the Indians loved this humble, white-haired missionary, whose long name was Father Fray Antonio de San Buenaventura Olivares.

The new expedition set to work to secure the settlement with prayers and guns. While the military leaders built a fort, on May 1, 1718, Father Olivares established the Alamo, which he named Mission San Antonio de Valero. The little mission was only a hut made of poles, brush, hides, and mud, yet it served its purpose and quickly prospered. The Indians listened to Father Olivares, ploughed his fields, and harvested the crops of melons, pumpkins, and chili.

In the little Mexican village of Dolores, an event occurred in 1810 that greatly influenced the future history of Texas. On a September day in the parish church, Father Miguel Hidalgo y Costilla rallied his people: "Will you make the effort to recover from the hated Spaniards the lands stolen from your forefathers three hundred years ago?" Father Hidalgo's call to freedom for Mexico echoed in distant places. Emissaries carried his message to the United States, and the old priest's words stirred a young American adventurer named Augustus Magee.

Magee resigned his lieutenancy in the United States Army to become the leader of the Republican Army of the North, a motley force of volunteers that included Americans, Mexicans, Indians, outlaws, and practically anyone living between Texas and Louisiana with a gun to shoot. Magee's men swept into Texas, defeated the loyalist troops of Spain, and hoisted above San Antonio the green flag of the Republican Army of the North. The Spaniards sent a second army into the valley, and that also was defeated. A third Spanish army marched forth with heartfelt vengeance and met the Texan rebels in battle south of the Medina River. The Spaniards fought behind prepared breastworks, with superior forces. Brutally, they hacked to pieces the army of the revolutionists.

San Antonio heard of the Spanish victory. Families who had helped Magee and his rebels tried to flee to safety into French-held Louisiana, and the Spanish soldiers slaughtered unmercifully any party they overtook. Meanwhile the Spanish general, Joaquín Arrendondo, arrived in San Antonio. A horrible day and night followed. Into one granary three hundred citizens were herded like sweltering swine, and another eight hundred were penned in the Alamo. Arrendondo shot whomever he pleased—men, women, children—burned houses, and turned a deaf ear to wails and screams. In this cruel work, the general found an able ally in a young lieutenant, Antonio López de Santa Anna. His would be a name heard on another day in the Alamo.

But the seed of liberty, planted by Father Hidalgo and carried into Texas by the freebooters of Augustus Magee, did not die under the crushing heels of General Arrendondo or the ruthless Santa Anna. A cold December day in 1820 saw a flinty-faced Connecticut Yankee ride into San Antonio on a borrowed gray horse. Moses Austin had traveled through ice and snow from Little Rock, pursuing a dream of new settlement. Austin died soon afterward from the cold and the exposure he had experienced, but the hope of colonizing Texas with Americans lived on in his son, Stephen. The Americans came, and as the year 1835 wore to a close, voices muttered over campfires: "Boys, rub your steels and pick your flints!"

In Mexico the fierce, strutting Santa Anna had become dictator of a country no longer bound to Spain, and desired to drive the American settlers out of Texas. Mexican patriots who opposed the tyrant-dictator joined with Americans; together they raised a new cry:

"Viva Texas!"

Santa Anna's brother-in-law, General Martin Perfecto de Cos, ruled the city of San Antonio, but even though his troops were reinforced, he could not hold the place against hard-riding soldiers of the new Texan Army. The defeat of Cos enraged Santa Anna. Perhaps he remembered the day when he and Arrendondo had humbled San Antonio. Now he was coming back—with an army of many thousands.

The bleak month of February, 1836, settled over the Alamo. Still another month must pass before the Republic of Texas could convene its delegates to declare independence. In a yet-unborn republic there was scant hope of reinforcements reaching San Antonio. The small garrison of Texans still could flee, but to do so would give Santa Anna's army a chance to strike at some equally unprepared spot.

The defenders of San Antonio, 183 strong under William Barret Travis, tightened their belts, cleaned their guns, and waited calmly for Santa Anna's thousands. With Travis stood the great Tennessee Indian-fighter, bear killer and pioneer patriot, David Crockett, who once had said: "If there is anything in the world particularly worth living for, it is freedom." Now Travis's comrades-in-arms—men like tough, stubborn James Butler Bonham and the legendary Jim Bowie, who had invented his own knife for peeling bearskins—were ready to prove that freedom also was worth dying for.

Crockett reached San Antonio on the 19th of February. "We have a prospect of soon getting our bellies full of fighting, and that is victuals and drink to a true patriot any day,"

wrote Crockett, no more disturbed than if flipping a flea out of his ear. Three days later Santa Anna and his army were reported within two leagues of the city, and, these reports said further, the Mexican was trying to stir up the Indians to join his assault. Texans laughed because the Comanche tribe loathed the Mexican people! Cheerily, Crockett scribbled into his diary that evening: "We are up and doing and as lively as Dutch cheese in the dog days."

Next morning Santa Anna's troops were sighted. Travis held a council of war and came to a quick decision. Everyone in San Antonio—soldiers, women, children—must hole up in the Alamo. The single hut with which Father Olivares's mission had begun now had grown into a formidable bastion. A stone wall enclosed a two-story building where the monks had lived, and rows of adobe and stone houses had been provided as quarters for converted Indians. Arcaded cloisters, a deep well, a granary for storing corn and beans also stood behind the wall of the Alamo.

The men Travis led into this citadel carried a large national flag with thirteen stripes of red and white and a big five-pointed star on a blue background that had a letter between each point spelling the proud word: TEXAS. In the distance the blood-red flag of the enemy flapped menacingly. Santa Anna dispatched

an emissary with the demand that the fort surrender unconditionally. Travis's answer was a cannon ball! Then Travis addressed a letter "To the People of Texas and all Americans in the world." "*I shall never surrender or retreat,*" Travis wrote. "I am determined to sustain myself as long as possible and die like a soldier who never forgets what is due to his own honor and that of his country. VICTORY OR DEATH."

The thirteen-day siege of the Alamo began. Poor Jim Bowie, desperately ill, crawled from his bed every day to cheer his comrades. The Mexicans rolled cannon within range and bombs burst over the fort. "They ain't doing any mischief," snorted Davy Crockett. Next Santa Anna tried to cut off the water supply. Crockett loved nothing better than "Betsey," his rifle, but Crockett swore that he'd give up Betsey and never pull a trigger again for one fair crack at that Mexican rascal—even at a distance of a hundred yards!

Then it was March. Within the Alamo provisions ran desperately low. Daily Santa Anna received more recruits, preparing for the final assault. But the Texan spirit would not break. In round figures, the defenders of the Lone Star reckoned they had killed three hundred Mexicans, but more cheering news was the discovery in a deserted house of eighty bushels of corn. If faith ever wavered, it was strengthened anew on March 2 when, in the little town of Washington on the Brazos River, the independence of Texas was declared!

For a time hope was held that reinforcements might come to the Alamo from the neighboring towns of Goliad or Refugio, but by March 3 this hope vanished. Travis rallied his boys around him. Even surrounded by Santa Anna's men and cannons, the square jaw of Travis jutted belligerently. They would fight to the last gasp. Three cheers rolled across the mission yard. Ailing Jim Bowie lent his voice to the common resolution: VICTORY OR DEATH.

The defenders of the Alamo knew that they already had chosen death. On March 4, Crockett wrote, shells from the Mexican guns fell like hail. Savagely, Santa Anna tightened his encirclement of the gallant bastion. From behind the blood-red flag, the encroaching cannon rocked and roared. The last entry in David Crockett's diary was dated March 5. Eloquently, it told the true story of the Alamo:

"Pop, pop, pop! Bom, bom, bom! throughout the day. No time for memorandums now. Go ahead! Liberty and independence forever!"

Santa Anna's cruel will was exerted; all the defenders of the Alamo lay in the dust. But time had been gained, and in two-fisted Sam Houston soon emerged a commander who fired the Texan troops with renewed vigor. Houston retreated before the

Mexicans until he reached the banks of the San Jacinto River. There, on April 21, he turned suddenly. From the throats of his soldiers sprang a cry that forever would mean a Texan had come to the limit of retreating:

"Remember the Alamo!"

On the banks of the San Jacinto, riding point-blank into enemy gun-

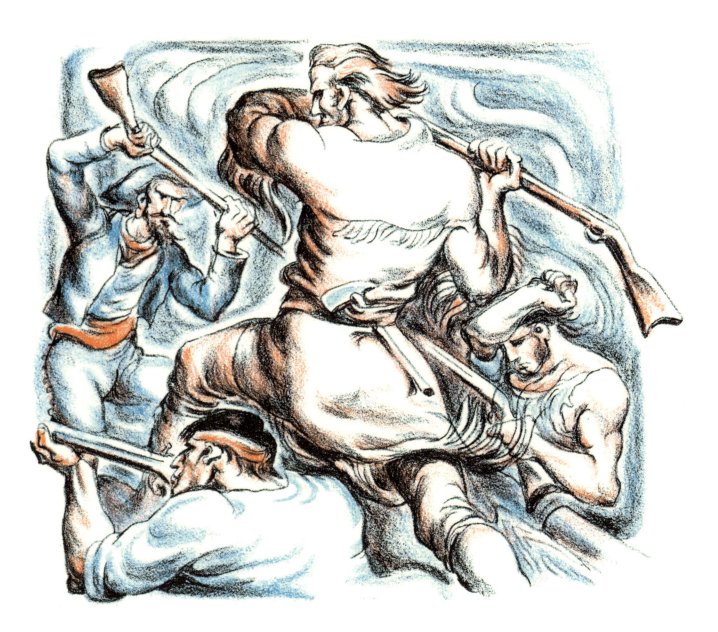

fire, Sam Houston's boys shouted their defiance and crushed Santa Anna's army. Autumn, mild and sweet, stole over Texas and into the green valley where the Alamo now stood enshrined. Peace and independence were the words the wind whispered. Sam Houston put aside his gun and took up the duties of President of the new Republic of Texas.

In 1845 Texas became our twenty-eighth state, and the Stars and Stripes flew over the domain that already had lived under the banners of Spain, France, Mexico, and the Texas Republic. In time a sixth flag—that of the Southern Confederacy—would wave over Texan soil. A river, over which large shipments of cotton could be inexpensively transported, would greatly influence that story.

24 · Mark Twain's Mississippi

The Boom Years of Steamboating, 1811-1873

THE RIVER was so full of sly tricks and fickle-headed fancies that the white man had a hard time learning what its secret was. Marquette and Joliet disproved two earlier theories. The Mississippi did not flow to the Atlantic, nor did it flow to the Gulf of California, providing a short route to China. In 1681 LaSalle solved the riddle—the Mississippi emptied into the Gulf of Mexico. The ability of the old river to keep everyone guessing—explorers, pilots, folk who thought they had lived on its banks only to discover later that channels had shifted and where they had lived there wasn't a river any more—was one of the features that made Mark Twain love the Mississippi.

"Nearly the whole of that one thousand three hundred miles of old Mississippi River which LaSalle floated down in his canoes," Mark said, as though it was the biggest joke in America, "is good solid ground now."

Each year the Mississippi emptied 406 million tons of mud into the Gulf of Mexico, inspiring one wit to call the river "The Great Sewer." Mark was a booster for even this habit of the Mississippi. In one of his stories a keelboatman named the Child of Calamity swore that Mississippi mud was nutritious. Said the Child of Calamity:

"You look at the graveyards; that tells the tale. Trees won't grow worth shucks in a Cincinnati graveyard, but in a St. Louis graveyard they grow upwards of eight hundred foot high. It's all on account of the water the people drunk before they laid up. A Cincinnati corpse don't richen a soil any."

The heyday of keelboatmen had waned when Mark Twain, whose real name was Samuel Langhorne Clemens, lived on the Mississippi in sleepy Hannibal, Missouri. By then the steamboat had taken over most of the river traffic, for speed was an American trait, and everyone had forgotten how they had laughed at the first idea of thinking a boat could navigate this tricky old river with hissing engines and fancy paddlewheels.

In 1807 Robert Fulton had sailed his steamboat on the Hudson River, and, impressed by this remarkable achievement, Governor Claiborne persuaded the legislature of the Louisiana Territory to authorize building a steamboat that could navigate the lower Mississippi. Robert Fulton and his young assistant, Nicholas Roosevelt, hustled to Pittsburgh to build the boat.

Nicholas Roosevelt sent men into the forests to cut timbers for the ribs and knees and joints, and was properly finicky about every board that went into a craft designed to bring steamboating to western waters. He didn't like the idea of white pine for the planking, the only lumber he could obtain without aggravating delays. Boatbuilders he could hire in Pittsburgh, but materials for machinery, and mechanics to knock it together, had to be brought from New York. After fretful weeks of labor the *New Orleans* was ready to launch. Her approximate cost had been $38,000.

Excitement bordering on scandalized alarm spread through Pittsburgh and up the valley of the Monongahela when it was learned that Mrs. Roosevelt intended to accompany her husband on the maiden voyage. No one ever had heard of such folly. Mrs. Roosevelt smiled and stood on the deck when, on a bright September day in 1811, almost everyone in Pittsburgh came down to the river to see the man and woman exploded into eternity. Instead, the *New Orleans* settled nicely in the water and, with a head of steam, clipped through the water

at a speed of eight to ten miles an hour. To the people along the banks of the Monongahela, success was even more astonishing than disaster. Cheer after cheer shook the air.

The big trial, however, came after passing Cincinnati, and the Child of Calamity would have blamed every bit of the trouble on coming near a city that had only clear drinking water! In late November, the *New Orleans* reached a point in the river where the rise of a falls had stopped with only five inches of draught at its shallowest part, and yet to get into the Indiana channel Nicholas Roosevelt had to risk navigating $38,000 worth of boat at this spot.

The steam boiler began to throb, the safety valve whistled, the paddle-wheels churned, and the big Newfoundland dog who had come along for the voyage crouched at Mrs. Roosevelt's feet as though afraid to look over his paws. In the water, black ledges of rock

glistened. The eddies swirled into white foam, then came up onto the deck in angry splashes.

No one spoke. The pilots motioned with their hands, indicating the direction that was needed. Then the tension eased. The *New Orleans* was through the perilous passage!

So steamboating came to the Mississippi, and when in 1857 Mark Twain, then about twenty-two, became an apprenticed pilot, the boom years of steamboating dominated life along the old river. How well Mark knew what a dead town Hannibal could be until ten minutes before a steamboat touched her dock, and how, ten minutes after the boat had departed, the town returned to its snooze. Even if he never did a bad thing in his life, Mark knew, God still wouldn't let him become a pirate, so the next best thing was to be a captain or pilot who set hearts bounding as town after town heard the magic cry:

"S-t-e-a-m-boat a-comin'!"

When soundings were taken of river depths, for two fathoms of water the boatman sang out, "Mark twain!" Listening, Sam Clemens acquired his pen name.

Mark's first experience as a cub pilot was aboard the steamer *Paul Jones*, out of New Orleans, and his instructor was the redoubtable Horace Bixby. Every point, every rock, every shallow along hundreds of miles of river, Bixby knew. He sang out each landmark once—"This is Nine-Mile Point" or "The slack water ends here abreast this bunch of China trees; now we cross over"—and expected Mark to remember this river lore forever. The youth didn't. Moreover, awakened in the night to take his second watch, he fell into a bad mood. So did Bixby—but let Mark tell the story his own way:

"It was a rather dingy night, although a fair number of stars were out. The big mate was at the wheel, and he had the old tub pointed at a star and was holding her straight up the middle of the river. The shores on either hand were not more than half a mile apart, but they seemed wonderfully far away and ever so vague and indistinct. The mate said:

'We've got to land at Jones's plantation, sir.'

"The vengeful spirit in me exulted. I said to myself, 'I wish you joy of your job, Mr. Bixby; you'll have a good time finding Mr. Jones's plantation such a night as this; and I hope you never *will* find it as long as you live.'

"Mr. Bixby said to the mate:

'Upper end of the plantation, or the lower?'

"'Upper.'

"'I can't do it. The stumps there are out of the water at this stage.

It's no great distance to the lower, and you'll have to get along with that."

" 'All right, sir. If Jones don't like it, he'll have to lump it, I reckon.'

". . . All I desired to ask Mr. Bixby was the simple question whether he was dumb enough to really imagine he was going to find that plantation on a night when all plantations were exactly alike and all the same color. . . . The stars were all gone now, and the night was as black as ink. I could hear the wheels churn along the bank, but I was not entirely certain that I could see the shore. The voice of the invisible watchman called up from the hurricane-deck:

"'What's this, sir?'

"'Jones's plantation.'

"I said to myself, 'I wish I might venture to offer a small bet that it isn't.' But I did not chirp. I only waited to see. Mr. Bixby handled the engine-bells, and in due time the boat's nose came to the land, a torch glowed from the forecastle, a man skipped ashore, a black man's voice on the bank said: 'Gimme de k'yarpet-bag, Mass' Jones,' and the next moment we were standing up the river again, all serene."

From such experiences Mark soon learned that there was more to piloting on the old Mississippi than met the eye. First was the necessity of a memory. "To know the Old and New Testaments by heart," he said, "and be able to recite them glibly, forward or backward, or begin at random anywhere in the book and recite both ways and never trip or make a mistake, is no extravagant mass of knowledge, and no marvelous facility, compared to a pilot's massed knowledge of the Mississippi and his marvelous facility in the handling of it."

Next, a pilot needed good, quick judgment, which was a matter of brains, and without "a good stock of that article" no one had a right in a pilothouse. Finally, a pilot must have courage, for the whole river was bristling with new dangers and new emergencies every moment of every trip.

Speeds of the runs between cities on the Mississippi created a national sport followed as avidly as today's major-league baseball standings, and the authority for records was Commodore Rollingpin's Almanac. In 1814 the *Orleans* had taken 6 days, 6 hours, and 40 minutes to make the 268-mile run between New Orleans and Natchez, Mississippi; in 1870 the *R. E. Lee* was making the same run in 17 hours and 11 minutes. From New Orleans to Cairo, Illinois, a distance of 1,024 miles, the run of the *J. M. White* in 1844 had taken 3 days, 6 hours, and 44 minutes; in 1870 the *R. E. Lee* cut the time to 3 days and 1 hour.

The *J. M. White* was deservedly renowned, for in 1844 she made the 1,218-mile run from New Orleans to St. Louis in 3 days, 23 hours, and 9 minutes. That record stood until 1870 when the *R. E. Lee* and the *Natchez* raced the same distance. The *R. E. Lee*, reaching St. Louis in 3 days, 18 hours, and 14 minutes, bested the run of the *Natchez* by 6 hours and 36 minutes. In 1868 the *Hawkeye State* made the 800-mile run from St. Louis to St. Paul, Minnesota, in 2 days and 20 hours, a record that stood. The *A. L. Shotwell* was another steamer of national prominence, although Mark Twain viewed dubiously the claim that "When the *Eclipse* and the *A. L. Shotwell* ran their famous race many years ago, it was said that pains were taken to scrape the paint gilding off the fanciful device which hung between the *Eclipse's* chimneys, and that for that one trip the captain left off his kid gloves and had his head shaved."

But even when the captains didn't shave their heads, a race between steamers of rival packet companies woke up the whole river. Boys waited eagerly at the landings for the great boats to appear, even though they knew that the stopover would only last the minute or two necessary to throw on more cord wood. Then off went the racers with tall columns of black smoke belching from their stacks, guns booming farewell, bands playing "Hail Columbia," and the crowds along the shore shouting themselves hoarse.

The Civil War cut off Mississippi steamboating in its prime, and just when fine boats like the *Natchez* and the *R. E. Lee* were reviving the old glory, along came the depression of 1873 to ruin everything. Doubtless the Child of Calamity blamed that sad tragedy on Cincinnati drinking water, too.

25 · By the North Star

The Underground Railroad, 1804-1860

ALONG THE MISSISSIPPI that Mark Twain loved, a flatboat in 1828 carried the young Abe Lincoln to New Orleans. William Herndon, who worked with Lincoln in his Springfield law office, recalled Lincoln's memories of that first trip to the deep South.

"One morning in their rambles of the city the trio passed a slave auction. A vigorous and comely mulatto girl was being sold. She underwent a thorough examination at the hands of the bidders; they pinched her flesh and made her trot up and down the room like a horse, to show how she moved, and in order, as the auctioneer said, the "bidders might satisfy themselves" whether the article they were offering to buy was sound or not. The whole thing was so revolting that Lincoln moved away from the scene with a deep feeling of "unconquerable hate." Bidding his companions follow him he said, "By God, boys, let's get away from this. If ever I get a chance to hit that thing [meaning slavery], I'll hit it hard."

Southern slave owners argued that slavery was not an American invention and therefore permissible because of its historical presence. In dim ages past, man had decided to put captured enemies to work instead of killing them; thus slavery had marked a stumbling step forward in civilization. The laws of Moses revealed that slaves existed among ancient Hebrews; the ancient Greeks purchased slaves from pirates; and at the height of Roman power there had been three slaves for every free man. The Portuguese discovered, sometime during the 15th century, the profit in selling captured African people, and imitators quickly appeared. A Dutch frigate, landing twenty African people at Jamestown in 1619, began on our own mainland the importation of human beings for profit.

However, around 1671, the Quakers in England developed an extreme opposition to slavery. Among nations, Denmark in 1792 was the first to stop its ships from carrying slaves (later that same year England outlawed the slave trade), and in 1808 the United States prohibited further importation of slaves. Slowly, man began to grope another step forward in his civilization, and recognize the extreme injustice in enslaving his fellow man. But history teaches nothing if not the fact that man progresses at an uneven pace and his gains are never constant around the world.

So would the force of history react on slavery. In 1833, slavery was abolished in all British colonies. American Quakers were jubilant. Now they were even more determined to free the slaves in America even if they must break the laws by which slavery was protected. Through the Underground Railroad, American Quakers had been brave liberators for years.

Imagine yourself in 1840 an operator for the Underground Railroad. You have come South by a circuitous

route, so that you will not be recognized from a previous journey to meet a band of slaves in the swamp behind a plantation. Men, women, and children, the young and the aged, the well-dressed and the ragged, crowd around you. A mother wants to rejoin her husband and son in Canada, who have already escaped; an older fellow, with ugly marks of a lashing on his back, pleads for a little peace before he dies; you must respect the spirit of a people who will run any risk to be free.

Your own risk is great, for you will be pursued, and, if caught, imprisoned, and perhaps beaten, hung, or shot. But you have learned from the experiences of other operators on the Underground Railroad, a great many tricks of slave-running. The untiring runner, Harriet Tubman, has taught you that it is best to start the journey north on a Saturday night, for the owner cannot advertise the escape of his slaves until the following Monday. Harriet also has taught you her grim rule of slave-running—if a slave loses heart and turns back, it is better to kill him than run the chance of betraying the others.

How to get the slaves north is a decision you must reach quickly. Again, experience is helpful, for many people have succeeded. The black man, Henry Box Brown, was shipped from Richmond to Philadelphia in a box, and carried every inch of the way by an unsuspecting Adams Express Company. You have learned, too, from the ingenuity of the Virginia slaveholder turned slave-runner, John Fairfield, who once helped twenty-eight slaves escape by organizing them into a funeral procession. But these are spectacular methods only

to be used in case of emergency; other ruses can be employed that have worked a hundred times under "normal" conditions.

Above everything, you must inspire confidence in the people who are going with you that they *can* escape and they will! They must understand that the Underground Railroad was first "incorporated" in 1804 and that as many as 3,000 persons may be engaged in its operation. They must know that at the established "stations" along the route others will be waiting with food, clothing, and money, with rowboats, horses, and carriages that have specially constructed secret compartments, and, if necessary, with white babies to carry so that fugitives may represent themselves as traveling servants.

Your point of starting decides which course on the Underground you must travel. One route will take you from Missouri northeast across Illinois, a second from Kentucky and Virginia across Ohio and western Pennsylvania, and a third from Maryland and Virginia across eastern Pennsylvania. You know that the Ohio "line" bears the heaviest traffic, and that under pressure any slave can be run from a border state to Canada in forty-eight hours.

You gather the band of slaves around you for final instructions. If bloodhounds pursue, onion rubbed on the body will throw off the scent. If circumstances force the band apart, remember to travel at night—by the North Star. If the sky is overcast, feel for the moss on the trunks of the trees and you will be going north. Move fast, keep under cover, say nothing unless you are sure you address a friend.

So the run begins. When the swamp ends, you pause, listening for the dogs. You look toward the North Star, then calculate the best road into the mountains, for generally mountain people run small farms that do not need slaves. You hurry those who fall behind, as every moment of darkness must count. Along the road, across fields, through forests, in rain or snow or full moonlight, you press on. But often you stop. You listen. A single dog's bark can spell disaster until you can find water to disguise your trail. With heavy heart, you realize how close the morning is. Where is the river? In the darkness a voice calls your name.

"Yes," you say.

"How many did you bring?"

"Ten."

"The boats are at the first cove. Tom and Sam will row. The loft of Sam's barn is cleared for them."

You find the cove and the boats. The oars dip softly. You breathe easier. Making the first station is always the most dangerous. Tomorrow night you will be in Ohio. There will be nothing to the run then!

How many slaves escaped by the Underground Railroad? Figures cannot be accurate because of the nature of the enterprise, but Governor Quitman of Mississippi estimated that between 1810 and 1850 at least 100,000 slaves, valued at more than thirty million dollars, were frequented out of the South. The "president" of the Underground was the Indiana Quaker, Levi Coffin, who alone was credited with helping 3,000 slaves escape. Valiant Harriet Tubman made nineteen trips on the Underground and led more than 300 slaves to freedom; John Mason, a fugitive slave from Kentucky, brought out 265; and over the Ohio route more than 40,000 slaves traveled.

As America approached the mid-century, many of the forces tearing at the nation were hidden. Texas gained its freedom and provided new territory into which slavery could spread, enraging those in favor of containing or abolishing slavery. The Louisiana Purchase, the Lewis and Clark expedition, the trails blazed by the fur trappers, opened a new empire, but where would the line be drawn between a nation half free, half enslaved? The Quakers, who did not believe in war, continued working diligently for the Underground Railroad. The Underground Railroad as well as the efforts of the Northern abolitionists like Garrison, Weld, and Harriet Beecher Stowe, helped to provide the spark that started the Civil War. Meanwhile, however, other chapters in American history were being lived. One of special significance belonged to New England.

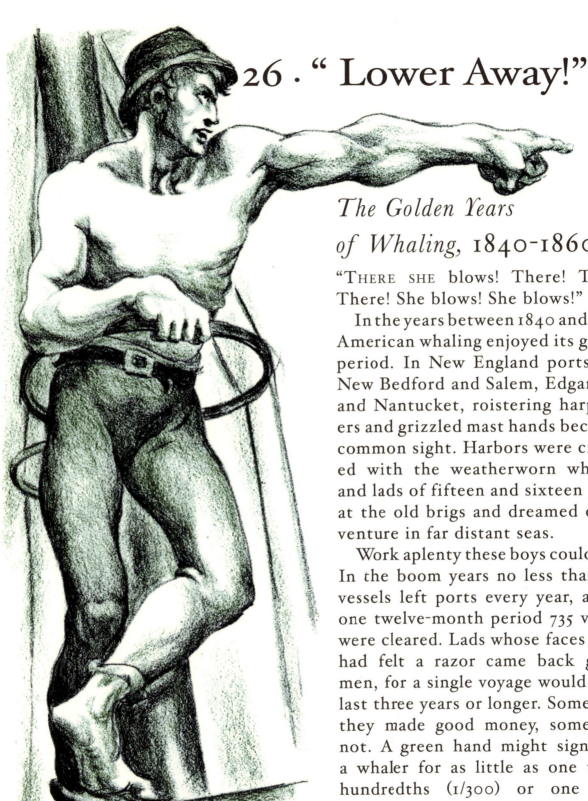

26 · "Lower Away!"

The Golden Years of Whaling, 1840-1860

"THERE SHE blows! There! There! There! She blows! She blows!"

In the years between 1840 and 1860, American whaling enjoyed its golden period. In New England ports, like New Bedford and Salem, Edgartown and Nantucket, roistering harpooners and grizzled mast hands became a common sight. Harbors were crowded with the weatherworn whalers, and lads of fifteen and sixteen gazed at the old brigs and dreamed of adventure in far distant seas.

Work aplenty these boys could find. In the boom years no less than 500 vessels left ports every year, and in one twelve-month period 735 vessels were cleared. Lads whose faces never had felt a razor came back grown men, for a single voyage would often last three years or longer. Sometimes they made good money, sometimes not. A green hand might sign onto a whaler for as little as one three-hundredths (1/300) or one four-hundredths (1/400) of the net profit earned from the sperm oil, whale oil, and whalebone brought home.

Principally, two types of whales

[165]

were hunted. The bowhead or Greenland right whale—so named because it was the "right" whale to find—was sought because of the horny plates in place of teeth that filled its mouth. Often a right whale, full grown to a length of sixty feet with one third of his body consisting of an enormous head, would yield two hundred of these elastic plates eagerly bought by manufacturers of corsets, collars, and hoop skirts.

Even more sought was the sperm whale, then found in the seas of temperate and tropical climates. In summer this whale usually migrated north, to the waters around Iceland and the Bering Strait, and about October moved south of the Equator. The sperm whale's length could be sixty or sixty-five feet, his weight seventy tons. The long, narrow lower jaw, more than one third the length of his body, contained from twenty to thirty fanglike teeth sometimes as thick as a man's wrist. Such a whale easily could swallow a man, although the strong digestive juices of the whale's stomach would soon end life for the unhappy fellow.

The sperm whale was full of tricks. When attacked, his powerful jaws could crush a whaleboat. Or to escape his pursuers he could dive to a depth of three fifths of a mile. Mother sperm whales, guarding their babies, grew especially pugnacious, and seasoned whalers told stories of frightened mother whales that turned on a three-masted ship and staved in its sides!

Yet the dangers of hunting sperm whales could not daunt Yankee owners from risking their ships, or young boys and grizzled harpooners from risking their necks, at the thought of the profits awaiting them. A great reservoir in the sperm whale's head, really part of its nose, contained an oil from which candles were made. Also in the intestines of sperm whales was found a grayish, musky-smelling substance called ambergris that was used as a base in making perfumes. A single ounce of ambergris brought a tidy sum, and one older sperm whale might yield as much as five hundred pounds. In addition, oil obtained from boiling the blubber of the whale had a steady market value and many uses.

Not only boys who grew up along the coast but also boys from farm and city dreamed of going down to the sea in stout-rigged whalers. One city boy was Herman Melville, who at seventeen appeared one day in New Bedford to seek his fortune as a seaman. Young Melville later found life aboard the *Acushnet* hard and cruel and beyond the endurance of his high-hearted spirit. In the Marquesas Islands, in the South Pacific, Melville deserted ship and took his chance among cannibals who often cooked and ate their

enemies. After four months, he escaped aboard an Australian whaler, but again life on ship seemed unbearable and he deserted.

In time Melville wrote *Moby Dick*, a story of the golden years of American whaling. The boy or girl who once voyages with Melville aboard his fictitious whaler, the *Pequod*, never forgets the hard, driving life that made famous the seamen of New England. Melville is Ishmael, the lad who wanted so much to "sail about a little and see the watery part of the world." There must have been many Ishmaels in the 1840s and 1850s, and perhaps there were harpooners like Queequeg, a cannibal turned whaler whose retreating forehead made Ishmael think of George Washington. Likely there were many mates like Stubb, from Cape Cod, a man of strong, silent, honest will; and like Flask, from Tisbury on Martha's Vineyard, who talked with reckless bravado except in the presence of the captain, when no one could have been more acquiescent.

But there could have been only one Captain Ahab, that strange man maddened by a hatred for Moby Dick, the white sperm whale that had bitten off his leg. Honest Stubb sensed first how wicked and ill-boding it was for anyone to seek vengeance as Captain Ahab did, so that he would search for years across all oceans to kill the white whale that had maimed him. Once, seeing Captain

Ahab upon his artificial leg made of whalebone, Ishmael thought: "On life and death this old man walked!"

Never would Ishmael forget that first time when, from high in the rigging of the *Pequod*, he heard the cry:

"There she blows . . ."

"Where-away?"

"On the lee-beam, about two miles off! A school of them!"

A sperm whale, blowing his spout with regularity, could never be mistaken. The *Pequod* was kept from the wind, so that the whales would not be alarmed and, with a mighty dive, make off in the opposite direction. Around Ishmael played the fast drama of whaling:

"The sailors at the fore and mizzen had come down; the line tubs were fixed in their places; the cranes were thrust out; the main yard was backed, and the three boats swung over the sea like three samphire baskets over high cliffs."

Across the deck came Captain Ahab's order:

"Lower away, then, d'ye hear? Lower away there, I say."

The thunder of the captain's voice made Ishmael leap, goatlike, into the boats below. The steady Stubb broke into a chant:

"Hurrah for the gold cup of sperm oil, my heroes! Three cheers, men—all hearts alive! Easy, easy; don't be in a hurry—don't be in a hurry! Why don't you snap your oars, you rascals? Bite something, you dogs! So, so, so, then—softly, softly! That's it—that's it! Long and strong."

Ishmael rowed with the others after the spouts of the sperm whales. Sometimes the vast swells of the sea would lift the boats on knifelike edges, then headlong, sledlike, the boats rushed down the opposite sides. Sometimes amid the curling and hissing of the waves came "an enormous wallowing sound as of fifty elephants stirring in their litter." Through the boat rose a loud shout: "Stand up!" Queequeg, harpoon in hand, sprang to his feet.

Again the boat tossed, the sail quivered. Then came the exultant cry: "That's his hump. *There, there*, give it to him."

Young Ishmael waited breathlessly:

"A short rushing sound leaped out of the boat; it was the darted iron from Queequeg. Then all in one welded commotion came an invisible push from astern, while forward the boat seemed striking on a ledge; the sail collapsed and exploded; a gush of scalding vapor shot up near by; something rolled and tumbled like an earthquake beneath us. The whole crew were half suffocated as they were tossed helter-skelter into the white curdling cream of the squall. Squall, whale, and harpoon had all blended together; and the whale, merely grazed by the iron, had escaped."

Ishmael helped right the whale-

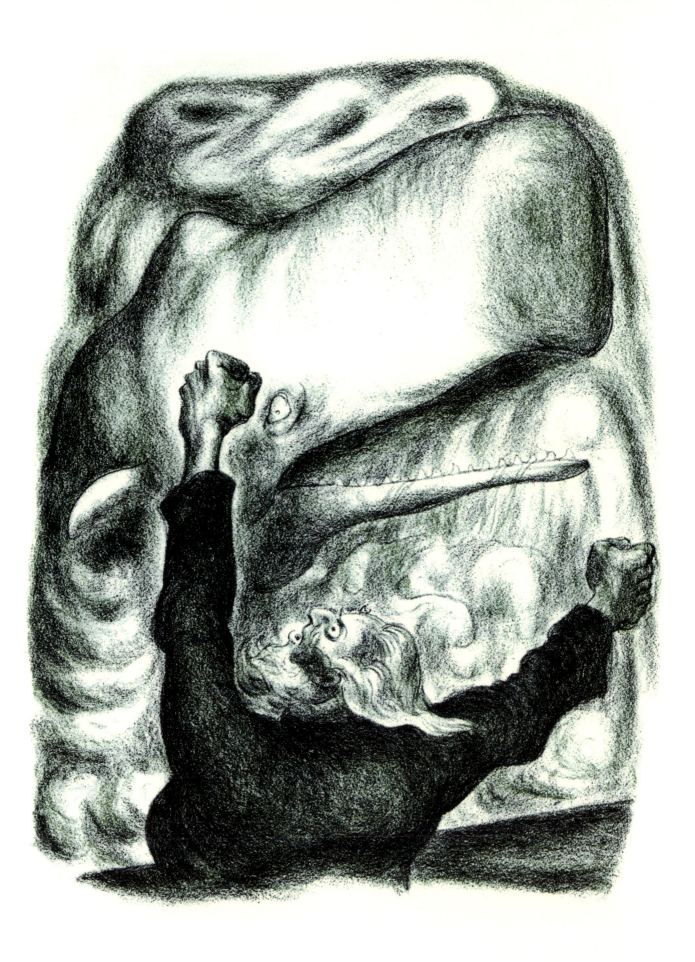

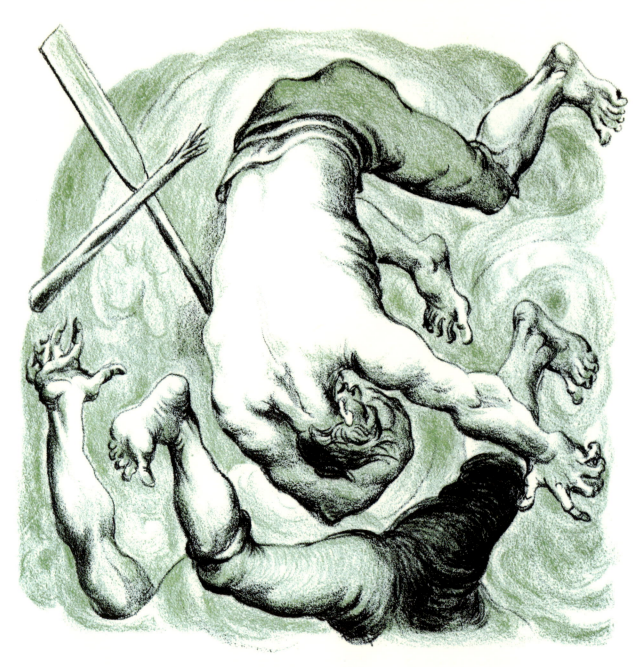

boat, retrieve the oars, and tumble back over the gunwale. Shivering cold, he returned to the *Pequod*. He knew now that whaling was no lark.

But American whaling prospered because the darted iron of a Queequeg more often struck its mark; the long line played out as the captured whale dove and twisted and raced and fought for freedom until on the sea appeared the gush of thick blood that meant death to the gallant adversary. Then, hauled to the main ship, the whale was lifted aboard by windlass. To cut off the great head sometimes took an hour and a half. When the blubber was peeled off the tail, the disjointed carcass was rolled into the sea to feed the sharks. A hole the size

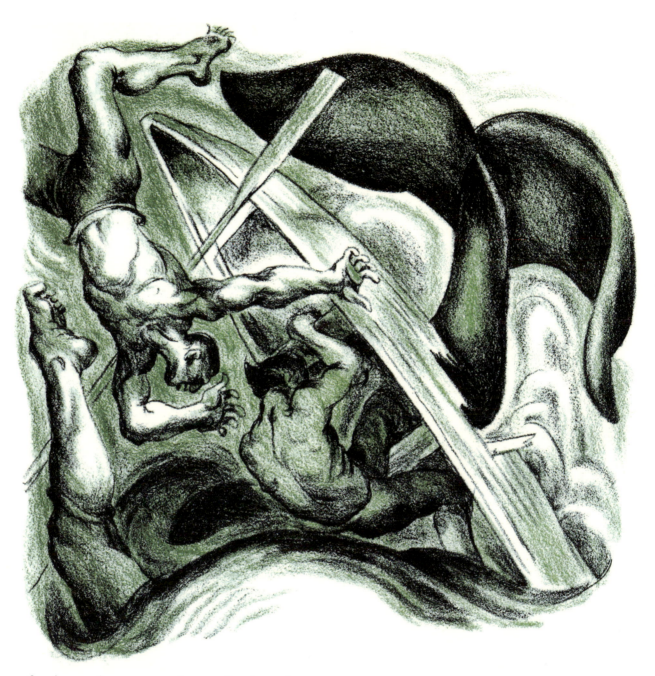

of a barrel was cut into the head to ladle out the semifluid that would be made into spermaceti candles. From fifteen to twenty barrels could be drawn from a large sperm whale.

Greediness ended the golden per-iod of American whaling. Fewer and fewer became the schools of sperm whales in the grounds where once they had been hunted so profitably. Whaling boats were sold, often for traffic off the coast of Africa where many years later, buried in the sands, could be found derelicts bearing such typically American names as *Yankee Trader*, *Maid of Salem*, and *Susan Adams*. Yet the quest for quick fortune had not ended in America. Soon the magic word would be "California!"

27 · Christmas at Donner Lake

The Settlement of California, 1846

"Push on over the mountain," the Indian guide advised. "It means death if more snow comes."

A moan spread through the party of California-bound settlers. Snow, mile after mile of dreary snow that had been falling since October, almost a month before it had been expected... snow choking the mountain roads so that the wagons couldn't be dragged through and the pack-laden oxen stumbled and fell; snow in the passes, waist-deep, where men and women clutched their children in their arms, trying to warm chilled flesh against chilled flesh. Always, the snow!

"It is only three miles to the summit," the Indian guide said. His grave, seamed face looked like the face of the Prophet Amos in the Bible.

Again, from the party of settlers, rose a sound of despair. Around them, under leaden skies, towered the menacing Sierras. Weak voices spoke:

"I can't go on."

Over the protest of the guide, it was decided to pitch camp. That night the dreaded snow fell. . . .

The year, 1846, was the year after explorers like John C. Frémont conquered California for the United States. Of the approximately five

hundred Americans who set out in 1846 to find new lives on the Pacific coast, none would tell a more tragic story than the group who failed to follow the Indian guide to the summit of the mountain. Originally, these settlers had started from Springfield, Illinois, under the leadership of George and Jacob Donner and James F. Reed; of the eighty-seven who left the quiet, rolling prairies, only forty-seven ever reached California alive.

The Reed girl, Virginia, blinked her eyes next morning against the terrible snow. They were trapped! She would never forget the behavior of the Indian guide when last night the first feathery flakes had hissed around the campfire. Wrapped in his blanket, he had gone to stand alone under a tree. He had stood there all night. Then, the nightmarish memory of an exhausted but disturbed slumbering through the darkness returned to Virginia. A shawl had been her only covering, and every few moments Mrs. Reed had bent over her, shaking the shawl so that the girl would not be buried alive.

'There's nothing to do but make the best of the devil's luck,' said Stanton, one of the leaders of the party.

But Stanton could not hide his heavy heart from Virginia, nor could she shield her misery from him. Somehow, on the shore of Donner Lake (then called Truckee Lake), by working together and trying to put on bright faces, a camp of three double cabins was built. The Reed half of the party were luckier than the Donner half, who had been caught in Alder Creek Valley below the lake, and who could only throw together brush sheds covered with pine boughs.

What cold, hard, busy days they were as the Breen Cabin, the Murphy Cabin and the Reed-Graves Cabin rose on the shore of Donner Lake! The men killed all the cattle and carefully packed the meat in the snow. The Indian guides lived in the same cabin with Virginia, the other Reeds, and the Graves family. It was a struggle for the girl to fight her way between cabins to visit her neighbors. When the storms struck, each group would be shut in the same dwelling for nine or ten days.

No one was particularly surprised when Baylis Williams died, for he had been sickly when the party started. But this first death at Donner Lake seemed a grim symbol. Before spring, starvation might kill all of them!

"We've got to get over the mountains somehow," Stanton declared. "We've got to have relief."

How many groups started for the California settlements and were hurled back by the howling storms, Virginia was never certain. Both winds and snows proved pitiless. But Stanton could be a stubborn man, and one day, mounted on snowshoes, he started out with a party of ten men and five women to cross the frozen Sierras. The sixth day out the gallant Stanton perished, one of the eight who would die. History has named his party the Forlorn Hope.

Meanwhile at Donner Lake, the long, freezing days passed. Hunger became the companion who slept and walked with everyone. The men crawled out after wood, scarcely having strength left to move.

One day when Virginia awoke, sluggish and shivering, her mother asked, "Do you know what day this is, Virginia?"

The girl shook her head.

"It's Christmas!" Mrs. Reed said.

Then that brave pioneer woman disclosed her surprise—the few dried apples she had saved, the beans, the bit of tripe, the small piece of bacon for a feast on this day that honored the birth of the blessed Jesus!

The cabin exploded with glee. Like long silent church bells that had awakened, laughter pealed from the throats of the children. No meal was ever cooked more carefully, or with more round eyes anxiously watching every bubble!

"Your Christmas dinner," Mrs. Reed cried at last.

Virginia crowded with the others around the crude table.

"Children," Mrs. Reed told them calmly, "eat slowly, for this one day you can have all you wish!"

Virginia savored each bite. Never would she lose the real meaning of Christmas now.

But the days that followed Christmas relapsed into the old, dreary pattern—each day growing a little worse, a trifle harder to bear. There were more deaths. More snows. More winds howling through the melancholy pines. More whimpering sounds of hunger.

"We are all starving," aged Mrs. Breen said one day.

Mrs. Reed's lips stiffened. She would not see her children starve! She would cross the mountains herself and bring them bread!

Bravely, without a guide, Mrs. Reed started on her mission, accompanied by her friend Eliza, Virginia, and stout-hearted Milt Elliott, who wore snowshoes and made the tracks for the women to follow. Eliza collapsed the first day and turned back to the cabin. Virginia, her mother, and Milt pressed on, sometimes really crawling instead of walking, and choking with discouragement when they reached the summit, for all they could see were mountains and more mountains and more mountains!

The nights were hardest for Mrs. Reed, Milt, and Virginia. The moaning pines cried out in utter loneliness. In the distance, beyond the campfires, wild beasts screamed.

Virginia awakened one morning, at first baffled and then stricken with a new fear. Indeed, this was no terrible dream—she was in a deep well of snow melted by the campfires during the night!

Milt took the lead now. "Careful," he said. "Watch every move. If we start an avalanche down here, we'll all be buried alive!"

Step by step, Milt dug a stairway to the surface. The party climbed out. Poor Virginia cried, her foot was so badly frozen.

"There is nothing to do but go back to the cabin," Mrs. Reed said wearily.

But it was lucky they did. Soon

the snow fell heavily once more. The three would have perished in the mountains.

So Virginia returned to still other days cooped up in the cabin. Mornings the snow must be shoveled out of the fireplace before a frail fire, that really warmed no one, could be built. All that remained to eat were the raw hides on the roof, which Mrs. Reed boiled, but looking at the stuff, Virginia felt revolted.

"It's just like a pot of glue!" she cried.

Mrs. Breen stepped into this emergency, slipping Virginia bits of meat that the woman had saved. If they all must die in the end, Virginia often wondered, why did they fight so desperately to keep their low ember of life aglow?

Elsewhere, a great event took place. Seven members of Stanton's party—the Forlorn Hope—crossed the mountains. Their gaunt bodies and pinched faces told their bleak story to the California settlers. Men stayed up all night, killing cattle, drying beef, making flour. A relief party of seven, under Captain Reasen P. Tucker, struck out through the Sierras for Donner Lake. On the evening of February 19, 1847, Tucker's group reached the cabins. From the cracked lips of Mr. Breen came four words:

"Relief, thank God, relief!"

In time Virginia arrived in Yerba Buena, as San Francisco was first called. Behind her in the snows of Donner Lake were many of her friends who had died, none more precious than Milt Elliott. But the story of the conquest and settlement of a great continent is often written in blood and its pages stained by bitter tears.

28 · A Word That Burns Like Fever

Gold Is Discovered in California, 1848

THE STORY of California before the tragic winter suffered by the Donner Party was filled with intrigue and conflict. Only the Indians lived in peace beside the towering mountains and hostile deserts. Beginning with the explorer, Juan Rodríguez Cabrillo, who in 1542 anchored in San Diego Bay, the white man brought seeds of jealousy that bore bitter fruit.

The Spaniards were not impressed with California, although in 1579 when England's Sir Francis Drake sailed along its coast, Spain's interest revived. Spain's first military posts were built at the sites of San Diego and Monterey, and beside the forts rose Franciscan missions; then, in a period of fifty years (1769-1819), nineteen other missions were established. When Mexico threw off its Spanish shackles, it claimed California and viewed with suspicion foreign interlopers. Within less than one hundred miles of San Francisco, Russian fur trappers had erected Fort Ross, but by 1841 the Russians had grown homesick and sold their land. *Americanos*, however, proved more tenacious, beginning with fur trapper Jedediah S. Smith who reached California in 1827, and completing a cycle of "invasion" when Kit Carson guided Frémont's expeditions in 1842, 1843, and 1845.

If Mexican tempers shortened at the increasing number of American settlers, American tempers were no longer. In 1844 Frémont reappeared with a band of soldiers to build a fort and stand guard over the rights of his countrymen. Crossly, the two governments talked war. An offshoot of the rising bad feeling came in 1846 when Americans routed the Mexicans from their fort at Sonoma and hoisted a homemade flag bearing a lone star, a grizzly bear, and the brave words "California Republic."

Among the early settlers was Captain John A. Sutter, who in 1839 established the first white man's post in inland California, which he named New Helvetia. Nine years later a town had been laid out, but renamed Sacramento; at nearby Sutter's Fort, the captain operated a sawmill. Then one day in 1848 an employee named John Marshall rushed into Sutter's private quarters.

The captain was puzzled by Marshall's strange manner.

"What is it, Marshall?"

"Can anyone hear us?"

"No."

Suspiciously Marshall peered around the room and under the bed.

"Tell me your trouble," Sutter insisted.

Marshall opened his hand and placed before the captain particles he had found in a ditch. He spoke a word that often burns like fever in the minds of men:

"Gold!"

Marshall's secret could not be kept, yet the first news of the discovery was not really believed. In Monterey an old-timer swore that the gold talk was a ruse whereby the United States was trying to trick Californians into thinking that, once they kicked out the Mexicans, heaven would fall into their laps. A messenger was sent to the American Fork, where the discovery had been reported, and when he returned, bringing specimens of the yellow treasure, gold fever swept Monterey. By nightfall husband and wife were packing their belongings, the blacksmith had dropped his hammer, the farmer left his sickle, the baker shut his oven. Said an eyewitness: "All were off for the mines, some on horses, some on carts, some on crutches; and one went in a litter."

Wherever the trade winds blew they seemed to verify the news of the discovery of gold in California, and within the next twelve years 260,000 fortune seekers arrived. Some jolted and bounced across mountains and plains in "prairie schooners," as covered wagons were called; some risked long sea voyages and jungle diseases crossing the Isthmus of Panama. Seamen carried the news to the ports of the world, and returned with excited prospectors.

California changed almost overnight. A shack rented for $100 a week, a small, one-story building sold for $40,000, a night's lodging on a cot cost $15, a weeks-old New York newspaper brought $1 a copy. Prices of food and clothing soared to dizzy heights in San Francisco and to dizzier heights in the gold fields where everything had to be carried by mule-

back. Easy money brought the gamblers and desperadoes; a tree limb and a rope administered swift punishment for the two unforgivable crimes, claim jumping and horse stealing.

Prospecting the gold fields properly was called "the big gamble," for where one man would "hit a strike" that brought him $100 a day, others would be lucky if they could show that much for a month's toil. Moreover, gold prospecting proved a hard, bitter, lonely life. Watching from hillsides dotted with the red, white, pink, and orange blossoms of wildflowers, the Sierra grouse must have wondered at the strange creatures in ragged shirts and scrubby beards who had invaded their wilderness.

A miner's "claim," which he "staked off," usually covered an area of forty square feet, and could only be held for ten days unless he remained on the spot. Generally, from four to six miners worked as a company, giving their claim some such names as "Bunker Hill" or "Illinois" to indicate their true home. The surface soil—miners called it "top dirt"—was worked in a "Long Tom" which was a trough about twenty feet long and eight inches deep. The "Long Tom" was made of wood except for a six-foot section of perforated sheet iron, called the "riddle," beneath which rested the "riffle box." Three or four men shoveled top dirt into the trough, water washed it down to the riddle, and here another man kept the dirt in motion with a hoe. Gold, being very heavy, sank to the bottom, and passed through the holes of the riddle into the riffle box.

Many miners disdained working top dirt, wanting to reach as quickly as possible the richer deposits in the "bedrock." First they "sank a shaft"—actually a process like digging a well—until they struck the bedrock. Now began the search for "crevices" containing the precious ore. This work they called "drifting coyote holes," which meant they dug passages from the main shaft to other sections of the bedrock. Thus they honeycombed the hill. A coyote hole was followed until the goal was reached or the air became so impure it extinguished headlamps and forced out the diggers.

Such was the backbreaking labor of real prospecting. The reward could be a fabulous fortune or almost nothing. Yet the word that burned like fever continued its hold on the minds of men. In 1858 the discovery of gold in Colorado started a second rush to "Pike's Peak or Bust"; in 1859 a silver strike at the incredibly rich Comstock Lode started the rush into Nevada; and in 1897 gold in the Yukon lured thousands across the snows to pay $10 a plate for ham and eggs.

One effect of the discovery of gold in California was its swift growth in population so that in 1850 it was admitted to the Union as our thirty-first state. Meanwhile the War with Mexico had been fought from 1846-1848, which made this event possible; and the fact that California had been admitted on the condition that slavery was forever prohibited on its soil indicated other clouds of storm gathering over the nation.

29 · Proving Ground

The War with Mexico, 1846-1848

THE LEAN, gangling Midwesterner with the gaunt, sad face spoke in sharp, biting tones. Fellow Congressmen listened, some with smiles, others with scowls. Whigs like Abraham Lincoln, who now had the floor, believed that this war was unnecessary. Democrats in the Administration argued that Mexico had "shed American blood on American soil." Congressman Lincoln ridiculed this claim. Where was the spot on which this blood had been shed? Would the President please locate it and ease the minds of Americans who feared that they had been tricked into a cruel war?

Critics like Lincoln succeeded in making James Knox Polk probably the most hated man ever to hold the Presidency of the United States. During the four years (1845-1849) that Polk served as our eleventh President he achieved every objective he sought, yet his unpopularity increased. Words such as "narrow," "ungenerous," and "cold," often applied to Polk's personality, explain in part the unhappy memory history retains of him, but the deeper reason for the dissatisfaction with Polk was dramatized by Lincoln's speech in Congress in 1848.

Mexico refused to recognize the legality of the action by which in 1845 Texas was finally annexed to the United States. However, this dispute may have been settled more peacefully if Americans had talked less about their "manifest destiny" as a nation to expand into the lands of the West and exhibited more understanding for the troubles that beset our neighbor to the south. A series of revolutions had afflicted Mexico with one unstable government after another and had produced, through the loss of American lives and property, claims against Mexico amounting to about three million dollars.

President Polk realized that Mexico had no way of meeting these claims. He offered to cancel the debt if Mexico would recognize the Rio Grande, instead of the more northerly Nueces River, as the boundary between the two nations; and, in addition, offered to pay twenty-five million dollars if Mexico would sell California and New Mexico. Our ambassador to Mexico, John Slidell, attempted to negotiate these terms at a time when another revolution swept the country. Neither Mexico's old nor new president wanted to be placed in the light of buckling down to the United States. Slidell returned to Washington in a huffy mood. Mexico deserved to be "chastised."

American troops, stationed at the Nueces River, were ordered forward to the Rio Grande. Here, on April 25, 1845, Mexican soldiers, who honestly believed they defended their homeland, defeated a small band of American cavalry. Polk claimed that the United States had been "invaded," a charge that Lincoln and the Whigs ridiculed. Moreover, Northern opponents of slavery, viewing Polk as the tool of Southern "slavocracy," suspected that a conspiracy existed to obtain more land for spreading slavery. Polk haughtily ignored all critics. On May 13, 1846, Congress declared war.

Stationed at Jefferson Barracks in Missouri at this time was a young West Point graduate who disliked the army and wished he could be a teacher of mathematics. Friends of the young second lieutenant heard him criticize sharply the war that now forced him to become a soldier. Thus, grudgingly, began the military career of possibly the greatest general in the nation's history. His name was Ulysses S. Grant.

One of the significant aspects of the War with Mexico would be the number of future national leaders it produced. A young engineer, Robert E. Lee, surely would be heard from again. Other Americans who received their "baptism of fire" in Mexico included William Tecumseh Sherman, George B.

McClellan, George Gordon Meade, Thomas "Stonewall" Jackson, and John C. Pemberton, whose names would become household words.

The Mexican War also served as a proving ground for future Presidents and Presidential aspirants, giving us General Zachary Taylor, our twelfth President (1849-1850); General Winfield Scott, who was defeated for office by another general, Franklin Pierce, our fourteenth President (1853-1857); John C. Fremont, the unsuccessful Republican candidate in 1856; Grant, our eighteenth President (1869-1877); and Jefferson Davis, President of the Confederate States of America.

U. S. Grant—his friends called him "Sam," short for "Uncle Sam"—was typical of the young West Pointers who learned in Mexico the difference between war taught from a textbook and war on a battlefield. Under Zachary Taylor, Lieutenant Sam Grant met the Mexicans in the war's first real action at Palo Alto, a battle fought eight miles northeast of Brownsville, Texas. Awaiting attack, Sam couldn't speak for the feelings of General Taylor, but he could speak for himself: he had never heard a hostile gun and was sorry he had ever enlisted. Knowing he was anything but a hero, he watched, on the morning of May 8, 6,000 Mexicans forming into lines of battle. The tall grass where Sam waited reached almost to his shoulders; the lances of the Mexican cavalry, he thought, looked sharp as darning-needles.

Then Sam Grant fought in his first battle:

". . . The Mexicans immediately opened fire upon us, first with artillery and then with infantry. At first their shots did not reach us, and the advance was continued. As we got nearer, the cannon balls commenced going through the ranks. They hurt no one, however, during this advance, because they would strike the ground long before they reached our line, and ricochetted through the tall grass so slowly that the men would see them and open ranks and let them pass."

At the top of a hill, the battle grew more furious. Grant clutched his flintlock musket. The surrounding chaparral often appeared impenetrable, and, Grant thought, "at the distance of a few hundred yards a man might fire at you all day without your finding it out." Once a cannon ball passed near Grant, took off the head of a soldier, and ripped away the lower jaw of a captain. Sam Grant tightened his hold on the musket.

The Americans defeated the Mexicans at Palo Alto, and next day won a second victory at Resaca de la Palma, where Sam Grant captured a Mexican colonel—not too spectacular a deed, since the colonel wanted to be taken! Grant's admiration for Taylor grew. The general wasn't much for dressy uniforms (which pleased Grant, somewhat on the slouchy side himself), but he had a sharp eye for sizing up a situation, moved quickly on his own initiative to meet emergencies in battle, and wrote his own orders in crisp, simple language. In Taylor, Grant saw the pattern of the general he would some day make.

From September 21 to 23, Taylor stormed the Mexican fortifications at Monterey, hoping to bring the war to a close. Here, riding for ammunition relief, Sam Grant displayed the stature of the soldier he had become. A boy who had grown up in Ohio knowing how to handle horses like an Indian, he rode exposed to withering Mexican fire—clinging to the side of the horse farthest from the enemy, one foot in the cantle of the saddle, an arm over the neck of the animal. He started at a full run, clung and prayed, and came through without a scratch!

After Monterey, Taylor pressed on to Saltillo and Victoria, important towns in northeastern Mexico. When still there was no peace, a second American army, under Winfield Scott, to which Grant was attached, launched a campaign against Mexico City. American victories at Cerro Gordo, Churubusco, and Chapultepec brought General Scott to the gates of his objective.

February 2, 1848, saw peace emissaries of the United States and Mexico meeting in the little village of Guadalupe Hidalgo, near Mexico City. The territory granted to the United States covered more than 525,000 square miles, which, in time, became the states of California, Nevada, and Utah, large parts of New Mexico and Arizona, and sections of Colorado and Wyoming. Later we paid Mexico fifteen million dollars.

But while Guadalupe Hidalgo ended tensions between the United States and Mexico, tensions at home became more strained. Were the

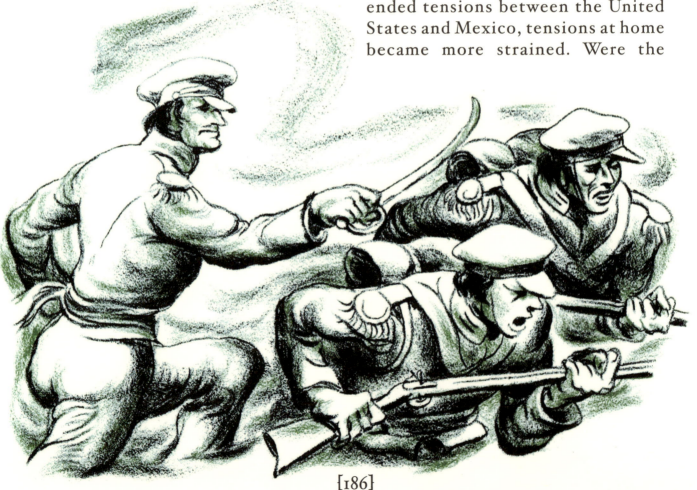

new lands to be free or were they to increase the domains of the slave owners? The Compromise of 1850 made California a free state, and under the principle of "popular sovereignty," gave New Mexico and Arizona, as territories, a choice between slavery and freedom. No one was really satisfied.

Congressman Lincoln returned to Illinois, and seemed to retire from public life. But there was a reason why one friend said that melancholy dripped from him as he walked.

There was reason, also, why, on looking back, the War with Mexico seemed like "the dress rehearsal" for the bloodier conflict yet to be fought.

30 · "The Tall Sucker"

Lincoln Debates with Douglas, 1858

"When I came of age, I did not know much," Abraham Lincoln once said. "I could read, write, and cypher to the rule of three, but that was all."

Lincoln's greatness stemmed from his dogged honesty. Always, he was as plain, unaffected and down-to-earth as the log cabin on the South Fork of the Nolin Creek in Hardin County, Kentucky, where on February 12, 1809, he was born.

At first, growing was the thing Abraham did best. When still in his teens, he reached his full height of six feet, four inches, and coarse black hair standing on end made him appear even taller. His homely, dark-skinned face relaxed into a grin at jokes about how his thin, big-boned body had grown to resemble an ax handle.

His early years were not easy. His father, Thomas Lincoln, fretted over rights to his farm land and decided, when Abraham was seven, to move the family to Indiana. Here property could be bought directly from the government. Moreover, Thomas Lincoln disliked slavery and Indiana was a free state.

Arriving too late in the fall to build a weather-tight dwelling, the Lincolns lived through the first winter in a "half-faced cabin" constructed, of logs and poles on three sides, while, on the fourth, a fire burned day and night. Well would Abraham speak of his Indiana home as "an unbroken forest"; bears and other wild animals roamed the woods, and the land was uncleared. An ax was placed in his hands, and he said humorously that until he was twenty-three he was "almost constantly using that most useful instrument."

In 1818, Abraham suffered tragedy at the death of his mother, Nancy Hanks Lincoln. Today we believe that the common frontier disease, "milk-sickness," was caused by cattle eating white snakeroot or rayless goldenrod and passing on a poison through their milk. In 1818, "milk-sickness" meant only high fever and quick fatality.

Young Abraham helped his father carry the crude coffin into the woods. Autumn touched the trees with a blaze of color; the boy's eyes reflected nothing but the dullness of his grief. His stricken heart could not rest until

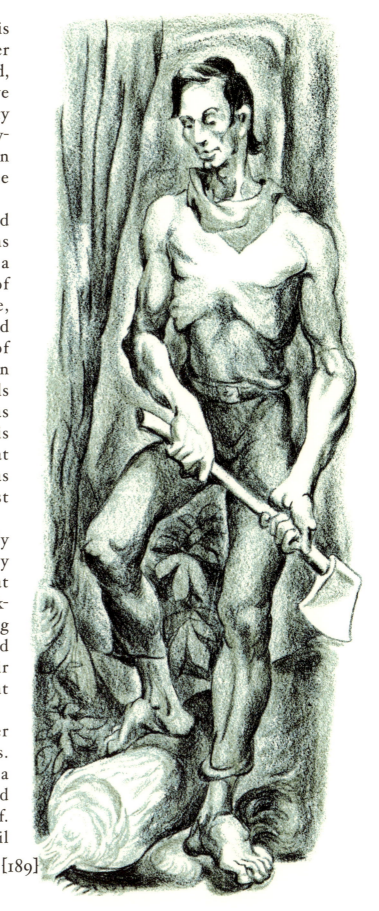

[189]

months later when a traveling preacher repeated the burial service over the lonely grave on the backwoods farm.

The future seemed bleak. Between boy and father little real companionship existed. Twelve-year-old Sarah Lincoln tried valiantly to keep the wilderness home in order. The cheerlessness mounted. Then Thomas Lincoln married Sarah Bush Johnston, a widow with three children. A new freshness, like the bursting of spring, swept the darkness from the Indiana years. Abraham's stepmother always understood him, always loved him, always encouraged his craving for learning and shared the ambitions that Thomas Lincoln couldn't comprehend.

Poor luck at farming and dread of milk-sickness lead the Lincolns to move to Illinois in 1830. Abraham, who already had traveled to New Orleans on a flatboat loaded with farm produce, wanted to strike out and stand on his own feet. He was strong. He could be a blacksmith.

In 1831, he came to the mud-and-log prairie village of New Salem. For six years it was his home as he tried storekeeping, running a post office, and picking up odd jobs as a surveyor. Lincoln, in his own words, described these experiences in New Salem:

"Before long, strangely enough, a man offered to sell, and did sell, to Abraham and another as poor as himself, an old stock of goods, upon credit. They opened as merchants; and he says that was *the* store. Of course they did nothing but get deeper and deeper in debt. He was appointed postmaster at New Salem—the office being too insignificant to make his politics an objection. The store winked out. The surveyor of Sangamon offered to depute to Abraham that portion of his work which was within his part of the county. He accepted, procured a compass and chain, studied Flint and Gibson a little, and went at it. This procured bread, and kept soul and body together."

During the New Salem years Lincoln also fought in the Black Hawk War and was elected captain of his company, but his entire military career consisted of "charges upon the wild onions," and "a good many bloody struggles with the mosquitoes."

Abe Lincoln's infectious wit—he laughed gracefully at himself—explained his immense popularity. He held his own wrestling with the huskiest roughnecks, mooned on the steps of the local tavern with pretty Ann Rutledge, and swapped stories with whoever felt like talking. He wanted to be a lawyer, but knew he would need a better education, so he borrowed books, often walking the long miles between New Salem and Springfield for that purpose, "and went at it in good earnest." In 1836 he received a license to practice law. By this time he had blossomed into an affable young politician and two years previously had been elected to the state legislature.

A pattern of life had emerged for Lincoln. Now he moved to Springfield, and married dark-eyed, spirited, Kentucky-bred Mary Todd. His home life was cheerful and comfortable, and in time he became the indulgent father of four sons. His simple, direct manner brought him a good reputation as a lawyer, for a jury of twelve farmers always understood Lincoln when he stated an argument; and since in those days courts were widely separated across the sparsely settled prairies, he devoted six months of each year to "riding the circuit." Yet he enjoyed this life, and his circle of political friends grew. In 1846 he was elected to Congress and like the staunch Whig he always had been took his stand against Polk and the War with Mexico.

After the term in Congress, Lincoln seemed to withdraw from political life. Friends noticed how he had changed. He seemed to be lost in his own thoughts, and at home or riding the circuit his long nose was forever thrust between the pages of a newspaper. Always he appeared to be absorbed in some personal quandary—to be seeking the answer to some puzzling, intense problem.

Actually, Lincoln sensed the crosscurrents pulling at the nation. He read the arguments that the black man was an inferior being only slightly above a brute and therefore deserved no legal rights. He pondered *Uncle Tom's Cabin* by Harriet Beecher Stowe that struck straight at the heart of this slavery argument by presenting the black man as a human being—as one of God's creatures. He read also of a slave named Dred Scott, who claimed his freedom on the ground that his master had taken him into Illinois and the Wisconsin Territory, in both of which slavery was illegal. But the Supreme Court of Missouri declared that Dred Scott was not free since he had returned voluntarily to a slave state. Lincoln pondered the case, his face sadly reflective.

Then a political event brought Lincoln out of his seeming retirement. In 1820 Congress had adopted the Missouri Compromise, which prohibited slavery in new territories north of an east-and-west line that was an extension of Missouri's southern boundary. To Lincoln this law permanently limited slavery. But in 1854 Congress passed the Nebraska Bill whereby settlers in territories could decide whether or not they wanted slavery. Lincoln could no longer keep quiet. The new law was wrong for the country. It must be reversed.

The full impact of Lincoln's opposition was not felt until 1858 when he ran on the ticket of the new Republican Party for the United States Senate. Political advisors, reading the speech he planned to give on accepting the nomination, were frankly worried. He was ahead of the times, some said; he would lose votes, others argued; what Lincoln proposed to say impressed one critic as a "fool utterance."

Lincoln stood firm. He would give the people the plain facts. If he must be defeated for telling the truth, he was content. He said, in part:

"A house divided against itself cannot stand. I believe this government cannot endure permanently, half slave and half free. I do not expect the Union to be dissolved—I do not expect the house to fall—but I do expect it will cease to be divided. It will become one thing, or all the other. Either the opponents of slavery will arrest the further spread of it, and place it where the public mind shall rest in the belief that it is in the course of ultimate extinction; or its advocates will push it forward till it shall become alike lawful in all the States, old as well as new, North as well as South."

Opposing Lincoln for election to the Senate was Stephen A. Douglas, who had fathered the Nebraska Bill. Douglas was called "The Little Giant" and "The Little Steam Engine in Britches." A favorite political nickname for Lincoln was "The Tall Sucker" and "Honest Abe." As these two candidates clashed, they literally represented the long and short of the slavery quarrel.

Across the state of Illinois, as the campaign progressed, Lincoln and Douglas hammered at each other in a series of seven debates. Large crowds appeared everywhere to cheer or jeer as the candidates each spoke for an hour and a half. Newspapers reported the arguments in detail. Nationally as well as in Illinois the great debates claimed an avid following.

"The Little Giant" was a vigorous orator, quick-witted, clear-headed, who could seize on a small molehill

of loose thinking and build it into a mountain of seemingly malicious intent. Douglas was meticulously dressed compared to Lincoln's awkward physical presence, but his weakness was that he never prepared to say where he stood on slavery and was harmed in trying to be all things to all people. But "The Tall Sucker" used his humor as a double-edged sword, cutting away the fat of fancy words and revealing the bare bones of every point argued.

Douglas defended his Nebraska Bill on the principle of "Popular Sovereignty." It was no such thing, snapped Lincoln—"Squatter Sovereignty" was the right term. Then Lincoln lashed into the Dred Scott decision. No matter what settlers wanted, the decision opened all territories to slavery. How ridiculous, asked Douglas, could Mr. Lincoln become? If the people did

not protect slavery, it could not endure in a territory. Lincoln questioned the morality of slavery, insisting that he looked upon slavery as "a moral, social, or political issue," while Douglas cared not whether slavery was voted up or down.

"Our progress in degeneracy appears to me to be pretty rapid," Lincoln stated. "As a nation we began by declaring that 'all men are created equal.' We now practically read 'all men except negroes.' When Know-Nothings* get control it will be 'all men except negroes and foreigners and Catholics.' When it comes to this I shall prefer emigration to some country where they make no pretense of loving liberty—to Russia, for instance, where despotism can be taken pure, without the base alloy of hypocrisy."

On and on the candidates spoke till Douglas's husky voice scarcely could be heard, while Lincoln's high, penetrating tones still rang passionately. Yet Lincoln knew from the beginning that because of the manner in which districts were apportioned in Illinois he would lose the election.

During the debates however, Lincoln had grown into a national figure. Succeeding months would see him taking his ideas to voters in Ohio, Indiana, Iowa, Wisconsin, and Kansas. In 1860 he would tell a New York audience in his famous Cooper Union speech: "Let us have faith that right makes might."

Within a few months, Abraham Lincoln became the sixteenth President of the United States. Across large areas of the country, young lads rode day and night to carry this news.

*The Know-Nothings were a political party of the 1850s that campaigned against immigrants, Catholics, and slaves.

31 · How the News Reached Nevada

Riding the Pony Express, 1860

"THIS LOOKS like the job for me," the tall boy said. "That's the one I mean, there at the bottom of the page."

Squinting against the hard, bright glare of the sun, a companion read aloud the newspaper advertisement:

> WANTED—Young, skinny, wiry fellows not over 18. Must be expert riders, willing to face death daily. Orphans preferred. Wages $25 per week. Apply, Central Overland Pony Express.

The words, "willing to face death daily," described exactly the nature of the fast mail service that, on April 3, 1860, was established between St. Joseph, Missouri, and Sacramento, California. Eighty crack riders—the most daring horsemen in America—covered the 1,966 miles of plains, prairies, and mountains between these points. Along the route of the Pony Express were 190 stations and more than 300 station-keepers and assistants to keep the 400 horses in the service running the mail at top speed.

"Young, skinny, wiry fellows" who rode for the Pony Express lived on the fine edge of their nerves twenty-four hours a day. The rider on duty recognized neither day nor night. His job, all the time, was to keep his mount driving ahead. Rain or snow, pounding sleet or sweltering heat, dry summer or wet winter didn't alter the pattern of his job. At least fifty miles—sometimes one hundred or more, if relief failed him—was the stretch he must cover before he rested, whether the route led down level prairie road or over mountain crags.

The express rider dressed sensibly for his job. His clothes fitted snugly, and a rider galloping through the moonlight like some ghost in a legend said that he was "flying light." A jacket and skullcap, pants tucked in boot tops made him look precisely what he was—a race rider!

Though the route of the Pony Express often passed through lands where hostile Indians or bandits lurked, the rider carried no weapon. He couldn't spare the weight! He had only one responsibility—to carry the mail, at five dollars an ounce, twenty ounces to a pouch. Even his horse was stripped to the barest equipment and letters were written on tissue paper. For security, the mail was wrapped in oiled silk, locked in a leather pouch, and strapped under the rider's thigh.

A run started with the driver often ignoring the stirrup, but catching the horn and being jerked into the saddle as the horse started. Riders called this a "Pony Express mount." Then, at top speed, the rider fled

ten miles to the next station and a fresh horse. Occasionally a rider made twenty-five miles an hour and a good day's run was 250 miles. At first the Pony Express delivered the mail once a week, but later twice-a-week delivery was offered.

A strong admirer of the Pony Express was Mark Twain, who, in *Roughing It*, painted a graphic picture of the exciting moments when a driver approached a station:

" *'Here he comes!'*

"Every neck is stretched farther and every eye strained wider. Away across the endless dead level of the prairie a black speck appears against the sky, and it is plain that it moves. Well, I should think so! In a second or two it becomes a horse and rider, rising and falling, rising and falling—sweeping toward us nearer and nearer—growing more and more distinct, more and more sharply defined—nearer and still nearer, and the flutter of hoofs comes faintly to the ear—another instant a whoop and a hurrah from our upper deck, a wave of the rider's hand, but no reply, and man and horse burst past our excited faces and go swinging away like a belated fragment of a storm!

"So sudden is it all and so like a flash of unreal fancy that, but for the flake of white foam left quivering and perishing on a mail sack after the vision has flashed by and disappeared, we might have doubted whether we had seen any actual horse and man at all, maybe."

The father of the Pony Express was Senator William H. Gwin, and the financial backing to establish the service came from Russell, Majors and Waddell, a rich firm of freight carriers. Gwin's idea was to use a route that would shorten the trail traveled by the coaches of the Overland Mail to the south. So the Pony Express followed the famous California Trail—along the Platte in Nebraska, through South Pass in Wyoming, along the edge of the Great Salt Lake in Utah, then on to Nevada's Virginia City and Carson City before daring the final precipices of the Sierras to California and Sacramento!

Ten days were required for the first Pony Express riders to cover the 1,966 miles, but later the speed was cut to eight or nine days, beating the time of the Overland Mail coaches by ten or twelve days. Rightfully did Pony Express riders feel proud of their record—only once in all the 650,000 miles ridden by the "young, skinny, wiry fellows" was the mail lost!

Every Pony Express rider could be called a hero, and was, in Mark Twain's words, "a little bit of a man, brimful of spirit and endurance." But one rider later acquired a fame above the others. No one could outshine him at handling or riding a horse, fighting Indians, or hunting buffalo. Born in 1846 in Scott County, Iowa, the boy who joined the Pony Express gave his name as William Frederick Cody. Soon the Great Plains—and in time thousands of circus-goers throughout America and Europe—would know him as Buffalo Bill.

The completion of the telegraph from coast to coast ended the Pony Express in October, 1861, and left its backers financially ruined. Before that, however, it made, for special reasons, a history-making run—in just six days—from Fort Kearney, Nebraska, to Fort Churchill, Nevada. At every station, riders shouted the same news. Old Abe Lincoln had been elected President!

32 · Johnny Reb

The South Fires on Sumter, 1861

THE WAR had many names. In the North, it was called the Rebellion, the Insurrection, and the Civil War; in the South, it was the War Between the States and the War for Southern Independence. Basically the conflict involved stongly held views that were irreconcilable. The North fought for the Union and abolition. The South fought for states rights and the ability to do with their "property" as they wished.

Johnny Reb, the Southern brother, grew up depending on black servants to mend his clothes, to see that he scrubbed behind his ears, to hustle him off to school, and to comfort him when he was hurt or sick. Slaves cooked the food he ate and at night, they turned down his bed, lighted the lamps, and latched the door. In the fields, slaves planted the cotton, or picked and baled it for market. A black man drove the carriage that took Johnny's family to church; a slave cleaned out the stables and milked the cows; a slave carried the carpetbag to train or steamboat when Johnny left on a journey.

To Johnny, slavery was as normal a part of life as the beautiful blooms on the magnolia trees, or the Spanish moss that festooned the forests around the sleepy bayous in Mississippi and Louisiana, or the bite of a catfish, the yap of a hound dog on a coon hunt, and the quail that flashed among the ragweed and partridge peas on a Virginia hillside. On Sundays, the local minister quoted from the Bible to prove to Johnny and his parents that slavery was not sinful. At

school, at home, Johnny learned that the black man was an inferior being, who owed him faithful service and to whom *he* owed protection, food, shelter, and clothing.

Slavery could not work unless Johnny was raised to believe in the oppressive code that the white man is superior and the slave must know his place. This belief decreed that Johnny was the master; his work must be done, his will obeyed. Slaves who behaved themselves Johnny liked and often loved. But since the black man was an "inferior being", to Johnny there was no point in over-taxing black people with education and running the risk of making slaves "uppity." Johnny believed that it was not Johnny's fault that years ago slave traders had stolen these people from their homes, that now at least they lived better and ate better. Johnny was sincere in these convictions, but was blind to the fact that his entire way of life and the Southern economy was built upon the backs of other men.

Politically, Johnny's mind was firmly settled. The Underground Railroad should be smashed, the fugitive slave laws enforced. The doctrine of "state's rights" was the foundation of national existence, for states that had voluntarily formed the Union were justified in withdrawing from that association when the need arose. Johnny brushed aside, impatiently and bad-temperedly, the so-called Northern do-gooders with their books like *Uncle Tom's Cabin* and their troublemakers like the militant abolitionist John Brown who would arm the slaves and turn them on their masters. Johnny Reb's case with the national government was clear and, he thought, unarguable: either he would be left alone to live as he liked or he would fight for his right to do so.

The election of 1860 drew the issue clearly. The leading Democrat, Stephen A. Douglas, had said in his debates with Lincoln that a territory could prohibit slavery even before it was organized as a state. To Johnny such talk was heresy, and when the Democrats nominated Douglas for the Presidency, the Southern wing of the party bolted and named John C. Breckinridge of Kentucky as a Presidential candidate. Even then, not all factions were satisfied and the Constitutional Union Party had been formed with John Bell of Tennessee for its standard-bearer. The result of the vote in 1860 told its own story:

Candidate	*Electoral Vote*	*Popular Vote*
Lincoln	180	1,866,452
Breckinridge	72	849,781
Bell	39	588,879
Douglas	12	1,376,957
	303	4,682,069

All of Lincoln's electoral vote, and nearly all his popular vote had come from Northern states. Clearly Lincoln was a "sectional" President.

A shudder ran through the South,

and swift, angry action followed. Lincoln would not be inaugurated until March 4, 1861, and Johnny Reb intended to make clear before then exactly where "The Tall Sucker" stood with the South. On December 20, 1860, South Carolina voted to secede from the Union. In January 1861, Mississippi, Florida, Alabama, Georgia, and Louisiana followed South Carolina out of the Union. In February Texas seceded, and conventions were forming for similar revolt in Virginia, Arkansas, North Carolina, and Tennessee. So, in March, 1861, within a week of each other, two Presidents were inaugurated—Abraham Lincoln as leader of the United States of America and Jefferson Davis as leader of the Confederate States of America.

Johnny Reb's mood suddenly was cheery. By George, he had stood on his own feet! He wasn't afraid of the devil or Lincoln or the whole bloody abolitionist North! Lincoln appealed to "the mystic chords of memory, stretching from every battlefield and patriot grave to every living heart and hearthstone all over this broad land," but Johnny Reb's ears were deaf to such poetry. Lincoln also had spoken toughly. The national government intended to "hold, occupy and possess" the forts, arsenals, and customhouses belonging to the Union. These words Johnny Reb understood. Again, his dander rose.

April, sweet with the scent of blossoms, found Charleston, South Carolina, tense with expectancy. Above Fort Sumter, in Charleston harbor, waved the defiant flag of the United States. Within was only a small garrison of men under Major Robert Anderson. In order to avoid what might be considered an act of war, Lincoln had decided to send provisions to Anderson but not to reinforce his small force.

Johnny Reb's temper snapped, and much of his good sense deserted him. To send Anderson provisions, instead of removing him and his plagued Yankees from the territorial waters of South Carolina, was a hostile act! A Southern general with the long name of Pierre Gustave Toutant Beauregard commanded the armed forces in Charleston. On April 11, he demanded the surrender of the fort. "My sense of honor and my obligations to my Government prevent my compliance," Major Anderson replied.

Charleston heard this news grimly. Clocks in Charleston homes, clocks on the steeples of Charleston churches passed the hour of midnight. It was April 12, 1861—a chill day approaching, with a threat of rain. Hardly anyone slept. Along the streets, soldiers moved. Rebel guns turned on Sumter, and Johnny Reb seized the cannon's lanyard, eager to pull it and have the fight started. At 3:30 A.M., Johnny received his orders. In one hour he could fire.

The clocks ticked on; then at the appointed time, in the ironclad battery on Cumming's Point, Edmund Ruffin of Virginia yanked the lanyard and the first gun roared. Over the harbor rose the shell, a fearful messenger of war, that, exploding, released echoes which would rumble over the land for the next four years. No gun replied on Sumter. Major Anderson simply waited—waited and prayed.

The dawn spread over Charleston. A quickening wind ruffled the water in the harbor and soon whitecaps broke against shore and fort. Johnny Reb suddenly noted the time. It was 7:00 A.M. One of the barbette guns on Sumter at last had been fired! The battle had been joined, and almost with relief of conscience Johnny returned to the dogged task before him.

Rain fell shortly thereafter, continuing until eleven. The sun, breaking through at last, illuminated a strange scene. On the roof tops of Charleston, ladies in hoop skirts watched the duel of the guns. Some spectators waved handkerchiefs, some clutched each other in their arms, some looked away and wept.

Confederate guns ringed Sumter. The bombardment, though it lasted thirty-six hours, was never in doubt. Major Anderson's guns had neither the range nor power seriously to damage the city's batteries. Sumter burst into flames and men could be seen rushing with buckets of water trying to put out the fire. The cannon of Charleston roared anew—at the wharf particularly, where the bucket brigade was centered.

Then all the guns fell silent. Soldiers and civilians alike watched breathlessly. Pull by pull, at Sumter the Stars and Stripes were being lowered. Next day President Lincoln asked the North for 75,000 troops.

33 · The Secret of the Old Desk

From Bull Run to Gettysburg, 1861-1863

BILLY YANK went to war no less confidently than Johnny Reb. Gaily singing "We'll Hang Jeff Davis to a Sour Apple Tree," Billy grabbed his musket and claimed that he would take the Confederate capital of Richmond, Virginia, in ninety days and reunite the Union.

At the same time that Lincoln was morally opposed to slavery, he believed as President, that his primary duty was to preserve the Union. "A house divided against itself cannot stand."

Near Bull Run, a small creek in northeastern Virginia, on July 21, 1861, Billy Yank suffered his first rude awakening. At first the Yankees, trying to turn the left wing of the Rebel army, believed the North had gained

the victory. But throughout the early fighting Stonewall Jackson's brigade never budged from the hill it held. Then, reinforced, Jackson's brigade charged. The Yankees reeled back in disorder, their casualties mounted to about 2,800 against 2,000 for the Confederates, and the supposed victory turned into dismal defeat.

Bull Run taught Billy Yank a new tune. The war would be neither short nor easy for either side. The South was full of fight and its generals were capable. Before the final surrender at Appomattox in 1865, 2,667,000 men would fight for the North, and 110,000 would die in action or of wounds, while another 250,000 would die of disease or starvation. The Confederate enlistments would number 1,400,000; their dead in action or from wounds, 75,000; their dead from disease or starvation, 90,000.

To no one more than to the man who lived in the White House, was this reality a sad blow, the price unduly severe. From month to month, at times from hour to hour, the melancholy deepened in Lincoln. Gravely he labored as Commander-in-chief to find a general who could lead the North to victory and thus preserve the Union.

The first choice for the supreme commander had been a Virginian,

but Robert E. Lee could not fight against his native state. In one of the loneliest, most heartfelt rides in history, Lee rode across the bridge from Washington to Arlington, Virginia, making the reluctant choice. The general Lincoln needed indeed existed, but it took a long time to find the man who as a young second lieutenant had so much admired the fighting style of Zachary Taylor. Meanwhile, before Grant emerged as the man who could win, heartbreak mounted for Lincoln as he padded around the White House at night in carpet slippers.

In a church in Washington, during the war, there was a little room off the chapel. Sometimes during prayer meetings the door to the room stood ajar, but no one was allowed near the room and whether or not the room was occupied remained a mystery. Then, one winter's night, a boy followed the footprints in the snow from the door that led from room to yard. So he knew the secret of where, some evenings, Lincoln could be found.

The spiritual strength in Lincoln was enormous, and surely he had need for every bit of such strength he could muster after the saddening Bull Run. The Peninsular Campaign under General George B. McGlellan in 1862 ended in failure instead of the capture of Richmond. Under General John Pope, the North suffered a second disastrous defeat at Bull Run in August of that same year.

June, 1862, saw Lincoln appear one day in the old War Department building. He asked for some paper and said he had something special to write. Then the President sat at a desk, holding pen against his cheek and looking out the window. He did not seem to do much writing.

For days Lincoln returned at intervals to resume his work, and at night what he had written was locked in a desk where it could not be read. Always, the composition came slowly. Lincoln chatted at times with the telegraph operators or gazed with fascination at a spiderweb. Some days he seemed most interested in reading what he had written and filling the margins with question marks.

In his inaugural address the President had said: "I have no purpose, directly or indirectly, to interfere with the institution of slavery in the States where it exists. I believe I have no lawful right to do so, and I have no inclination to do so." Now Lincoln had changed his mind.

Doubtless military considerations led the President to go day after day to the old desk, working slowly and thoughtfully at the writing of the Emancipation Proclamation. Again, once the slaves were proclaimed free, foreign powers could not very well aid the South and thus sanction an institution now generally condemned by mankind. However, Lincoln felt he could not issue his proclamation until the North could claim a military victory.

On September 17-18, 1862, at Antietam Creek, near Sharpsburg, Maryland, the Union Army threw back Lee's first attempt to invade the North, and this bloody battle gave Lincoln the opportunity he sought. On September 22 came the first indication of his intention—a warning really to the South of what was in store if it persisted in the war. On January 1, 1863, the proclamation was issued, declaring that all slaves in the states then in rebellion "are, and henceforward shall be, free."

Actually the Emancipation Proclamation, applying only to those states fighting the Federal government, freed few slaves, but it won great respect for the North with foreign nations and led in time to the adoption of the Thirteenth Amendment to the Constitution, whereby slavery everywhere in the country was abolished.

The war, however, went on grimly, and the shadows around Lincoln's eyes, the lines in his grave face, deepened. December 13, 1862, saw Lee retrieve his initiative, lost at Antietam, with a smashing victory at Fredericksburg, Virginia; again, in early May of 1863 Lee forced the Union out of Virginia with another crushing victory at Chancellorsville.

Lincoln's despair was understandable. The fighting force Lee was defeating time and time again was the Army of the Potomac, and on paper North America had never known a greater concentration of power. At full strength, 125,000 men fought with the Army of the Potomac; whenever the army moved it was as though a city like Albany or Columbus or Indianapolis had arisen one morning and walked away complete in every detail—clothing, food, medicine, ammunition, horses, wagons, people.

Lincoln still looked for a general who could win. Lee, emboldened, moved into Pennsylvania, threatening both Washington and Philadelphia. The Army of the Potomac under still another general, George G. Meade, pursued the wily Virginian and at last caught up with him at Gettysburg. For the first three days of July, 1863, the hills and ridges south of Gettysburg shook with the roar of savage battle before Lee, defeated, lumbered back to Virginia. Meade failed to pursue the fleeing Confederates. He was not the general Lincoln needed.

The North, wildly celebrating the victory at Gettysburg, received the following day the equally jubilant news that Grant had captured Vicksburg, and, as Lincoln would say, the Mississippi now could flow "unvexed" to the sea. Everyone believed that these two victories, in the east and west, must end the war. But Johnny Reb tightened his belt. He seemed madder than ever. But July had produced one climactic result. In Ulysses S. Grant the North had produced the general that Lincoln wanted. "He fights," the President said, paying him a Commander-in-chief's highest tribute.

On November 19, 1863, a military cemetery was dedicated at Gettysburg. Edward Everett, perhaps the country's most polished orator, was to give the main address, Lincoln to speak but briefly. It is untrue that Lincoln scribbled his remarks in a few moments. The President pondered deeply what he would say. Why did we fight this war? What did it mean? Lincoln said:

"Fourscore and seven years ago our fathers brought forth on this continent a new nation, conceived in liberty, and dedicated to the proposition that all men are created equal.

"Now we are engaged in a great civil war, testing whether that nation, or any nation so conceived and so dedicated, can long endure. We are met on a great battlefield of that war. We have come to dedicate a portion of that field as a final resting-place for those who here gave their lives that that nation might live. It is altogether fitting and proper that we should do this.

"But in a larger sense, we cannot dedicate—we cannot consecrate—we cannot hallow—this ground. The brave men, living and dead, who struggled here, have consecrated it far above our poor power to add or detract. The world will little note nor long remember what we say here, but it can never forget what they did here. It is for us, the living, rather, to be dedicated here to the unfinished work which they who fought here have thus far so nobly advanced. It is rather for us to be here dedicated to the great task remaining before us—that from these honored dead we take increased devotion to that cause for which they gave the last full measure of devotion; that we here highly resolve that these dead shall not have died in vain; that this nation, under God, shall have a new birth of freedom; and that government of the people, by the people, for the people, shall not perish from the earth."

34 · When the World Ended

Sherman's March to the Sea and the Surrender at Appomattox, 1865

EMMA FLORENCE LECONTE lived in Columbia, South Carolina. Emma had been thirteen when Fort Sumter fell. "The joy—the excitement—how well I remember it," the girl wrote in her diary. "We women ran trembling to the verandah—to the front gate, eagerly asking news of the passersby. The whole town was in a joyful tumult!"

Now Emma was seventeen. What four long years of war had meant she could reduce to a single sentence: "No pleasure, no enjoyment—nothing but rigid economy and hard work—nothing but the stern realities of life." At first the gallant Lee had done so well, and then with the early summer of 1863 the terrible change had come—on July 3rd the smashing Northern victory at Gettysburg, the very next day the humiliating defeat for the South at Vicksburg!

Since then the Confederacy had fought on, but Emma could not be fooled. The world of the South was ending. Lee fell back before Grant in Virginia, that Sherman wrecked Atlanta and marched across Georgia to Savannah destroying all in his path. Even the hope for an honorably negotiated peace between North and South seemed dim to Emma: "A sea rolls between them and us—a sea of blood."

Grim, gray, cold, January of 1865 settled upon Columbia. Emma looked at her unbleached homespun frock, her coarse stockings, her crude shoes of calfskin and thought that before the war she

had given away better clothes to her slaves. Now calico sold for sixteen dollars a yard! Truly, only the extortioner in the South gained anything from the years of war!

Some nights a haze hung over the moon. Fears grew stronger then. Sherman, who once had boasted he would "bring every Southern woman to the wash-tub," would turn next on South Carolina. The North rued South Carolina since it was the first state to secede from the Union.

Was William Tecumseh Sherman the brutal genius of destruction that the South believed him to be? It was true that all his life he had disliked his red hair, and once had tried to dye it, only to have his head turn a hideous shade of green, but otherwise, he had been like any other boy growing up in Ohio. At sixteen he had entered West Point and afterward had spent four years at an army post in Charleston. He had loved the South, said that his happiest years before the war were spent here, and at the outbreak of hostilities had been superintendent of the Louisiana military college in Alexandria. No one wanted less than Sherman to see the war come. "Men are blind and crazy," he told his daughter Minnie.

Sherman did not fight to free the slaves; he fought to save the Union. Sherman bore no grudge against the South; he simply denied its right to secede, and intended to keep on fighting till it gave up that right even if, as he expected, the war took twenty years!

Grant and Sherman were a team—perhaps this fact as much as any accounted for the military success that came to the North after the summer of 1863. Once when Grant had been severely criticized and had threatened to resign from the army, Sherman had persuaded him to change his mind. Afterward the two generals fought side by side at Vicksburg. There they learned a new kind of war. Previously it had been believed that before an army could move into battle it must first establish a base of supplies and protect the highways, railroads, and rivers by which those supplies could be moved up to the fighting front. At Vicksburg, however, Grant abandoned his base and decided "to live off the country" as he moved. This surprise fooled the Confederates, permitted Grant to interpose his forces between two Rebel armies, and wrest the victory that ultimately gave the North control of the Mississippi River.

The emergence of Grant at Vicksburg as a great general led to his appointment as supreme Commander of the Northern armies. He conferred with his old friend Sherman, whom Grant considered as fine a general as the Union had, and together they planned the

1864-1865 campaign to end the war. The plan itself was called the "anaconda policy," after the anaconda snake that squeezes its victim to death. While Grant drove Lee's army before him toward the Confederate capital of Richmond, Sherman's army jumped off from Chattanooga, and, living off the country, raced along the edge of the mountains to Atlanta. Later had come the idea of the march to the sea by which Sherman sought to get behind Lee and catch him in the jaws of a gigantic military nutcracker. For six weeks, dashing across Georgia, Sherman and his army simply disappeared, cutting off all communication with the world until they reached Savannah. Sherman's army, Grant said, resembled a ground-mole: "You can here and there trace his track, but you are not quite certain where he will come out till you see his head."

In Columbia, however, Emma LeConte made no allowance for the possibility that Sherman's movements fitted a predicable military pattern. The fear that Sherman planned a special devastation for South Carolina grew like a hard core within her. Then on St. Valentine's Day Emma knew the truth:

"What a panic the whole town is in! I have not been out of the house myself, but Father says the intensest excitement prevails on the streets. . . . It is true some think Sherman will burn the town, but we can hardly believe that. . . . I have been busily making large pockets to wear under my hoopskirt—they will hardly search our persons."

Sherman's army continued to advance on Columbia. Terror mounted within the city. Then on the 17th of February the Yankees were there, "before them flying a panic-stricken crowd of women and children who seemed crazy." At the window Emma watched the Confederate flag pulled down from the State House and the flag of the United States raised. She turned away, weeping.

General Sherman insisted that he gave no orders to burn the city that night, but Southerners continue to blame him for the fire that destroyed their home. About seven o'clock in the evening Emma stood on the back porch of her home. Below her, she said, the whole southern horizon "was lit up by campfires which dotted the woods." Elsewhere pink light touched the skies. Some houses had been fired.

With the passing of another hour, the wind howled in a gale. Flames jumped from house to house, and suddenly Columbia was "wrapped in one huge blaze." Emma drew a picture of the terrorizing scene:

". . . Imagine night turning into noonday, only with a blazing, scorching glare that was horrible—

a copper colored sky across which swept columns of black rolling smoke glittering with sparks and flying embers, while all around us were falling thickly showers of burning flakes. Everywhere the palpitating blaze walled the streets as far as the eye could reach—filling the air with its terrible roar. On every side the crackling and devouring fire, while every instant came the crashing of timbers and the thunder of falling buildings. A quivering molten ocean seemed to fill the air and sky. The Library opposite us seemed framed by the gushing flames and smoke, while through the windows gleamed the liquid fire."

Three days later Sherman's army pushed north, leaving behind 366 burned acres, 1,386 homes and stores in ruins.

In Virginia, Lee fought as valiantly as ever, but his army was greatly reduced in size, and strategically Grant laid siege to Petersburg. Richmond, Grant's goal, was only twenty-one miles away. On April 1, a Union cavalry force under Little Phil Sheridan defeated the Rebels in the battle of Five Forks. Grant pushed his attack on Petersburg, and when the brave defense of that city crumbled, drove Lee in hopeless retreat while the Yankees entered Richmond. At the end of

that day, Lee was heard to confess, "Then there is nothing left me but to go and see General Grant and I would rather die a thousand deaths." So on April 9, Grant and Lee met at Appomattox Court House to arrange the surrender of Lee's Confederate forces.

Lee, who had been courageous in victory, now could be noble in defeat. Confederate soldiers choked up at the sight of this kindly, understanding leader, whom they called with affection "Uncle Robert."

Lee, dressed in his best uniform including a scarlet silk sash, mounted his horse, Traveler, and proceeded solemnly to the meeting place. Grant entered and the two men shook hands.

"I have come to meet you here, General Grant, to ask upon what terms you would accept the surrender of my army."

Grant graciously and generously stated that the officers and men might go home on parole and that they might keep their arms and horses. This was as President Lincoln would have it.

"There is just one thing," Lee said. "Our privates in the cavalry

also own their horses."

"In that case," said Grant, "all the men who claim to own a horse or mule may take it home with them to work their farms."

"That will have a very happy effect," said Lee.

The men walked to the porch and Lee mounted his horse. Grant raised his hat in salute to Lee. The Virginian raised his hat also.

The Union was preserved. The slaves were free. The time of malice was over and with charity and goodwill the nation would be rebuilt.

Sadly, President Lincoln who had paid so dearly to preserve the Union, fell to an assassin's bullet on Good Friday, April 14, 1865, just five days after Lee's surrender.

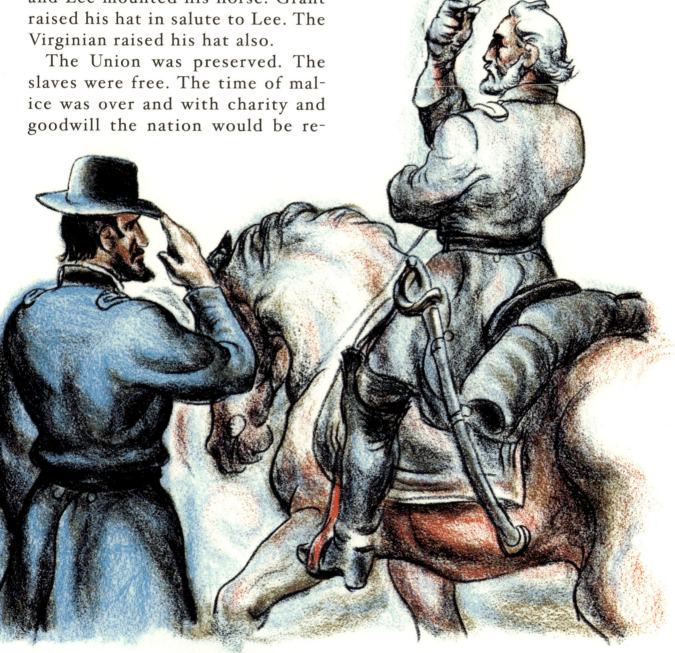

35 · "Ou! Bum! Haugh!"

The First Game of Intercollegiate Football, 1869

SPORTS AND their development are significant in the history of any country that believes its youth must cultivate sound minds in sound bodies. This basic American belief began to develop shortly after the end of the Civil War, and in 1869 American intercollegiate football was born.

Across College Field, in New Brunswick, New Jersey, that November, wind lifted a cloud of reddish dust. Atop a wooden fence that sometimes swayed tipsily, partisans of the two colleges, Rutgers and Princeton, hooted derisively and slapped their sides to keep warm. At opposite ends of the field the rival teams received earnest advice from those supporters who had not possessed the luck to find a seat on the fence.

Early in the 19th century, farm children often whiled away the long winter afternoons kicking an inflated pig bladder. Some time around 1835, during a soccer game at Rugby School in England, a student picked up a ball that had been kicked to him and ran with surprised teammates in dogged pursuit. To these incidents is credited the inspiration for American football, but the first intercollegiate game was a far cry from the football we now know. Before the contest in 1869, the Rutgers and Princeton captains agreed upon ten rules that reveal the difference:

1. The ground must be 360 feet long and 225 feet wide.
2. Goals must be 24 feet wide.
3. Each side must number 25.
4. No throwing or running with ball; if this is done, it is a foul and the ball then must be thrown perpendicularly in the air by the side causing the foul.
5. No holding of the ball or free kicks allowed.
6. A ball passing beyond the boundary by the side of the goal shall be kicked in from the boundary by the side which has that goal.
7. A ball passing beyond the limit of the side of the field shall be kicked in horizontally to the boundary by the side which kicked it out.
8. No tripping or holding of players.
9. The winner of the first toss has the choice of position; the winner of the second toss has the first kick-off.
10. There shall be four judges and two referees.

In the tense moments before the game started, whenever the Rutgers boys glanced at Princeton's Big Mike, their hearts skipped. "Look at that fellow," they grumbled. "He's a regular Goliath!" Big Mike—his name was J. Michael—was a rawboned Kentuckian whose head towered above every head on the field. Some said that he had fought in the Civil War.

Uneasily, the Rutgers players still watched Big Mike when the teams deployed onto the field. Two members of each side took their positions as "captains of the enemy's goal," and their task was to guard the opposing goal posts and hope they could intercept any well-directed kick. The remaining members of each team were divided into groups of eleven and twelve players. One group guarded the ground in their own half of the field, and were called the "fielders"; the other group, or "bulldogs," carried the attack and pursued the ball anywhere on the field.

Princeton chose to make the first "mount" or "buck" of the ball—rather an odd circumstance, Rutgers supporters complained, since the agreement had been to start the ball against the wind. Big Mike scowled ferociously and came with a rush. But the kick was bad, the ball swerved, and the Rutgers lads pounced on the wobbling "mount." Then, really without design, the shorter Rutgers lads fell into a mass formation similar to the famous flying wedge that would distinguish football in later years. Thus protecting the ball, Rutgers carried it down field by short kicks and dribbles and drove home the first goal.

Each score was called a "game," and after each score the teams rested. The Rutgers partisans on the fence, with their team leading 1 to 0, hooted deliriously, pounded the old boards with their feet, and started a cheer which, the local newspaper said, sounded like "Ou! Bum! Haugh!"

Meanwhile a calculating gleam smoldered in Big Mike's eyes, and, when play resumed, everyone understood why. The Kentuckian soon made mincemeat of that flying wedge!

"Can't anybody stop that first-class nuisance?" growled Leggett, the Rutgers captain.

Apparently no one could—nor could the fence, which Big Mike struck on one of his crushing drives, spilling spectators into the air like leaves from a tree. The Princeton Goliath carried the attack against the Rutgers enemy as though he were a guerrilla chieftain still fighting the Civil War! Once a stunned Rutgers player began to kick the ball the wrong way—toward his own goal—and was saved from an inglorious fame by the alert counterattack of his own teammates.

"To describe the varying fortunes of the match, game by game," reported the Rutgers undergraduate newspaper, "would be a waste of labor, for every game was like the one before. There was the same headlong running, wild shouting and frantic kicking. In every game the cool goal-tenders saved the Rutgers goal half a dozen times; in every game the heavy charger of the Princeton side overthrew everything he came in contact with; and in every game, just when the interest in one of those delightful rushes at the fence was culminating, the persecuted ball would fly for refuge into the next lot, and produce a cessation of hostilities until, after the invariable 'foul,' it was put in straight."

Grittily Rutgers fought back against Big Mike and the Princeton team until the score stood at 4 to 4.

"See here," said Leggett, the Rutgers captain, "those fellows are so much taller than we that when we keep the ball in the air they have all the advantage. So kick it low and make them crawl for it!"

With that speech Leggett invented the first football "system"! Rutgers quickly ran up the next two goals and won the game, 6 to 4. But Princeton's revenge came in a return match on its home grounds when Big Mike and his fellow warriors won handily, 8 to 0. A third game was scheduled, but college authorities intervened and the contest was called off. Football, they said, interfered too much with studies!

36 · "The Bones of Men and Animals"

Life on a Cattle Drive, 1867-1884

IN 1867 the rails of the Kansas Pacific Railroad reached Abilene, Kansas, and produced a new American phenomenon—the "cow town." During the next seventeen years similar towns—each a rip-snortin', gun-totin', brawling locality that acquired fame and infamy—included Wichita, Kansas; Miles City, Montana; Ogallala, Nebraska; Cheyenne, Wyoming; and Sidney, Nebraska.

When, after weeks of driving a

herd, cowboys came to Abilene or Miles City or some other cow town, they were ready to forget the dreary hardships of the trails. Saloons that sometimes advertised beer for sale by the washtub, dance halls, and gambling dens; the dusty main thoroughfare with its hitching posts, bank, hotel, and inevitable "New York Store"—all beckoned the cattle drivers to throw away their cares and money. Usually they required little nudging. Within a few hours after delivering the cows to the stockyards, the drivers were deep in fun or trouble.

Lawlessness flourished, for the "bad men" of the Old West were no myths. The easy money of the cow towns naturally attracted desperadoes like William H. (Billy the Kid) Bonney, the Younger and James brothers, Sam Bass, Big Harpe and Little Harpe, John Ringo and Boone Helm. Yet, generally, the crooks, card-sharps and trigger-happy hotheads avoided Abilene where the town marshal was James Butler (Wild Bill) Hickok.

Wild Bill strode the streets of Abilene, long hair flowing around his shoulders, six guns thrust in waistband with butts pointed inward for a quick, double cross-draw, and dark eyes flashing with suspicion. Born on May 27, 1837, in LaSalle County, Illinois, Wild Bill had fought Indians, driven a coach for the Overland Mail, served as a

Union scout and sharpshooter during the Civil War, and had cleaned up Hays City before coming to Abilene.

Anyone fool enough to draw against Hickok invariably signed his own death warrant, and, always a gentleman, Wild Bill provided a funeral for all victims. He could whip out a six-shooter, fire from the hip, and kill an opponent before the other had pulled the trigger. Using two guns at once, Wild Bill could drill tin cans on opposite sides of the road. The bad men took the hint and steered clear of Abilene.

Between layovers at the cow towns, men who drove the herds to the stockyards worked at a hard, lonely business. Hardships and dangers were many, yet the herds were kept moving and in the period from 1867 to 1884 more than five million head of cattle traveled from Texas to shipping points in the North. The first of the famous routes over which the cows were driven was the Chisholm Trail, and it is probably true that this trail is celebrated in more than a thousand cowboy verses and songs. The Chisholm Trail began at the Red River in Texas, crossed the Colorado at Montopolis (just below Austin, Texas) and ran seven hundred miles to Wichita and Abilene.

Other famous routes included the Old Shawnee Trail, which came into Kansas at Baxter Springs; the Middle or West Shawnee Trail that branched off at the Canadian River and led to Junction City, Kansas; the Pecos Trail which joined its west and southwest paths at Horsehead Crossing on the Pecos River; and the mean Panhandle Trail over the mesas of the Staked Plain.

Cowboys hated most that part of the long drive over the unwatered plain. As Andy Adams, among the greatest of Texas cattlemen, once said, "the bones of men and animals that lie bleaching along the trails abundantly testify" to the fact that the "plain had baffled the determination of man." Once Andy Adams, driving through this region when the breaks all went against him, started the cattle grazing by daybreak "before the sun could dry out what little moisture the grass had absorbed during the night." A week of oppressive heat had begun to tell. Several times a day the cattle were allowed to lie down and rest for an hour or more; then, by mid-afternoon, "thirst made them impatient and restless, and the point men were compelled to ride steadily in the lead to hold the cattle to a walk."

Yet the danger was just beginning. Guards were doubled at night; the herd remained restive. A cowboy would be doing well to get an hour's sleep a night, there was so much to watch. The cook, however, kept open house all the time—the chow was plentiful and tempers remained even because of contented stomachs. Also the cowboy always

had the comfort of his music:
> *What keeps the herd from running,*
> *Stampeding far and wide?*
> *The cowboy's long, low whistle*
> *And singing by their side.*

On this drive, Andy Adams knew that something more than a long, low whistle and a song would be needed. Another hot day and night without sight of water made holding the herd in check a twenty-four-hour job. A few clouds might have made the dif-

ference, Andy thought; the lead cattle were wandering aimlessly and had to be turned constantly. With fresh horses, the boys finally had the cows spread out on the trail, but before a mile had been covered, the leaders again turned, and, Andy said, "the cattle congregated into a mass of unmanageable animals, milling and lowing in their fever and thirst." But worse trouble was ahead, Andy discovered:

"We threw our ropes in their faces, and when this failed, we resorted to shooting; but in defiance of the fusillade and the smoke they walked sullenly through the line of horsemen across their front. Six-shooters were discharged so close to the leaders' faces as to singe their hair; yet under a noonday sun they disregarded this and every other device to turn them and passed wholly out of our control. In a number of instances wild steers deliberately walked against our horses, and then for the first time a fact dawned on us that chilled the marrow in our bones—*the herd was going blind.*"

There was nothing to do but depend on the instinct of the herd. The cattle were going back to Indian Lakes, where two days before they had found water. They would travel day and night, ceaselessly seeking relief. Nature itself drove them, and when the cows reached Indian Lakes, Andy found that instinct still ruled:

"Wading out into the lakes until their sides were half covered, they would stand and low in a soft moaning voice, often for half an hour before attempting to drink. Contrary to our expectation, they drank very little at first, but stood in the water for hours. After coming out, they would lie down and rest for hours longer and then drink again before attempting to graze, their thirst over-powering hunger. That they were blind there was no question, but with the causes that produced it once removed, it was probable their eyesight would gradually return."

So ended a possible tragedy. This time, happily, the plain was cheated of more bleached bones.

37 · The Golden Spike

East Joins West at Promontory Point, 1869

THE lowing herds of cattle, driving up from Texas over the Chisholm, Shawnee, Pecos, or Panhandle trails, symbolized the change that expanding railroads were bringing to America. The story of how, by rail, the United States joined East with West begins in 1827 when a charter was granted to build the Baltimore and Ohio. Charles Carroll, the last surviving signer of the Declaration of Independence, laid the cornerstone for the line on July 4, 1828, and two years later the country's first railroad to carry passengers and freight operated its horse-drawn cars over thirteen miles of track.

Complications verging on both the comic and tragic filled the early days of American railroading. For example, a dispute over whether the tracks of the B. & O. should attempt to go over street gutters ended when someone asked how cars that balked at this hindrance ever expected to cross the Allegheny Mountains. Later Evan Thomas startled fellow citizens of Baltimore by building the *Meteor*, a sailing car. Due to the prevailing breezes, the *Meteor* could be used only for eastbound traffic, and then required a stiff northwest wind.

The South Carolina Railroad introduced service by steam across 136 miles of track between Charleston, South Carolina, and Hamburg (opposite Augusta), Georgia. Named the *Best Friend of Charleston,* this engine, built in New York City and shipped south by packet, was the first practical locomotive produced in America.

The *Best Friend* made her official run in January, 1831. Bands played, two hundred passengers boarded the gaily painted cars, and newspapers insisted that "great hilarity and good humor prevailed throughout the day." Then, in mid-June, the *Best Friend* built up too great a head of steam and tossed her exploding boiler twenty-one feet. About to put a second locomotive into service, harried officials searched for some way of allaying the uneasiness of passengers. Their solution was to separate locomotive from passengers with two intervening cars. In the first car they placed bales of cotton, in the second a brass band!

In the decade before the Civil War, railroading boomed in spite of angry farmers who shook pitchforks at passing trains they believed would kill their livestock, or the protests from those who believed dazzling speeds of fifteen or twenty miles an hour injured human health. American homes were cluttered with plates, cups, and even whiskey bottles decorated with railroad scenes. The plains country—Kansas, Nebraska, the Dakotas, Minnesota—especially felt the impact of steam and rails. Thousands of European immigrants, imported to lay the roads, stayed to become the backbone of new settlements springing up along the rails.

A great American dream, interrupted by the war, was the building of a transcontinental railroad. By January, 1866, that dream had revived. Building eastward from Sacramento, the Central Pacific Railroad by then had completed fifty-six miles of track and, building westward from Omaha, the Union Pacific had laid about forty miles.

Americans everywhere followed this great drama of railroading. The builders sent back to loved ones at home exciting messages: "The grain fields of Europe are mere garden patches beside the green oceans which roll from Colorado to Indiana." They wrote, too, a poetic saga of prairie farming: "Further on, huge plows, drawn by eight oxen, labored slowly along, each furrow being an added ripple to the tide which is sweeping up over all these rich regions—a tide whose ebb the youngest will never know."

Gigantic problems of construction had to be overcome. As the tracks pushed west, all building materials and commissary supplies were hauled overland from Iowa, and for those building east, materials were brought across the Isthmus of Panama or around Cape Horn. Moreover, as the tracks from East and West drew closer, an unexpected hazard developed. The tracklayers for the Central Pacific were mostly Chinese laborers and those for the Union Pacific were mainly Irish immigrants. Guerrilla wars have thrived for centuries on such rivalries.

"Our Irishmen," wrote Grenville M. Dodge, chief engineer of the Union Pacific, "were in the habit of firing their blasts in the cuts without giving warning to the Chinese men on the Central Pacific working right above them. From this cause several Chinese men were severely hurt. . . .One day the Chinese men, appreciating the situation, put in what is called a 'grave' on their work and, when the Irishmen right under them, were all at work, let go their blast and buried several of our men. This brought about a truce at once."

To do the complete job, the Central Pacific had to lay 689 miles of track, the Union Pacific 1,086 miles.

First to push into new country were the "graders," about 2000 in numbers, who often found the ravines filled with unpredictable Indians. Grading outfits worked with guns stacked at the side of the cut, and often it was a race between Indians and workmen to reach the weapons. Behind the graders followed the 1500 "tie-getters" or woodchoppers, whose axes, said a contemporary account, "are resounding in the Black Hills, over Laramie Plains, and in the passes of the Rocky Mountains."

Finally, came the "tracklayers" in parties of five, standing on either side of the cut. The one in the rear threw the rail on the roller, the next three seized it and ran it out. Two men, with a single swing, forced the rail into place and the chief of the squad called, "Down!" Every thirty seconds the same command, "Down!" "Down!" brought the sledges onto the spikes, ten to a tie.

May 10, 1869, found the tracks from east and west approaching a juncture at Promontory Point, deep in the Rocky Mountains of Utah. The crews converging from the two directions made a diverse picture—Irish in shirtsleeves, Chinese in blue blouses, Mexicans in sombreros, African Americans with glistening skins, even a few American Indians.

Laurel wood had been brought from California for the last tie. Nevada had sent a spike of silver, Arizona a spike of iron, silver, and

gold, California the "last spike" of solid gold. Across the nation every city awaited the telegraphic message that would mean East had joined West in Utah.

The first message flashed across the country's telegraph wires:

"To everybody. Keep quiet. When the last spike is driven at Promontory Point we will say 'Done.' Don't break the circuit, but watch for the signals of the blows of the hammer."

Soon another message rippled

over the wires:

"Almost ready. Hats off. Prayer is being offered."

Then a third message:

"We have got done praying. The spike is about to be presented."

Finally the wires said: "All ready now!" Across America church bells rang, people shouted, hats were thrown into the air. We were indeed a country indivisible!

38 · Prairie Tragedy

The Great Chicago Fire, 1871

DISASTER is a natural part of history. Often calamity is created by causes beyond the control of man as was the case when the Grasshopper Plague of 1874 devastated every sign of green vegetation from the Rocky Mountains to beyond the Missouri River. Science then knew nothing of the habits of Rocky Mountain locusts; suddenly one day the insects appeared, borne on a hot southwest wind. Within minutes they stripped field, orchard, or vineyard, eating everything to the ground or bark. Farms were ruined overnight.

Flood, tornado, and sandstorm

are periodic grim visitors to the Midwest and Southwest; hurricane and typhoon often ravage coastal areas. Fire, however, stands apart. As we know and use fire, it is a man-made source of light and energy. Too often we take fire for granted and think that we understand it. But fire out of control is a horrible, overwhelming force that consumes in an instant the achievements of a century.

The greatest tragedy of this kind in America was the Chicago Fire. Within a period of hardly more than twenty-four hours, 300 lives were lost, 90,000 were left homeless, and the property damage approximated $200,000,000.

Thoughtful Chicagoans felt apprehensive all through the late summer of 1871. There had been practically no rain or even a thunder shower. Wells dried up. Lawns in a city built largely of wood curled in browned, withered death. Prematurely, leaves turned color and drifted to the earth.

There were warnings of impending disaster: on September 30, a warehouse burned on 16th Street at a loss of $600,000; on October 7, a fire starting in a planing mill on Canal Street burnt out four square blocks, damaged several pieces of fire-fighting equipment, and left many of the city's firemen weary

after sixteen hours of battling the blaze. Wind swept Chicago. Then at 8:45 o'clock on the evening of October 8 another fire started in the O'Leary barn on De Koven Street.

Legend declares that Mrs. O'Leary's cow kicked over an oil lamp, but no one knows whether that story is true. Yet there is no doubt that in less than two hours the fire was out of hand in the tinder-dry city. Starting on the West Side of the prairie metropolis, about three eighths of a mile west of the South Branch of the Chicago River, by midnight the fire had reached that stream. An hour and a half later it had left the heart of the business district a mass of roaring flame. In an hour more it had jumped the river and raced into the North Side.

A strange phenomenon of the conflagration was the "fire-devils" it created. These were whirling masses of fire and superheated air, at times almost of a gale-like velocity, that hurled brands, sparks, and burning materials for distances up to three eighths of a mile. Horace White, editor of the Chicago *Tribune*, wrote for a Cincinnati newspaper a vivid picture of how the flames gobbled

up Chicago:

"Billows of fire were rolling over the business palaces of the city and swallowing up their contents. Walls were falling so fast that the quaking of the ground under our feet was scarcely noticed, so continuous was the reverberation. Sober men and women were hurrying through the streets from the burning quarter, some with bundles of clothes on their shoulders, others dragging trunks along the sidewalks by means of strings and rope fastened to their handles, children trudging by their sides or borne in their arms. Now and then a sick man or woman would be observed half concealed in a mattress doubled up and borne by two men. Droves of horses were in the streets, moving by some sort of guidance to a place of safety. Vehicles of all description were hurrying to and fro, some laden with trunks and bundles, others seeking similar loads and immediately finding them, the drivers making more money in one hour than they were used to see in a week or a month. Everybody in this quarter was hurrying toward the lake shore."

From the shore of Lake Michigan, the stricken people looked back. Both earth and heaven seemed ablaze. Some moaned that this was the end of the world.

Everywhere the homeless, bewildered crowds surged, and even the jail doors were thrown open so that prisoners might rush to safety. Many spent the terrible night in still unfinished Lincoln Park, which previously had been the City Cemetery. The bodies had been removed from the graves, but the holes were not yet filled in. Quickly the abandoned

graves were transformed into sleeping quarters by those lucky enough to seize them first.

The dawn on October 9 was scarcely recognizable. Dust filled with hot sparks saturated an air already dense with smoke. Substantial structures like the courthouse or the Chamber of Commerce Building melted away within minutes as a great wall of fire—usually 200 to 300 feet in length and perhaps 150 feet in height—enveloped them. People sobbed for the loss of their homes, thinking not so much of the buildings whisked from sight within seeming seconds, as of the books, the pictures, the collected treasures of their travels, the beloved mementoes of a lifetime.

Misery alone could not quell greed. When the fire had burned itself out, and at last a rain fell, looting became a problem. Thousands of special police were sworn in. Plunderers were shot or hung to lampposts. Day-and-night vigils were kept to guard against sparks. No fires could be lighted, even for boiling tea. Men in the street with lighted cigars were stopped and their cheroots extinguished.

But the goodness in the vast majority of people quickly prevailed. To shelter and to feed the 90,000 homeless seemed an impossible task, but all over America, and especially in the neighboring communities on the prairies, contributions of money, food and clothing were raised to aid a city where there was no longer rich or poor, but simply the destitute. A typical illustration of this spirit of brotherhood occurred in Rock Island, Illinois:

> TO THE PEOPLE OF ROCK ISLAND!
>
> *The Homeless and Starving Citzens of Chicago call for Cooked Food*
>
> Let every family in the City cook food and deliver it at the Court House (for the 1st and 2d wards), and at the Depot of the Chicago Rock Island & Pacific railroad Company, (for the 3d and 4th wards,) by five o'clock this evening. Boiled and Roast meats, hams, poultry and bread are particularly desired. It is necessary to send a car load by the evening train.

Many believed that in despair and discouragement Chicago would remain for years a ruin upon the shore of Lake Michigan. But within two short years the prairie city had been largely rebuilt. In 1870, the year before the fire, Chicago's population had been 300,000; in 1880, the figure reached 500,000 and by 1900 passed 1,000,000. Today Chicago is the third largest city in America.

Unburned was the cottage on the O'Leary property where the great conflagration had started!

39 · Only Comanche Survived

Custer's Last Stand, 1876

"IF I were an Indian, I often think that I would greatly prefer to cast my lot among those of my people who adhered to the free open plains, rather than to submit to the confined limits of a reservation, there to be the recipient of the blessed benefits of civilization, with its vices thrown in without stint or measure."

The author of these words was General George Armstrong Custer. He is today a national hero, the victim of one of the bloodiest incidents in our history, because many Indians agreed with him.

As the railroads spread across the country, leading settlers into wilderness where once only fur trappers had felt at home, the American attitude toward the Indians grew tinged with bitterness and impatience. Ironically, despite the fact that the Indians were the original inhabitants, the newcomers often looked upon them as interlopers and troublesome stepchildren. Especially in the Dakota Territory, in the mid-1870's, was the situation charged with explosive qualities.

General Custer, an experienced army man, sensed the danger. At twenty-one he had fought with the North at First Bull Run, at twenty-three he had become the youngest brigadier general in the history of the United States Army, and two years later, its youngest major general.

Custer was a wiry man, tough and intelligent. He knew when he came into the Dakota Territory that the treaty of 1868, signed at Fort Laramie, Wyoming, had created the Great Sioux Reservation as a permanent home for the Sioux and Cheyenne Indians. This area included the Black Hills, into which in 1874 Custer led his Seventh Cavalry on a scientific expedition. Rumors persisted that there was gold in the Black Hills. Custer supplied the proof.

Indian territory or not, the inevitable happened. Despite the Indian territory and the hazardous hardships of a Dakota winter, prospectors swarmed into the Black Hills. Dissatisfied with the rations issued on the reservation, Indians wandered beyond the limits of territory prescribed by treaty, and occasionally staged a raid on white settlements. The army warned the Indians to return to their reservation by January 31, 1876, an impossible order to obey for Dakota was swept by a cruel winter. On both sides, bad feelings rubbed like pieces of flint. On both sides, sparks fell among emotions crisp as tinder.

On June 21, 1876, the steamer *Far West*, headquarters boat of General Alfred H. Terry, was anchored at the mouth of Montana's Rosebud Creek. With Terry on board the *Far West* were Custer and General John Gibbon. Terry had a plan to catch the Indians between two forces, compel them to fight, and break their open defiance. Thus Gibbon was to lead the Seventeenth Infantry up the Yellowstone, cross to the south side, and march up the Bighorn and on to the Little Bighorn. Custer would take the Seventh Cavalry up Rosebud Creek, swinging down in a pincers movement on the Indians.

By noon next day Custer was ready to start. The pack mules were loaded with ammunition and a fifteen-day supply of hard bread, coffee, sugar, and bacon. At the last moment Custer issued an extra ration of salt in case the men should be compelled to live on horse meat. To each man went one hundred rounds of ammunition for his carbine, twelve rounds for his pistol. His horse was issued twelve pounds of oats.

Custer's men were in good spirits—but then they didn't know that at that moment Indians gathered along the Little Bighorn in great strength. A few were Northern Cheyenne, under Chiefs Two Moon and White Bull. Most, however, were Teton Sioux: the Ogallalas under Chiefs Crazy Horse, Low Dog and Big Road; the Uncpapas under Medicine Man Sitting Bull and Chiefs Gall, Crow King, and Black Moon; the Minneconjous under Chief Hump; the Sans-Arcs under Chief Spotted Eagle. How many in all? One can only guess—perhaps 12,000, perhaps 15,000 with as many as 5,000 warriors. Their camps covered three miles.

With six hundred soldiers, forty-four Indian scouts, and twenty or more packers, guides, and civilians, Custer pushed cautiously along the Rosebud. On June 24, the scouts reported the Indian trails turning westward toward the Little Bighorn River valley. Custer kept on doggedly through most of the night. At daybreak, scouts sighted the smoke of the Indian encampment but by the time Custer arrived to look, haze obscured the view. Moreover, word reached him that his presence had been discovered by the Indians. Custer decided not to wait until the 26th to join Gibbon's infantrymen. He must attack at once—before the Indians escaped!

Custer divided his force into three battalions. Three companies under Captain Frederick W. Benteen were sent to scout the left of the trail, while three companies under Major Marcus A. Reno and five companies under Custer followed opposite banks of a creek into the valley of the Little Bighorn. Two miles from the river the camp was sighted. Bluffs and the foliage of tall cottonwoods tricked Custer. He never guessed how many tepees were there. So Reno was sent ahead to charge the camp, while

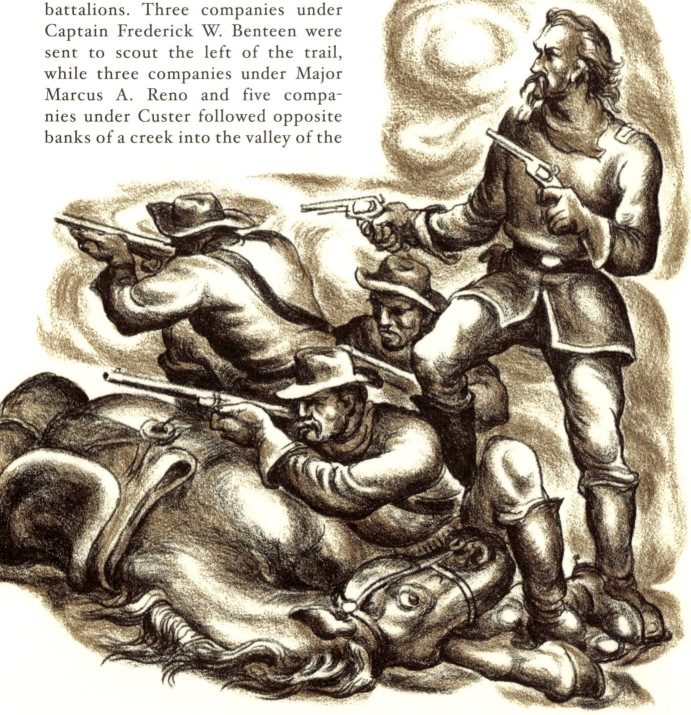

Custer turned to the right. He could have intended only one move—an attack on the Indian flank and rear in support of Reno.

The Indians swarmed out on Reno, who, dismounting his cavalrymen, pulled them back to the bluffs and watched them break into a panicky flight—every man for himself. Someone saw Custer waving his hat in encouragement. After that, no one saw him alive again.

Today in the Dyche Museum at the University of Kansas is the body of a horse. His name is Comanche. The horse lived to the age of thirty, and no one was permitted to ride or work him. At every military ceremony at Fort Riley, where Comanche was stationed, he was saddled, bridled, and paraded. Of the men and horses who rode with Custer after that last wave of the general's hand, it was Comanche alone that survived.

And the others? Only the Indians could say afterward what happened. Custer and his men were caught on a hill. Cavalrymen shot some of their own horses, using them as breastworks. The Sioux and Cheyenne warriors screamed and charged.

Likely Custer tried to swing to the left and the Indian encampment, where two ravines joined. Ogallalas under Crazy Horse cut off that course. Minneconjous under Hump howled around the embattled band. Outnumbered twenty to one, Custer must have known the slaughter would be complete. In the gullies, behind every knoll the Indians had him trapped—Uncpapas wriggling on their bellies, rising, firing, yelling; Sans-Arcs, Cheyennes starting the Cavalry's remaining horses stampeding into the valley, where Indian women waited to catch them.

At the end, the Indian youths and old men charged in to plunder what they could from the dead bodies of Custer and his men.

Later the Sioux rebellion was put

down, and, except for the Battle of Wounded Knee Creek in 1890, the Sioux would never fight again. The advance of the white man's civilization had crushed them. They accepted the fact. But the ghosts that haunt the valley of the Little Bighorn know how terrible was their vengeance before they made that hard, sad peace.

40 · Six Eggs

Booker T. Washington Builds a School, 1881

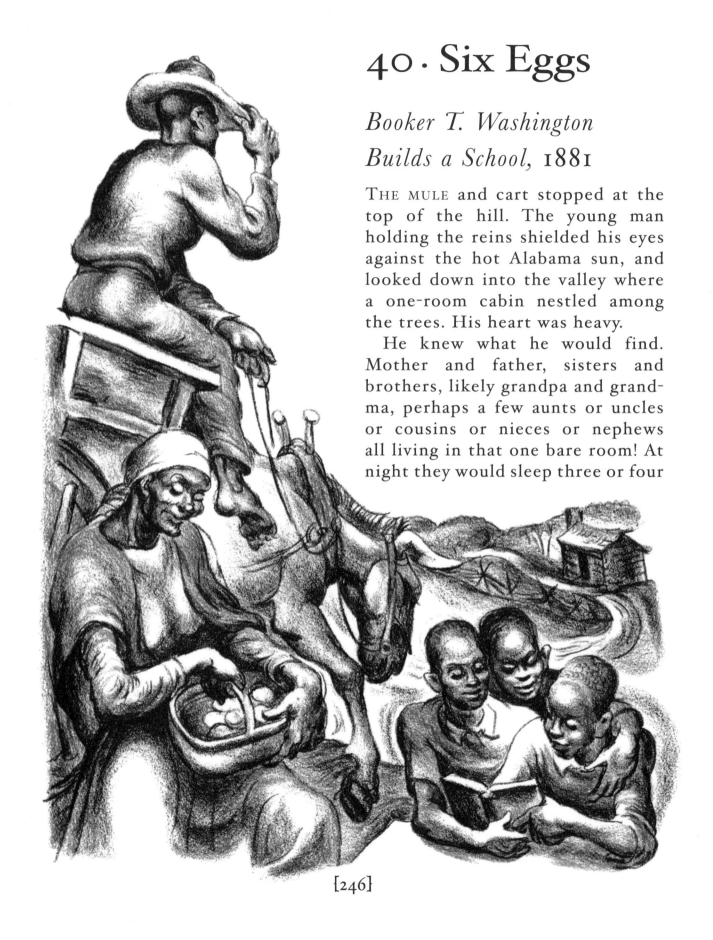

THE MULE and cart stopped at the top of the hill. The young man holding the reins shielded his eyes against the hot Alabama sun, and looked down into the valley where a one-room cabin nestled among the trees. His heart was heavy.

He knew what he would find. Mother and father, sisters and brothers, likely grandpa and grandma, perhaps a few aunts or uncles or cousins or nieces or nephews all living in that one bare room! At night they would sleep three or four to a bed, and the floor would have to do for the others.

The young man in the mule cart remembered an evening in a similar cabin when he had sat down to the inevitable dinner of fat pork and corn bread. There had been five persons at the table but only one fork. He hadn't known whether to reach first or wait until last.

Someday, the young man thought, he would write the story of his life and he would call it *Up From Slavery*. He would tell first how he, Booker T. Washington, had been born a slave in 1856. He would tell about the day he and his mother had walked across the plantation to the "big house" and there had heard read the Emancipation Proclamation. He would tell of the time he had walked three hundred miles to Hampton Institute in Virginia because he had wanted an education so badly.

Booker T. Washington would never relinquish this one big, overwhelming idea that the way for his people to rise above the poverty, the hardships, and the handicaps slavery had produced was through education. This conviction explained why he sat at the moment in a mule-drawn

cart on a hilltop. He was going to do something about bringing more education, better education to the newly freed blacks of Alabama!

For a time Booker T. Washington remained on the hilltop, thinking. How greatly his people needed new concepts and new values! For weeks he had been driving dry, rutted roads, or wet, boggy roads to see for himself how black people lived and how they were taught.

The schools themselves were truly disgraceful. Usually they were in session for only three, four, or five months. An abandoned log cabin hardly fit for hogs housed the typical classroom. The teachers possessed neither professional nor moral preparation for their work. Once he had seen two pupils in the front row holding a book between them, while two others peeped over their shoulders at the same book, and behind them stood a fifth little fellow on tiptoe peeping over the shoulders of all four. One book for five students—it was shameful!

Sadly, Booker T. Washington thought of how African Americans lived and how desperately they needed to be taught to recognize their own cultural blind spots. Never any staple in their diet but fat pork and corn bread, when there was land enough around every cabin to grow all the green vegetables they could ever use. But custom had taught them to plant cotton right up to the cabin door, and no one had told them to change the custom!

Sometimes, however, when they did change their customs, the result was worse than previous conditions. Booker T. Washington closed his eyes and recalled some of the cabins he had visited. He saw dingy, cramped dwellings without the barest necessities of life, and yet with a sewing machine or an organ or a showy clock that the family was buying on monthly installments. Think of living from hand to mouth—sometimes going without the fat pork and subsisting only on corn bread and black-eye peas cooked in plain water—for such things!

The young man flipped the reins. "Giddap, there!" he shouted at the tired old mule. He drove down the hill, more determined than ever.

Beginning in June, 1881, Booker T. Washington devoted five months to traveling through Alabama, especially through the country districts, eating and sleeping among the people he wanted to educate, and finally at Tuskegee he opened the doors of his own school. He had thirty students and was the only teacher. The greater number of his pupils already were public school teachers seeking to improve their educations, precisely the opportunity that Booker T. Washington had most wanted.

High humor—and heartbreak—

marked the first weeks of the school. Almost all prospective students that Booker T. Washington interviewed possessed a name with two or three middle initials, and when the schoolmaster asked what the letters meant, he was told that they were just part of the student's "entitles." Many said that they had studied "banking and discount," although they didn't know the multiplication tables. The bigger the textbook and the longer the name for a subject, the more they were impressed by it.

"I soon learned that most of them had the merest smattering of the high-sounding things that they had studied," Booker T. Washington said. "While they could locate the Desert of Sahara or the capital of China on an artificial globe, I found out that they could not locate the proper places for knives and forks on an actual dinner table, or the places on which the bread and meat should be set."

With a deep breath, Booker T. Washington turned to the task of making sense out of their education. He stressed plain good reasoning, fundamental subjects, basic morals. He stressed agriculture and religion. In the old shanty and deserted church that the black population of Tuskegee had loaned him for his school, he pounded away at his mission. Each day brought him new students.

A crisis arose. In order really to succeed the school required better, larger quarters. Nearby, an abandoned plantation was for sale and the price was only $500—dirt cheap, if one had the money, which Booker T. Washington didn't. The owner said that he would sell for half the money down and the other half within a year. The schoolmaster taught by day and worried by night. Finally he wrote to a friend, General J. F. B. Marshall, treasurer of the Hampton Institute. Would the Institute lend him the down payment? No, Marshall replied, the Institute couldn't make the loan, but he, Marshall, personally could!

Joyfully Booker T. Washington set to converting the plantation into a school. Even the henhouse was used for a recitation room.

In the end, however, the old worry returned. How would he pay off friend Marshall's loan? How would he meet the second payment of $250? The older people, who had

[250]

spent most of their years in slavery, gave generously, out of the little they had. Often they could give only five cents, and a quarter was a lot. Sometimes they gave a quilt or a quantity of sugar cane.

Discouragement became a crushing weight upon the shoulders of Booker T. Washington. His faith and his courage wavered. Then one day into his office hobbled an old lady on a cane. She was at least seventy years of age, but brittle and spry and spirited. She was dressed in rags, yet they were clean rags. Stopping before the schoolmaster, the old lady made a little speech:

"Mr. Washin'ton, God knows I spent de bes' days of my life in slavery. God knows I's nev'r had a eddication, but I knows what you an' Miss Davidson is tryin' to do. I knows you is tryin' to make better men an' better women of our people. I ain't got no money, but I wants you to take dese six eggs what I's been saving up, an' I wants you to put dese six eggs into de eddication of dese boys an' gals."

It was a beautiful speech, spoken from a beautiful heart. Booker T. Washington would never forget those words—not even after long years when his Tuskegee Institute was famous throughout the country, and educational theory and practice all over America benefited from his example of how academic study could be combined with industrial training. Around the world the founder of Tuskegee Institute carried to sympathetic audiences the problems of the black population. Never forgetting the goal that must be won with the six eggs, Booker T. Washington lived until 1915, a man highly honored in America, a man deeply loved. If only the old lady could have been alive then, she would have said:

"Mr. Washin'ton, you hatched dem eggs good!"

41 · America on Wheels

The Automobile to the Model T, 1893-1908

MANY factors determine not only how a country grows, but also where it will grow. The eastern coast of the United States, for example, is a lowland with mountains a few miles inland. Thus rivers flowing from the mountains to the ocean create waterfalls, a cheap source of power. This "fall line" can be traced by the sites of industrial cities from Bangor, Augusta, and Portland in Maine, to Augusta and Macon in Georgia.

As the settlement of a country

moves inland from the coast, its course is determined by the rivers, and the first railroads generally follow the same valleys since man, like water, seeks the route of least resistance. The story of the settlement of America was changed dramatically by the invention of the automobile. Towns were no longer dependent on the railroad for the acquisition of goods and services, so towns and cities sprang up everywhere.

The story of the motor car, and how it changed our national life, does not begin in this country. The automobile was a European invention. A captain in the French army, Nicholas Joseph Cugnot, hauled artillery with a steam-propelled tractor that he invented in 1769. Captain Cugnot's vehicle could attain a speed of three miles an hour—when it wasn't stalled every few hundred yards, building up steam. Next, near Camborne, England, on Christmas Eve, 1801, Richard Trevithick awakened neighbors to the excitement of a carriage bouncing along the road by

steam propulsion, and, in succeeding years, Trevithick's imitators were many. Speeds up to ten miles an hour were reported; the snorting steamers could chase chickens up hill as well as down.

As the number of steam coaches increased on British highways, so did the bad tempers of British pedestrians. The 1860's brought laws that steam-driven vehicles must be preceded during the day by a man on foot carrying a red flag and at night by a footman with a lantern. In one form or another, England continued these Red Flag Laws until 1896, and, as a result, other countries, especially France and Germany, went ahead in automotive production with such inventions as the four-stroke engine and a carburetor that vaporized gasoline. Meanwhile the steam-carriage craze saw steamers racing in Paris in 1888 at speeds up to twenty-five miles an hour.

In Springfield, Massachusetts, in 1893 neighbors were justifiably curious over the activities of the Duryea brothers, Charles and J. Franklin, who soon were scudding along the road in a horseless buggy, a one-seater, driven by chains running from engine to rear wheels. Elsewhere in America, at about this time, other neighbors were similarly curious. Kokomo, Indiana, had its Apperson brothers, who were building a car designed by Elwood Haynes; Cleveland, Ohio had Alexander Winton, an early automobile manufacturer; Lansing, Michigan, watched Ransom E. Olds pounding away in the engine shop his father owned. November 28, 1895, brought to Chicago, America's first automobile race. Starting in Jackson Park and bouncing through the streets of Chicago's North Side, the cars whizzed by at speeds up to ten miles an hour—that is, when they weren't stopped for repairs or, as in the case of the Duryea, to take on cakes of ice to cool the engine.

In Detroit, Michigan, lived a young machinist named Henry Ford, who for more than ten years had mulled over an ambition which he later described as the wish "to lift farm drudgery off flesh and blood and lay it on steel and motors." Ford wanted to build a tractor. The first vehicle he finished was a steam car that obtained its power from a kerosene-heated boiler, and with a wry smile he admitted its weakness: "Sitting on a high-pressure steam boiler is not altogether pleasant." For two years Ford experimented with various boilers before he faced the blunt truth. He was on the wrong track.

As a young apprentice, Ford had read in an English publication a description of a silent gas engine. Now, seeking some substitute for a boiler, Ford wondered about this engine even though in those days, as he said, "all the wise people demonstrated conclusively that the engine could not compete with steam." Luck played into his hands when he was asked to repair such an engine for the Eagle Iron Works. Soon he was building an engine for himself to make certain he understood the "four-cycle" principle whereby a piston traversed a cylinder four times to secure one impulse of power—one stroke drawing in the gas, the next compressing it, the third exploding it, and the fourth ejecting the waste gas. Ford found that his model engine worked well. His father, however, wanted him to become a farmer, and offered him forty acres of timberland if he would give up being a machinist. Ford, wishing to be married, accepted, but even with cutting timber and building a modest cottage for his bride, he still found time to think about engines.

"I read everything I could find," Ford said afterward, "but the greatest knowledge came from the work. A gas engine is a mysterious sort of thing—it will not always go the way it should. You can imagine how those first engines acted!"

By 1890, Ford was working on a double-cylinder engine, one cylinder to deliver the power and the other to carry off the exhaust, and the two driving a much lighter flywheel than any previously used. At first he planned to mount his engine on a bicycle, but abandoned the idea for practical reasons —with engine, gasoline tank, and necessary controls it was going to be difficult finding the bicycles! A job as machinist at forty dollars a month gave him a chance to leave the farm and to work nights on his engine in a brick shed in back of a new home in Detroit on Bagley Avenue.

"I cannot say that it was hard work," Henry Ford recalled. "No work with interest is ever hard."

Encouraged by Mrs. Ford, the machinist-turned-farmer-turned-machinist-again was always "certain of results." In 1896 he drove his first car—a kind of buggy with seat suspended on posts and coach body on elliptical springs. The vehicle had two speeds—one of ten and one of twenty miles an hour. The life of the motorist in those days was thoroughly eventful, Ford could testify:

"My gasoline buggy was the first and for a long time the only gasoline automobile in Detroit. It was considered to be something of a nuisance, for it made a racket and it scared horses. Also it blocked traffic. For if I stopped my machine anywhere in town a crowd was around it before I could start up again. If I left it alone for even a minute, some inquisitive person always tried to run it. Finally, I had to carry a chain and lock it to a lamp post whenever I left it anywhere."

Ford sold his first car for $200 and used the money to build another. In 1903 he finally organized the motor company that bears his name, and

in four years a cash investment of $28,000 had grown into $1,038,822! Ford rejected the then prevalent belief that the automobile was meant to be a rich man's luxury. He would build cars anyone could own and drive—and in an age that claimed few garage mechanics, that also could be easily repaired. Instead of building cars by bringing parts to a stationary frame, and thus constructing his automobiles with excessively expensive overhead, he conceived of the assembly line where the frame moved to the parts and no operation was lower than waist-high so that a man did not lose time stooping. Mass production, which would revolutionize American business, had been created.

In 1908, Ford completed plans for his Model T, a sedately black, four-cylinder automobile that could ride over an America that still needed to build roads for the age of motor-driven trans-portation. The Model T bounced over ruts and out of holes; it was the car that finally and permanently put America on wheels. Variously called the Flivver and the Tin Lizzie, the butt of thousands of jokes, the Model T came off the assembly line first by the thousand, and then by the million. "I will build a motor car for the great multitude," Ford had promised in announcing the Model T. The multitude climbed aboard and rode off—with puffs, coughs, and backfires.

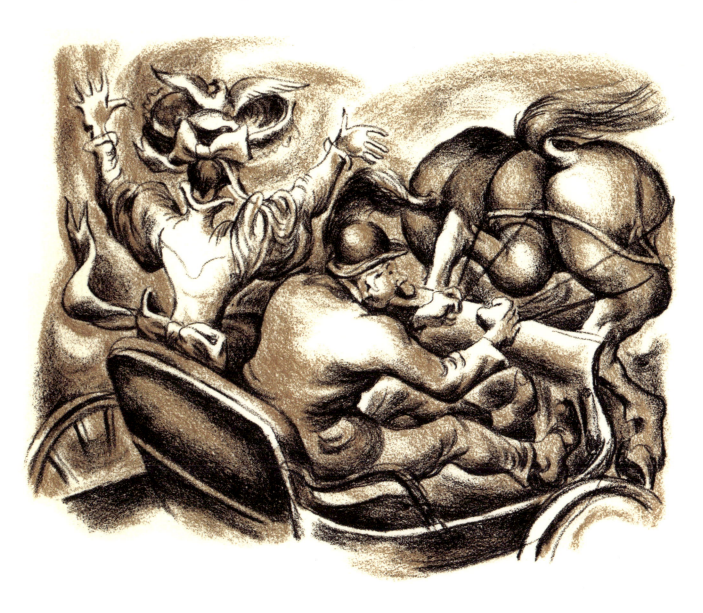

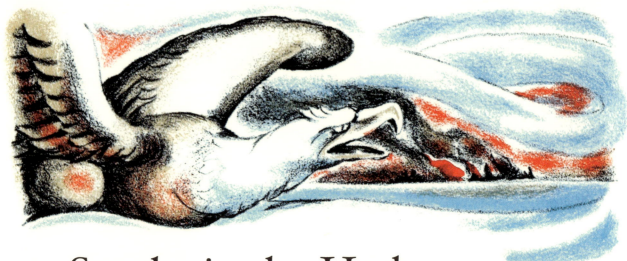

42 · Smoke in the Harbor

The Spanish-American War, 1898

AMERICA approached the close of the 19th century facing a major war for the fourth time in eighty-six years. There were homes where grandfather remembered his father talking of experiences in the Revolutionary War or of fighting with Andy Jackson in the defense of New Orleans. Grandfather himself had fought in the War with Mexico and his son in the Civil War. Now grandson spoke of how the Cuban people suffered under the harsh rule of their Spanish masters and how such tyranny on our very doorstep should be stopped. Grandfather must have sighed a bit sadly. The boys of each generation seemed yoked like oxen to caissons that were forever rolling to some new battlefield.

All this proved to grandfather was that where the country had changed in many ways, in one way it didn't change. Trackless wilderness had been transformed into farms and ranches and cities, linked together by railroads that ran from coast to coast. Fellows like Henry Ford tinkered with their horseless buggies, other fellows like Cyrus Field laid a telegraph cable across the Atlantic Ocean, and still other fellows like Andrew Carnegie took cheap water power and cheap immigrant labor and built an empire of steel where the Allegheny and Monongahela flowed together. Grandfather admitted it was every bit wonderful—the story of a country that had picked itself up by the bootstraps after a disastrous civil war and had moved ahead with the gigantic strides of Paul Bunyan—and yet here we were ending a century as we had begun it: talking war.

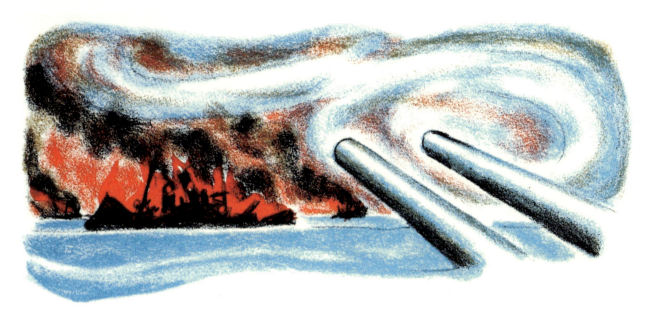

The more Americans read about Cuba the hotter tempers flared. The Spanish governor, Valeriano Weyler y Nicolau made a thoroughly convincing villain. When Cuban women and youngsters were herded like cattle into concentration camps, and died of starvation, no American could blame Cuban rebels for destroying cane fields and sugar mills owned by their Spanish masters. We ought to help the Cubans win their independence, Americans said in increasing numbers—among them Theodore Roosevelt, our Assistant Secretary of Navy, and Senator Henry Cabot Lodge.

William McKinley, our twenty-fifth President (1897-1901), honestly tried to avoid war, winning through negotiation the removal of Weyler as Governor of Cuba and a grudging consent to a form of self-government for the troubled island. Then, when the war talk seemed to lessen, the American warship *Maine* arrived in the harbor at Havana. From causes never explained, the warship exploded. A Spanish trick, shouted those who wanted war, and when Spain ordered an end to fighting in Cuba and attempted to walk a perilous diplomatic tightrope in keeping the peace, many Americans answered angrily: "Remember the *Maine*!" America now would be satisfied with no less than a free and independent Cuba. On April 21, 1898, Congress declared war.

The war lasted less than four months. In the Pacific, an American fleet entered Manila Bay in the Philippines, then a Spanish possession, and in the words of Admiral George Dewey engaged the Spanish fleet in "the misty haze of the tropical dawn." The nation thrilled at accounts of how Dewey held the fire of the American vessels until he had the enemy well within range, then, turning to his captain, said coolly: "You may fire when you are ready, Gridley."

[259]

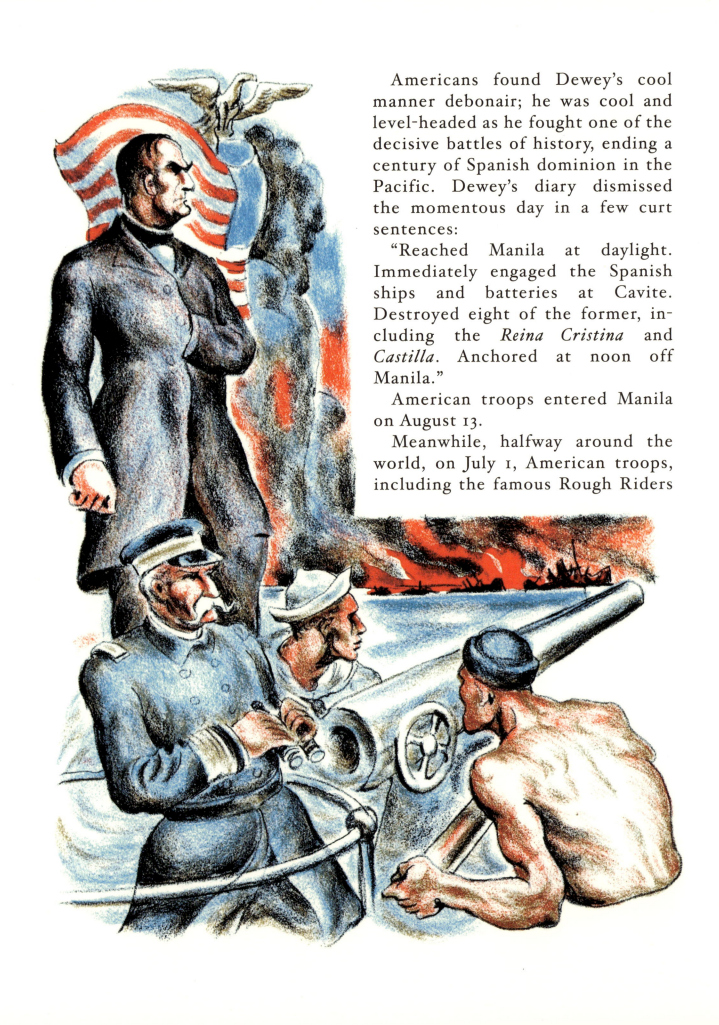

Americans found Dewey's cool manner debonair; he was cool and level-headed as he fought one of the decisive battles of history, ending a century of Spanish dominion in the Pacific. Dewey's diary dismissed the momentous day in a few curt sentences:

"Reached Manila at daylight. Immediately engaged the Spanish ships and batteries at Cavite. Destroyed eight of the former, including the *Reina Cristina* and *Castilla*. Anchored at noon off Manila."

American troops entered Manila on August 13.

Meanwhile, halfway around the world, on July 1, American troops, including the famous Rough Riders under Colonel Leonard Wood and Lieutenant Colonel Theodore Roosevelt, had met the Spaniards on Cuban soil and won the battles of San Juan Hill and El Caney. Again Americans thrilled to Colonel Teddy, hat in hand, shouting "To the charge!" and leading his Bluejackets up San Juan Hill. Grim fighting had followed, and American casualties were relatively high, but the country retained the romantic image of Teddy, who later became its twenty-sixth President (1901-1909).

Still the war had not ended. For a month before the land battles had been won, the United States Navy had stood off Santiago Harbor, blockading the Spanish fleet under Admiral Cervera. Sooner or later Cervera had to fight. American impatience mounted.

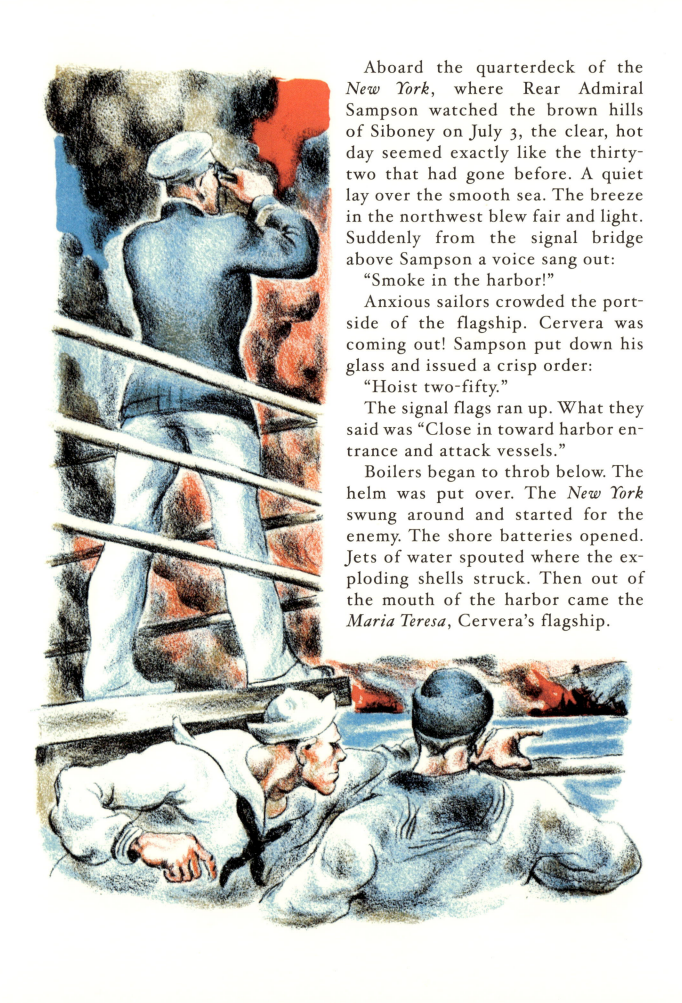

Aboard the quarterdeck of the *New York*, where Rear Admiral Sampson watched the brown hills of Siboney on July 3, the clear, hot day seemed exactly like the thirty-two that had gone before. A quiet lay over the smooth sea. The breeze in the northwest blew fair and light. Suddenly from the signal bridge above Sampson a voice sang out:

"Smoke in the harbor!"

Anxious sailors crowded the portside of the flagship. Cervera was coming out! Sampson put down his glass and issued a crisp order:

"Hoist two-fifty."

The signal flags ran up. What they said was "Close in toward harbor entrance and attack vessels."

Boilers began to throb below. The helm was put over. The *New York* swung around and started for the enemy. The shore batteries opened. Jets of water spouted where the exploding shells struck. Then out of the mouth of the harbor came the *Maria Teresa*, Cervera's flagship.

Hull hidden by the smoke of her guns, the *Maria Teresa* plunged forward. Round the hill of Morro, which hitherto had shielded them, came the warships of Spain—the *Viscava, Colon, Oquendo.* The guns on the decks of the *Iowa, Oregon, Brooklyn, Indiana, Texas,* and *Gloucester* barked and the spouts of water rose everywhere. Hard on the wake of the four big Spanish cruisers came two saucy torpedo-boat destroyers, banging away at the American blockaders with their fourteen- and six-pounders. Commented an eye-witness on board the *New York*: "It was as if marionettes now occupied the stage where a few minutes before great actors had played tragedy."

Smoke curled from the funnel of the *New York* as she led the chase after the escaping Spanish vessels. Firemen trying to get up the steam in the boilers heard the plea:

"Get those engines going. Get us there! Get us there!"

The guns at the harbor forts sent

shells whizzing over the decks of the *New York*. Should she answer? Sampson responded briskly:

"No, let us go on—on after the fleet! Not one must get away!"

The four Spanish cruisers clung to the curve of the western shore. The American battleships bore in stubbornly. The fleets were about a mile apart—hard to see through the smoke from the guns as they moved in parallel lines. Except for the belch of flame as the top decks fired, the water spouts as the shells exploded, it was difficult to tell that a battle raged. The Spanish ships now were massed together. Flash followed flash. Again, the observer couldn't always be sure whether Spanish guns fired or American shells exploded.

Suddenly, like a quarterback that has knifed through a line and is dancing merrily away from the startled secondary, the light cruiser *Gloucester* appeared among the heavy Spanish cruisers. How she had gotten there no one knew. Her armament was inferior, her batteries not really the equal of her adversaries. Yet on came the *Gloucester*, blazing away, under Lieutenant Commander Wainwright, the former executive officer of the *Maine*. Within minutes, it seemed, two Spanish cruisers were in flames, and limping for the beaches. Without apology, the little *Gloucester* was making herself the pride of Uncle Sam's Navy!

There was still a lot of fight in the Spanish fleet, but the turn had come, and in the end all four enemy cruisers were beached. The *Brooklyn* reported one man killed—that was all! The small cost of the victory was incredible.

At Paris on December 10, 1898, Spain and the United States signed a peace treaty that gave Cuba her freedom and made Puerto Rico, the Philippines, and Guam our possessions. For public property in the Philippines, Spain received twenty million dollars. That same year we annexed Hawaii. Many Americans felt uneasy—we were reaching too far and becoming too involved with the rest of the world. But the "anti-imperialists" waged a losing fight. We had become a world power, proud of our navy (which we proceeded to build into a navy second only to that of Great Britain) and before long we talked of the canal needed across the Isthmus of Panama to shorten the route to the defense of our new Pacific possessions.

With only one vote to spare, the United States Senate finally approved the treaty with Spain on February 6, 1899. As the 19th century drew to a close and we realized how we had grown from thirteen states along the Atlantic Coast struggling for national existence into a country that now was a world power, we could feel both a sense of pride and of wonder. At Gettysburg, Lincoln had said the world looked to us to prove that "government of the people, by the people, for the people, shall not perish from the earth." The nation had met that test, and, again to use Lincoln's words, had won "a new birth of freedom."

We felt that we were a world power not because of our army or navy, but because of our spirit. Ours was a heritage of freedom—a heritage that we wanted to share. And so, in 1900, writing to the Secretary of State on how we should deal with the Philippines, President McKinley said:

"A high and sacred obligation rests upon the Government of the United States to give protection for property and life, civil and religious freedom, and wise, firm and unselfish guidance in the paths of peace and prosperity, to all the people of the Philippine Islands. I charge this Commission to labor for the full performance of this obligation, which concerns the honor and conscience of their country, in the firm hope that through their labors all the inhabitants of the Philippine Islands may come to look back with gratitude to the day when God gave victory to American arms at Manila and set their land under the sovereignty and protection of the people of the United States." In this spirit, we began the new century.

43 · "Please Do Not Shoot the Umpire"

Modern World Series Baseball Begins, 1903

Soon after the beginning of the 20th century, an event of recurring and increasing interest in American life occurred—the first World Series. But to understand how baseball emerged as our national sport, it is necessary to go back to those days when veterans of the Civil War, returning home, protested at the change in the rules whereby a ball caught on the first bounce was no longer an automatic out. Previous to the end of the war, various forms of the game had been popular for as far back as anyone could remember. A print of

Boston Commons in 1834 shows a group of boys playing "rounders" or "One Old Cat," as the sport was then called. There could be as many "Old Cats" as there were bases and batters to run them, but the basic game was played with one base, a pitcher, catcher, and batter.

Alexander J. Cartwright, in 1845, gave baseball its first organized team and drew up its first standardized rules. The field was square, the bases set "42 paces equidistant," only underhand pitching was permitted, and of the eleven rules established by Cartwright, the most familiar today is "Three hands out, all out." Cartwright's New York Knickerbockers encouraged the organization of teams in other cities, and, with the formation of the Olympic Club in Boston, even New England teams gave up the practice of "soaking" or hitting the runner with the ball.

It was natural that baseball should suffer in the years from 1861 to 1865, but despite the elimination of the one-bounce rule, returning war veterans resumed the game with enthusiasm. Especially in Ohio, Illinois, Indiana, and Wisconsin did new teams sprout up like toadstools in a rainy season. The wonder of all was the organization in 1869—the same year that America discovered intercollegiate football—of the first professional team, the Cincinnati Red Stockings.

The Red Stockings were an incredible team. In one season they traveled 11,877 miles between California and Massachusetts, taking on all comers and winning fifty-six games, losing none, and tying one. "I'd rather be president of the Cincinnati Reds than of the United States," said its exultant boss, and numerous fans all over America agreed with him. Not until the Reds had run their winning streak to sixty-nine games was it finally broken by the Brooklyn Atlantics.

The Red Stockings made America avid for more professional baseball, and in 1871 the first league, the National Association, was founded. A 2-to-0 victory for Fort Wayne over Cleveland opened the league's activities on May 4, 1871, but the season's championship went to the Philadelphia Athletics with a record of twenty-two games won and seven lost. The Association was reorganized as our present National League in 1876, and the American League followed in 1901. By then the spirit of American baseball as a game heatedly played both on the field and in the grandstand was well expressed by a sign that in 1886 appeared in a Kansas City ball park:

PLEASE DO NOT SHOOT
THE UMPIRE
HE IS DOING THE BEST
HE CAN

The year 1903 brought the first modern World Series game. The National League champion that year, the Pittsburgh Pirates, surprised no one. Any team sparked by a hard-hitting, bowlegged shortstop like Honus Wagner, better known as "The Flying Dutchman," and by a twenty-five-game winner in pitcher Deacon Phillippe should be unbeatable. The American League champion, Boston, had its own aces in Big Bill Dinneen, a twenty-one-game winner, and outfielder Patrick Henry Dougherty, who in those days of the "dead ball" had a season's batting average of .332.

The series opened in Boston on October 1, and 16,242 fans each paid a dollar admission to see their heroes throttle the highly touted Deacon. In the first inning Pittsburgh pounded home four runs, and went on to win 7 to 3 while the Deacon scattered six hits. Boston's obvious nervousness was reflected in its four errors against two for the

Pirates. Before the series ended, the two teams committed a total of thirty-two errors (Pittsburgh finally won top honors with eighteen errors), giving proof at the start that the pressure of World Series baseball frequently produces anything *but* the best quality of play.

The attendance for the second game dropped to 9,415. Big Bill Dinneen strode to the mound, chewing a cud of tobacco that might have choked a horse, gave up three hits and no runs, while the redoubtable Patrick Henry Dougherty slammed two homers. Boston won, 3 to 0. The attendance next day leaped to 18,801 and the hungry-looking Deacon Phillippe, no mean chewer of the cud in his own right, went

forth to duplicate his opening victory. Actually the Deacon improved on his performance of only two days before, yielding four miserly hits in the late innings as the Pirates triumphed, 4 to 2.

The teams moved to Pittsburgh, and the pitching duel of the century was advertised—the Deacon versus Big Bill Dinneen. That only 7,600 fans would pay seventy-five cents to see the struggle of the titans was a disappointment. The game was not. The seemingly inexhaustible Deacon, though pounded for nine hits and frightened to the core by a three-run Boston uprising in the top of the ninth, squeezed out his third World Series victory, 5 to 4.

Pittsburgh's baseball fever soared. Next day 12,322 spectators watched their champions play like clowns and hit like kids in knee breeches. Boston won easily, 11 to 2, and, the following afternoon, won again behind Big Bill, 6 to 3. Now Pittsburgh put its full heart behind the Pirates. When for the sixth game the mighty Deacon Phillippe went to the mound, the cheers of 17,038 greeted him. So did the Boston bats. The Deacon didn't have enough that day, losing 7 to 3, nor did he have it in Boston on October 13 when, once more opposed by Big Bill Dinneen, he was pounded for eight hits as Boston won its fifth and decisive game, 3 to 0.

Still in the future was the great Babe Ruth, whose power at bat would remake the game with the introduction of the "live ball" and the parade of hitters trying to equal the Babe's mark of sixty home runs in one season. The highest salary that the Cincinnati Red Stockings had paid a player in 1869 was $1,400, whereas in time reports would place the Babe's salary at $80,000. When Ruth's boss complained that this was more money than was paid in a year to the President of the United States, the flippant Babe answered: "How many homers did HE hit last year?"

Part of the appeal of baseball has been its ability to tickle the American funny bone. A favorite quip in 1909 ran: "Washington—first in war, first in peace and last in the American League." Or in the 1920's: "Overconfidence may cost the Dodgers sixth place." But the statement that really expresses why America loves baseball belonged to Larry Doyle, star second baseman of the New York Giants in 1913.

"Gee," Larry said, "it's great to be young and a Giant!"

What American boy will deny it, though perhaps he *might* pick another team!

44 · "Wizard of Electricity"

The Miracle Man of Menlo Park, 1847-1931

"AL, WHAT in the name of mercy are you sitting on?"

Six-year-old Thomas Alva Edison squirmed uneasily. "Goose eggs," he said.

"But why?" his mother asked.

"I guess if an old goose can hatch out eggs so can I," the boy answered with a defiant tilt of chin.

Mrs. Edison didn't know whether to laugh or feel exasperated. Being the mother of a genius involved its own brand of hardships! She had already experienced her share of them since young Al had been born in Milan, Ohio, in 1847, and her crop of problems seemed to double and then treble when in 1854 the Edisons moved to Port Huron, Michigan.

"Al is a dunce," said his teacher in just about those few blunt words. Mrs. Edison took her son out of school, determined to teach him herself. Al might be a dreamer, indifferent to lessons that had not captured his interest, a bit sassy, but he wasn't stupid. His father offered the boy a quarter for each intelligent report Al gave on a book he had read, and the lad was accumulating his own small fortune. If anyone in Port Huron possessed a better memory

than Al, his mother would like to see that fact proved!

What new curiosity would lead Al into his next trouble no one could ever predict. Who, for example, could have guessed that while Al watched a balloon filled with gas floating through the air he was thinking of how, if a person could inflate his stomach with gas, he might do the same thing? Or that he had sufficient gifts of persuasion to lure a friend into trying this fascinating experiment? At Al's urging, the poor fellow downed a triple dose of Seidlitz powders.

[271]

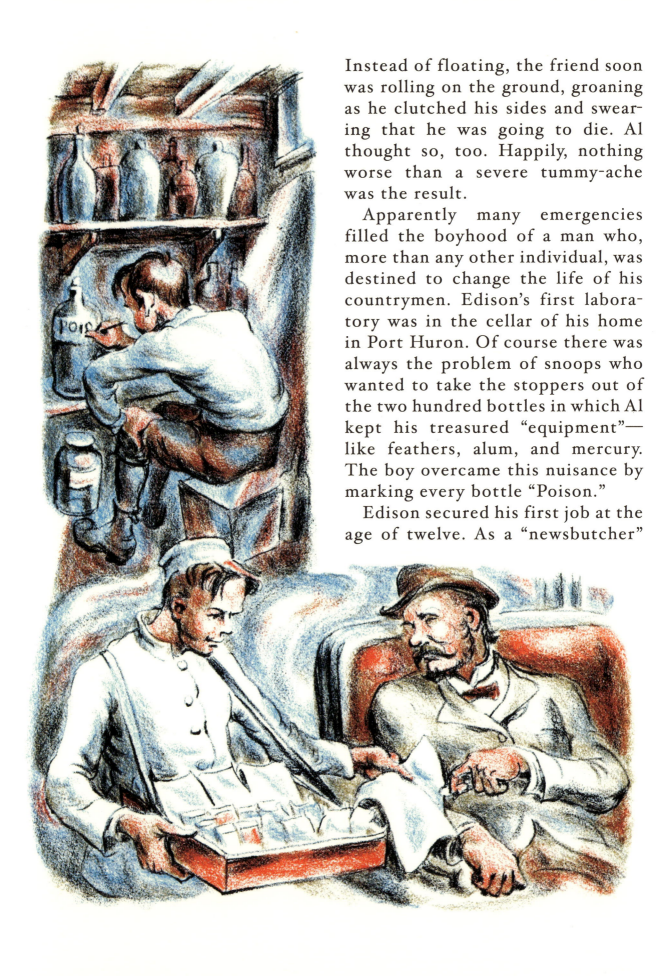

Instead of floating, the friend soon was rolling on the ground, groaning as he clutched his sides and swearing that he was going to die. Al thought so, too. Happily, nothing worse than a severe tummy-ache was the result.

Apparently many emergencies filled the boyhood of a man who, more than any other individual, was destined to change the life of his countrymen. Edison's first laboratory was in the cellar of his home in Port Huron. Of course there was always the problem of snoops who wanted to take the stoppers out of the two hundred bottles in which Al kept his treasured "equipment"—like feathers, alum, and mercury. The boy overcame this nuisance by marking every bottle "Poison."

Edison secured his first job at the age of twelve. As a "newsbutcher" on the Grand Trunk Railway, selling newspapers, sandwiches, candies and peanuts, Al did not neglect his education. A visit to the public library with a tape measure had convinced him that by reading a foot of books a week he could learn everything known to man. Next, setting up a printing press in the baggage car of his train, he branched out as a publisher with the *Weekly Herald*, the first newspaper published on a moving train. He also cluttered the baggage car with his laboratory equipment. Then one day a bottle of phosphorus overturned and flames leaped through the car. The exasperated conductor could endure no more. Out went Al, printing press, laboratory!

Two other incidents, while working with the Grand Trunk Railway, greatly influenced Edison's future. Once when he slipped boarding a train, the brakeman who jerked him to safety damaged Al's hearing organs. But deafness didn't worry Edison—it was so much easier to concentrate! On another occasion he saved the life of a child playing on a railroad track. The lad's father was a telegrapher who taught Edison the art of sending and receiving messages, and for five years Al supported himself at this craft.

By working the night shift, Edison had all day to give to his experiments. Electricity fascinated him. His first of more than one thousand patents was issued in 1868 for an electrical vote recorder that Al thought would be a great help in Congress. No one in Congress had the least interest. Undaunted, Edison built a stock ticker, and this time he found a customer.

"My patents on this invention should be worth three thousand dollars," muttered Edison on his way to the meeting where the sale was to be negotiated. "Anyhow, I shouldn't take a penny less than two thousand dollars."

At the meeting Edison was asked his price. He tried to tell his prospective purchasers what he wanted, but a fine case of nerves overcame him. Not one word would emerge! He hemmed, hawed, shifted with embarrassment. Suspicion settled over the others, until, impatiently, one said:

"It's no use asking us a big price. We have made up our minds what we will pay—and not a cent over. Forty thousand dollars is our limit."

Edison now was twenty-two years of age. With his unexpected windfall, there was only one career he wanted. So, as a professional inventor, he established the first of the many laboratories where he worked, although his principal workshops were at West Orange and Menlo Park, New Jersey. He was a tireless worker, thinking nothing of toiling eighteen hours at a stretch, forget-

ting to eat unless reminded to do so, sleeping on a table with a pile of books for a pillow, and then at times not really sleeping but closing his eyes and meditating how to make his newest invention simple to use, without parts that might need repair. Sixty years of such toil produced results no one could have imagined. Whole industries grew out of the products of Edison's creative mind. Every home in America in one way or another—and usually in several ways—was affected. Not only America, but also the entire world became indebted to this "Wizard of Electricity."

In Menlo Park there burns today the Eternal Light as the symbol of one of Edison's greatest gifts to humanity, the incandescent lamp. During 1878 and 1879, Edison worked to discover some substance which, when heated by electricity to give off light, would not burn to ash. Thousands of materials, ranging from platinum to human hair (fiery red hair, too, pulled from the beard of the father whose child Edison had once saved), were tested until the carbon filament was finally demonstrated the best. The months of toil led to a tense moment on October 19, 1879, when the light was at last turned on. Earlier incandescent lamps had flickered out in a short time. How long would the carbon lamp burn? For forty hours the light glowed brightly—and man saw how, if he wished, night might be transformed into day!

The phonograph and motion-picture machine surely have had far-reaching influence on our lives, and as early as 1914 Edison was experimenting with the two to produce talking pictures. Edison's early interest in telegraphy continued as other of his inventions included the automatic repeating telegraph and the printing telegraph. All sorts of electrical devices and appliances

came from his lively brain—the storage battery, telephone transmitter, electric motors and dynamos, mimeograph and dictating machines, among hundreds more.

At the Paris World Exhibition in 1889, Edison traveled to the City of Light to demonstrate his many remarkable inventions, but most importantly, the incandescent lightbulb. He also exhibited his phonograph, and created a motion picture film of the moving sidewalk at the Exhibition! He was eager to climb the Eiffel Tower and signed the guest book with a heartfelt tribute to its designer and engineer as follows:

> To M. Eiffel the Engineer, the brave builder of so gigantic and original specimen of modern Engineering from one who has the greatest respect and admiration for all Engineers including the Great Engineer, the Bon Dieu,
>
> Thomas Edison

Edison was tireless in his pursuit of new thoughts and ideas. At the age of eighty-three he was still seeking a new patent, this time for a process of extracting rubber from goldenrod!

On the golden anniversary of the incandescent lamp, notables from all over America, including Herbert Hoover (our thirty-first President, 1929-1933), gathered at Greenfield, Michigan. Here Henry Ford had reconstructed as a national shrine the laboratory where Edison had worked on the lamp at Menlo Park. Smiling shyly, Edison repeated the historic experiment of October 19, 1879. The boy whose teacher had once called him a dunce had proved, through his life's work, something all American youth well can remember. Once Edison's interest was aroused, he never stopped studying, thinking, learning!

Thomas Alva Edison died on October 18, 1931, at ripe age of 84. President Herbert Hoover ordered the lights of the White House and of the nation dimmed in honor of the American son who had lit the world.

45 · "Nails in the Coffin of the Kaiser"

The United States in World War I,
1917-1918

"... THE WORLD must be made safe for democracy. Its peace must be planted upon the tested foundations of political liberty. We have no selfish ends to serve. We desire no conquest, no dominion. We seek no indemnities for ourselves, no material compensation for the sacrifices we shall freely make. We are but one of the champions of the rights of mankind. We shall be satisfied when those rights have been made as secure as the faith and the freedom of nations can make them...."

The man who addressed these words to Congress on a solemn April day in 1917 was Woodrow Wilson, the twenty-eighth President of the United States (1913-1921). His full name was Thomas Woodrow Wilson and he had been born December 28, 1856, in Staunton, Virginia. From his Scotch-Irish ancestors he inherited a strong will and deep religious convictions that made his stubborn chin his most characteristic feature. As president of Princeton University, he had said that his job was to change the university from "a place where there are youngsters doing tasks to a place where there are men thinking." Wilson's brilliant mind, his dedication to a high, serious purpose in all he did, won the trust of the people, who elected him governor of New Jersey and then President.

Wilson belonged to his age—a troubled age, both in America and throughout the world, when all of a sudden the globe seemed to shrink in size. Almost prophetically, one of Wilson's first acts as President was the opening of the Panama Canal in 1914. Once weeks and even months had been consumed in the voyage from the Atlantic to the Pacific around Cape Horn. Now the distance had been reduced to hours.

A new force had entered our lives that we did not fully understand. The labors of men like Henry Ford, the genius of Thomas A. Edison, had helped to produce a revolutionary change. Men and their ideas had begun to travel not in miles but in minutes. Our scientists were growing better wheat on the plains of Kansas and the same wheat was growing on the steppes of Russia. So, men could enrich the lives of other men halfway around the

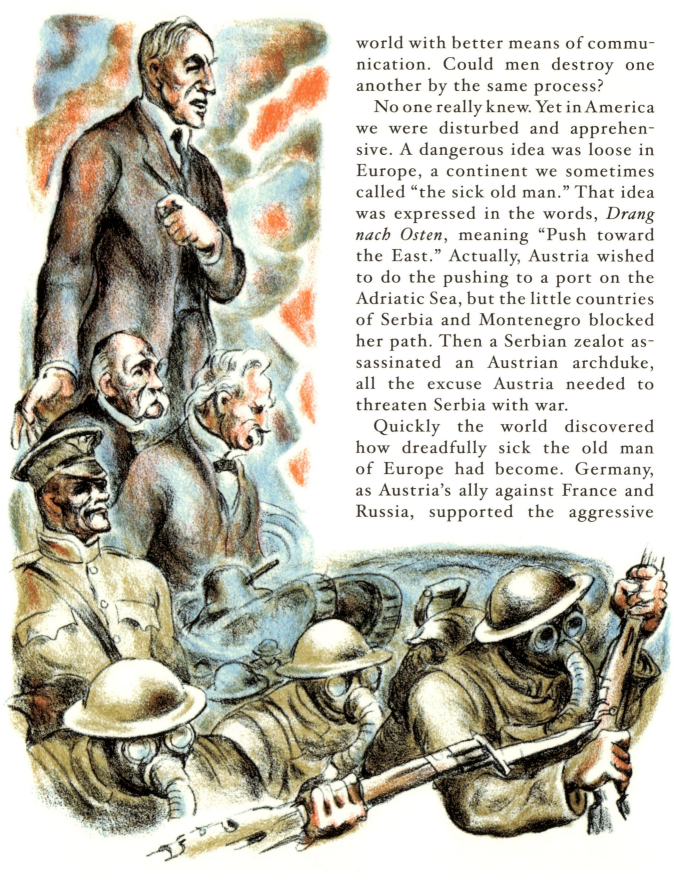

world with better means of communication. Could men destroy one another by the same process?

No one really knew. Yet in America we were disturbed and apprehensive. A dangerous idea was loose in Europe, a continent we sometimes called "the sick old man." That idea was expressed in the words, *Drang nach Osten*, meaning "Push toward the East." Actually, Austria wished to do the pushing to a port on the Adriatic Sea, but the little countries of Serbia and Montenegro blocked her path. Then a Serbian zealot assassinated an Austrian archduke, all the excuse Austria needed to threaten Serbia with war.

Quickly the world discovered how dreadfully sick the old man of Europe had become. Germany, as Austria's ally against France and Russia, supported the aggressive action toward Serbia. So, expecting only a quick, easy, local war, Austria ignited the powder keg of jealousies and fears on which the sick old man rested. Beginning on July 28, 1914, and continuing until November 11, 1918, Austria's quick little war ultimately claimed the lives of eight million soldiers. The Central Powers included Germany, Austria, Turkey, and Bulgaria; in time the major nations among the Allies would number nineteen, with the brunt of the early fighting falling upon Great Britain, France, Belgium, and Russia.

America, under Wilson's leadership, tried to remain strictly neutral, but the American people were not hesitant in taking sides. With the British navy controlling the seas, the Allies depended on American factories and farms to support its armies in the field. The Central Powers saw clearly what was happening—the United States had become the storehouse of the Allies.

Tension mounted when Germany unleashed vicious submarine attacks against American ships. Each new headline telling of an-

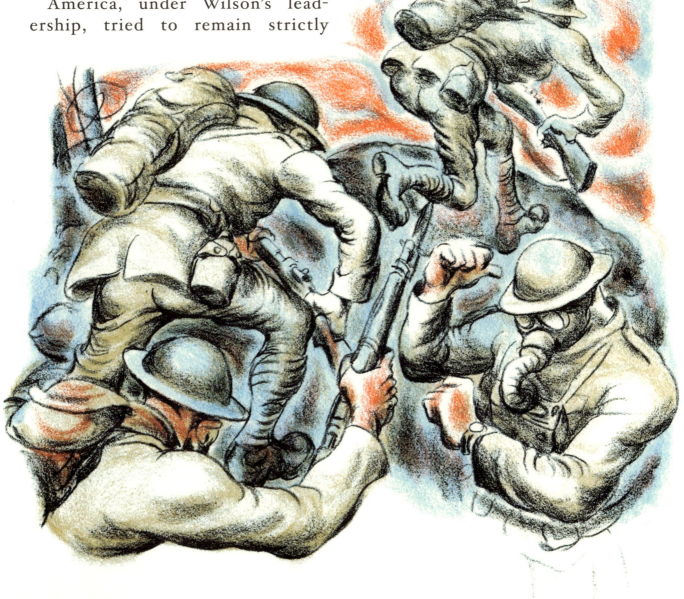

other United States vessel lost to the hidden enemy in the water inflamed tempers in America. Finally, on April 2, 1917, President Wilson went before Congress. "We have no quarrel with the German people," he said. We were going to war against "little groups of ambitious men who were accustomed to use their fellow men as pawns and tools."

To join in a conflict that surpassed any nightmare the minds of men yet had conceived, khaki-clad Americans—doughboys, we called them—embarked for Europe singing "We won't be back till it's over, over there." The whole nation throbbed with patriotism. "A war to end war," we cried, feeling that we were engaged in a crusade. We quoted Wilson's eloquent words to Congress, and felt that the will "to make the world safe for democracy" sprang from ideals deep-rooted in the character of the people we were.

To almost all Americans, the war became deeply personal. It justified any sacrifice. So we accepted undreamed-of taxes. Factories and shipyards worked day and night. Farmers felt no less involved than the boys at the front as they plowed and harvested to feed the Allies. We supported Liberty Loan drives, school children collected pennies to buy war savings stamps and scrounged in trash cans for tons of tinfoil somehow needed to win the war, mothers and sisters knitted millions of socks and sweaters, and everyone sang about "K-k-k-katie" who would be waiting at the k-k-k-kitchen door when Johnny came marching home.

Our national hero became John J. Pershing who, as our commanding general, shaped and trained within eighteen months an army of two million men. In affection we called Pershing "Blackjack"—a nickname derived from the fact that he once had commanded a regiment of African American troops—and we liked the story of how, arriving in France and visiting the tomb of Lafayette, Pershing had said, "Lafayette, we are here!" (Actually someone else said it.) Black Jack would lick the Huns in a hurry, we boasted. Americans didn't do things the slow way!

Our cockiness wavered when experience taught us the tough fighting quality of the German army. Our resentment against the German submarine or U-boat, which had brought us into the war, found us striking our most effective blow during the early months of the conflict in the North Sea. Here the American navy under Admiral William Sowden Sims stretched a network of mines from the Orkney Islands to the Norwegian coast, through which few of the deadly, hated U-boats could penetrate.

The American mine-layers went out in groups of ten, and at every trip left about 5,400 mines in the North Sea to harry the U-boats. Without lights or signals, the squadron would pick a dark, misty night for slipping from Moray Firth into the open sea. Gunners stood watch at the batteries, and soon, if the expedition went well, British destroyers appeared to escort the mine-layers. Dawn found the little American vessels forming into two columns, each about five hundred yards from the next. The destroyers circled around. The squadron plunged onward into the waters of the hidden enemy.

Out from the sides of the ships stretched the paravanes—that is, underwater outriggers intended to protect the craft from German mines. Somewhere at headquarters, mathematicians had calculated the location of the Star Point—that spot in the ocean where operations were to begin. Seven or eight miles from Star Point, the mine-layers wheeled into a new formation. Two went in front, eight followed in a straight line. Eyes fixed on the flags at the stern. When suddenly a red flag was hauled down, the signal meant: "First mine over."

The sailors worked smoothly and cheerily. "Okay," they called. "Let's get going. More nails in the coffin of the Kaiser!"

The mine-layer plowed ahead at full speed. Toward the stern glided a black object, perhaps five feet high. At the edge of the deck this object seemed to pause, then with a great lurch fell headfirst. Water splashed upward in a gigantic geyser. At once the object sank until specially contrived anchors stopped it at the depth desired. There it lurked—a lethal surprise for any U-boat that rammed it. Meanwhile the minelayer swept on, dropping more of these "eggs." Certainly the labor was monotonous. Wars are not won with romance.

Late March, 1918, brought the start on land of an all-out German offensive to divide the Allied army in France and then to destroy its separate parts. From Ypres southward for fifty-one miles the cannon roared, the tanks rumbled, the men moved through the slime of trenches. For ten bloody, stubborn days of fighting without parallel, the Allies retreated. For a time the assaults stopped, while the German army, twenty-seven miles deeper into France, hauled up heavy artillery. Again the drive opened—swept on, stopped, was renewed in four other waves. Through late May the Allies reeled under the German pressure. "We are fighting with our backs to the wall!" cried British Field Marshal Haig. Paris must fall, many believed.

By May 31st the Germans had reached the banks of the Marne. In the heartbreaking battle of Belleau Wood, out of 8,000 American marines engaged, 6,000 were killed. Meanwhile the tired French were yielding at Château-Thierry, and Americans were rushed to that sector of the front. Check the deadly advance of the Germans, the Yanks were told. Fall back slowly, in good order. But at Château-Thierry, after falling back for a time, American tempers snapped. Counterattack—rout the Heinies—give it to 'em, Yank... wthat was the sudden cry. On July 2 the Germans were out of Château-Thierry. Paris was saved. Desperate fighting still remained—especially at Saint Mihiel and in the Argonne Forest in September and October—but the spark that fired the final Allied victory was struck at Château-Thierry.

With the Armistice on November 11, 1918, America erupted into a celebration that surpassed any outpouring of joy the nation ever had known. We tried to forget the terrible cost of the war in lives—we had ended war and made the world safe for democracy. We sang and paraded. We believed in a future of peace on earth. That dream is no less beautiful today than it was in 1918. The way ahead seems a bit harder, but the hope has not been surrendered. It will never be.

46 · Tommy and His Crystal Set

America Discovers Radio, 1920-1930

"Tommy, what is this mess?"

"Gee, Mom, I needed the box, and I didn't want to waste the oatmeal, so I cooked it."

"You cooked the whole box?"
"Gee, Mom, how did I know there was a bucket of cooked cereal in one of those things? I had to have something round to wind my radio coil on, and that box was just right."

Doubtless Tommy's mother threw up her hands in despair. All over America, in the early 1920's, mothers gave up combatting the clutter of copper wire coils, dry cell batteries, plugged-in earphones, easy-to-take-up-in-the-carpet-sweeper quartz crystals, and boxes of all shapes and sizes as Tommy and his father discovered the thrill of the homemade radio. Living rooms reeked with the smell of the shellac that went onto the cardboard containers before the wire could be wound. Tommy's eyes were round with excitement.

"Gee, Mom, it's everywhere!"

"What is, Tommy?"

"Voices. Music. In the air, I mean. You can hardly believe it!"

What the miracle of radio meant to America could be shown in one simple figure:

	1920	1930
Home-owned radio sets	0	10,000,000

Behind the simple crystal-set receiver that Tommy and his father built lay a story that began in the

1800's when the English scientist, James Clerk Maxwell, discovered that both light and sound traveled in waves. Moreover, Maxwell found, electrical discharges could produce electromagnetic waves that could be sent through space. Next the story of radio shifted to Germany where in 1888 Heinrich Hertz used a machine called an oscillator to produce such waves. Science then named the discharges from the oscillator "Hertzian waves"; today we call them radio waves.

At that time, in many parts of the world (proving once again how little-isolated man had become), the puzzle of radio began to fit together. In France, Edouard Branly built an apparatus known as the coherer for receiving Hertz's waves, in Russia a Professor Popoff used the coherer to detect waves at a distance, and in Italy young Guglielmo Marconi used it to devise a system of wireless telegraphy.

In America a brilliant scientist, Reginald A. Fessenden, read of Marconi's success in 1896 of sending messages from ship to shore and three years later of sending them across the English Channel. Fessenden, however, saw new applications to

old theories and worked toward the development of radiotelephony. In 1900 he began transmitting actual speech experimentally; in 1906 he broadcast phonograph music as well as speech. Meanwhile research that Edison had done twenty years before led an Englishman, John Ambrose Fleming, to invent the vacuum tube, which two Americans, Lee De Forest and Irving Langmuir, greatly improved. What, more than anything, the emerging miracle of radio seemed to prove was the great truth dominating the 20th century everywhere. Men shared common aspirations and common abilities, which they could use for good or evil.

In the fall of 1920, America's first broadcasting stations, WWJ in Detroit and KDKA in Pittsburgh, began operation. Whereas KDKA's broadcast of the election results by which Warren G. Harding was elected our twenty-ninth President

(1921-1923) was properly an event of historic significance, it was radio's coverage of the Democratic National Convention in 1924 that found America sitting with its earphones strapped to its head. The Democrats that year were hopelessly split between factions favoring William G. McAdoo of California and Alfred E. Smith of New York. Day after day the convention dragged wearily on, as both sides refused to budge; yet America seemed to be fascinated at the drama. Here was the American process at work, American history in the making, with the voices making it coming directly into American homes! The experience profoundly affected America, as with astonishing patience it listened through 103 ballots until John W. Davis finally emerged as the compromise candidate.

In the elections of 1924, Calvin Coolidge easily won a continuing four years as our thirtieth President (1923-1929), the Democrats tried to patch up their political differences, and America built more radio sets and felt it had glimpsed the wonder of the age. But at this very time C. Francis Jenkins, an American scientist, and John L. Baird, an English scientist, had other ideas. What Jenkins and Baird proposed to do was based on research in the 1880's carried on by a German, Paul Nipkow.

Between a powerful light and an object Nipkow placed a revolving disk in which he had punched spiral rows of holes. With this "scanning disk," Nipkow allowed the light passing through only one hole at a time to shine on the object. Thus the revolving disk revealed parts of the object in sequence, passing from top to bottom. In 1925, using the principle of Nipkow's scanning disk, Jenkins and Baird employed vacuum-tube amplifiers and photoelectric cells to produce images that could be recognized. The further miracle of television had been born!

A hundred years before, America had lived on a frontier that had seemed to pose problems of conquest that might be far beyond the reach of man. But that struggle was an old story now. Another frontier had opened—the frontier of science. We began to ask, "What would our forefathers think of America today?" We had no doubt they would feel awed. We, too, felt a growing sense of awe.

47 · "Which Way Is Ireland?"

Lindbergh Flies to Paris, 1927

IT WAS not yet daybreak. A soft rain fell as the taxi stopped at the airport. The tall, lean young man who stepped out crossed his fingers for luck.

"Think you'll get off?" the driver asked.

"According to the weather reports I should."

"Mister," the driver said, "I'll sure be rooting for you."

Charles A. Lindbergh smiled. Ever since the news had leaked out that he intended to fly his Ryan monoplane, *The Spirit of St. Louis*, nonstop from New York to Paris, everyone in America had been pulling for him. It was true that two Englishmen, Alcock and Brown, had flown nonstop from Newfoundland to Ireland in 1919, but Lindy was going alone.

Moreover, Lindy's boyishness, his shy smile, his modest reserve made him an engaging personality. Think of this kid going up there all by himself, a lone eagle, to dare a feat like that! If he succeeded, no one knew how far aviation might go in the next few years!

Newspapers gave columns of space to Lindy's background. His father, Charles Augustus Lindbergh, Sr., had represented Minnesota in Congress from 1907 to 1917. Lindy had studied two years at the University of Wisconsin, then learned to fly. He had served in the United States Air Service Reserve and the Missouri National Guard and flown air mail between Chicago and St. Louis. In 1919 a New York hotel owner, Raymond Orteig, had offered a prize of $25,000 for the first New York-to-Paris nonstop flight. Lindy was young (he didn't look his twenty-five years), ambitious, a doer-of-big-things. Ten days before, he had set a new transcontinental record, flying from San Diego, California, to New York in 21 hours and 20 minutes. Now he wanted to win that $25,000 prize.

Americans awakened on the morning of May 20, 1927, to hear on early radio newscasts that Lindbergh had reached the airport, his plane had been fueled and rolled to the runway for the take-off. The rain had stopped at dawn, though the sky remained overcast. Then came the news flash: at 7:40 A.M. the motor of *The Spirit of St. Louis* was started, at 7:52 the Lone Eagle had raised his hand in a wave of farewell and roared away! Thereafter, across the nation, few radios were silent. America tried hard to work, to carry on normal patterns of living, but the effort was not very effective. Millions spent the day wondering about the lad, listening for the news bulletins, and praying for the success of his flight.

Halfway down the runway, Lindy knew that the Ryan would get off the ground despite the heavy load of extra fuel he carried. He lifted the nose of the plane, clearing a tractor by fifteen feet, a telephone wire by twenty, then dipped to the right to avoid some high trees. In moments he was soaring safely across Long Island Sound, Paris-bound.

For the next few hours the flight was lived on two levels—one over the radio, the other within *The Spirit of St. Louis*. The Lone Eagle had passed over Cape Cod, the newscasters shrilled; he was flying low, at times not more than ten feet above the trees and water. At Cape Cod, Lindy saw that the haze had lifted. Between Cape Cod and Nova Scotia reports were broadcast of fishing boats that had sighted the little airplane, purring smoothly ahead. Lindy also saw the boats—and the dark storm areas. Occasionally he flew through cloudbursts. Again, an excited news flash: the roar of the plane had passed over Newfoundland. Again, ships along the way had sighted and reported the course of the Lone Eagle. To Lindy, looking down, the scene impressed him most because of the caked ice which disappeared when he approached the coast.

At St. John's, Lindy veered east—the next land Ireland! His eyes, searching the ocean, saw no ships, though, bleak and silent, many icebergs drifted below the wings of the droning monoplane. At about 8:15 P.M. darkness settled down with a thin, low line of fog over the sea. Surprisingly, the white outlines of the icebergs were still visible. The fog thickened.

Lindy put *The Spirit of St. Louis* in a climb. Two hours later he was flying at 10,000 feet and just skimming the tops of storm clouds. A thick haze hung all around him. Now and then he glimpsed a star directly overhead, but the experience was rare. He couldn't see the moon at all.

The lean, tall young man didn't try to kid himself. Some of the storm clouds ahead towered thousands of feet above him. Stubbornly, he nosed the mono-plane into one of them, then, with a leaden heart, realized the truth. Sleet was collecting on the plane! Lindy kept his wits. He had to turn, fly back, find clear air again! Hereafter he flew around storm clouds!

Then he saw the moon, and the ordeal lessened. At about 1:00 A.M. New York time, dawn broke over the ocean, raising the temperature and removing the danger of sleet. Sunrise found the clouds more broken, although there remained fog through which at times he flew only by instruments. The fog came in patches, and those fog patches played tricks. Time and again, if a man didn't hold on to his senses and remember he was flying over the mid-Atlantic, the fog patches could have been mistaken for the shore lines of islands. Trees seemed to stand out in perfect outline against the horizon.

Lindy, however, understood that the "islands" were simply mirages. During the day, two boats reported seeing him, but Lindy never saw them. From the cockpit of *The Spirit of St. Louis* all that the ocean revealed were endless whitecaps produced by a constantly strong wind, a few birds, a number of porpoises. The first proof that the plane approached the coast of Europe came when Lindy saw fishing boats grouped within a few miles of each other. He flew low over the first boat, seeing no sign of life, but over the second a man's face peered through the cabin window. Lindy circled, came low over the boat, throttled down his engine, leaned out, and shouted:

"Which way is Ireland?"

Of course he couldn't be heard!

To an America that had waited anxiously by the radio, now came the news flashes that were answers to the nation's prayers: Lindy sighted over

Cape Valencia and Dingle Bay, Lindy over Plymouth, the English Channel, Cherbourg, and then the Lone Eagle landing safely at Le Bourget Field, Paris! Eyes filled with joyous tears. Lucky Lindy, sang a nation that had never embraced a hero in greater affection.

Many remembered that a mere twenty-seven years before, the 20th century had opened with people still saying, "God never intended men to fly." In 1903 Samuel Pierpont Langley had attempted to launch a heavier-than-air craft from a houseboat on the Potomac, but the machine had dropped into the river and critics had scoffed, "Langley's Folly!"

Almost at the very moment that a grief-stricken Langley tried to understand why his flying machine had failed, two brothers, who ran a bicycle shop in Dayton, Ohio, arrived at Kitty Hawk, North Carolina. Orville and Wilbur Wright had been planning to build a machine that would fly from that day in 1899 when Wilbur had written for all available literature on the subject to the Smithsonian Institution, carefully explaining that "I am an enthusiast, but not a crank."

Self-educated in the principles of aviation, the two bicycle builders worked diligently for the next three years with gliders, gas engines, a homemade wind tunnel for testing

wing strain. Sister Katherine helped brother Orville sew wing covering. There wasn't a place in their Dayton home that didn't seem cluttered with one part or another of their plane. An intensive study of weather and geography led to the selection of the sand dunes of Kitty Hawk for the first big test.

The date was December 17, 1903. The wind from the north blew at twenty to twenty-five miles an hour. Engine and propellers were worked out for a few minutes, then at 10:35 A.M. Orv "got on the machine." The rope was slipped off, the plane glided along its track, increasing to a speed of seven to nine miles, then lifted into the air! On the first trial, Orv stayed aloft about twelve seconds, Wilbur did approximately the same on the second run; on the next, Orville wobbled in a bad gust of wind and came down after rising to twelve or fourteen feet; then on the fourth trial, Wilbur stayed aloft fifty-nine seconds and flew over a ground distance of 852 feet!

Word flashed across the country that at Kitty Hawk, man had at last flown. Generally, editors disbelieved the story and few papers carried the news. But the great age of the air had been born—the age of aviation, radio, television. By the time Lindbergh flew the Atlantic, our imaginations were well adjusted to the wonders that the future could bring. Again, distance had been reduced—distance in the new terms of time.

48 · "War Is a Contagion"

Japan Bombs Pearl Harbor, 1941

IN 1914, thoughtful men had worried over "the sick old man of Europe"; by 1937, sick old men seemed to dwell all over the world. Six years earlier, Japan had seized Manchuria, the first step in its intended conquest of Asia. In 1935, the dictator of Italy, Benito Mussolini, had carried war into Africa with the invasion of Ethiopia, and in 1936, the dictator of Germany, Adolf Hitler, ignored treaty promises and marched troops into the districts west of the Rhine River. The following year, Japan carried its aggression into China.

On October 5, 1937, President Franklin D. Roosevelt arrived in Chicago to dedicate a bridge. The President's remarks that day made newspaper headlines around the world.

"War is a contagion, whether it be declared or undeclared," he said. "We are determined to keep out of war, yet we cannot insure ourselves against the disastrous effects of war and the dangers of involvement."

Blunt words and bold acts were characteristic of Franklin Delano Roosevelt, who, as our thirty-second President (1933-1945), occupied the White House longer than any man in history. Not since Lincoln had any President been so devoutly loved or so intensely hated. Not since Lincoln had any President occupied the supreme office in a period of greater national peril. In the hearts of the plain people of America, the small wage earner, no President ever had been held in greater affection. They returned him to office for unprecedented third and fourth terms.

Roosevelt's own background had been one of wealth and security. Born on January 30, 1882, at Hyde Park, New York, young Franklin's education was received from private tutors in America and Europe and later at Groton School, Harvard University, and the Columbia Law School. As the junior member of a distinguished law firm, Roosevelt did not seem to put his heart into that profession, but the chance in 1910 to run on the Democratic ticket for the State Senate from a district that was always solidly Republican brought out a jaunty, competitive spirit.

In 1910 an automobile was still a novelty that attracted crowds, and Roosevelt, gaily bouncing over dusty roads, ignored seasoned politicians who said he couldn't win. He appealed especially for the support of farmers, and they did not fail him. Elected by a good majority, he tangled at once with party bosses who wanted to influence legislative action, and quickly became known as a fighter for decent government. Roosevelt's political star rose rapidly thereafter. Under President Wilson he served as Assistant Secretary of the Navy and in 1920 was his party's vice-presidential candidate in the campaign against Warren G. Harding.

Roosevelt's political advisors were far from depressed by that defeat. Someday, they felt certain, Franklin would be President. Then in the summer of 1921 he contracted infantile paralysis, and the dream seemed smashed. When the fever passed and it became clear that he could not walk, the future seemed to promise only quiet years at Hyde Park with his books, his stamp collection, his navy prints. Slowly the jaunty, competitive spirit returned. In the pool at Warm Springs, Georgia, he struggled to rebuild his weakened legs. He crawled on a sandy beach to strengthen his muscles in arms and shoulders. His infectious smile flashed; he knew that he was coming back. In 1928 and 1930 he was elected governor of New York, proving anew that he was a vote-getter almost without equal. In 1932 he won the Presidency by an electoral vote of 472 to 59.

A severe depression swept the country. Three weeks before Roosevelt's inaugural, a banking panic, starting in Michigan, raced wildly across the nation. A people, sick with despair, looked anxiously to a new

President to save them by some miracle. Again, the jaunty, competitive spirit did not fail. "All we have to fear is fear itself," he said. National spirit rose as the people listened.

Through the first term in office Roosevelt fought depression and unemployment. Many of his legislative programs were bitterly attacked; yet Roosevelt, perhaps through necessity, revolutionized the American concept of the function of government, seeing it as a proper means for bettering the conditions of those who were "ill-fed, ill-clothed and ill-housed." Despite his critics, the program slowly produced a recovery. In 1936 he was returned to office with the electoral vote of every state but Maine and Vermont.

Yet as the nation healed, the world continued to sicken. From 1937 to 1940 the contagion of war left its pockmarks across the face of Europe. Germany seized Austria, invaded and subdued Poland, gobbled up Denmark and Norway, swept over Belgium and the Netherlands, drove 300,000 exhausted British troops onto rescue boats at Dunkirk, forced France to her knees in surrender, and held Hungary, Rumania, and Bulgaria in terrorized bondage. Germany's ally, Italy, conquered Greece and much of North Africa. An isolated England lay at the mercy of German bombers that came by day and night to pound her cities and ports into useless rubble.

The cruelty of the Nazi concentration camp and gas chamber, the insane doctrine of superior race by which Hitler destroyed and enslaved the Jews of Europe, the vulgar displays of arrogance with which Hitler and Mussolini strutted before news cameras as conquerors of Europe and Africa, disgusted Americans. In December, 1940, President Roosevelt boldly announced that America could not escape a historic role: "We must be the great arsenal of democracy."

On August 3, 1941, Americans were told that President Roosevelt, aboard his yacht *Potomac*, had sailed out of New London, Connecticut, for a few days of restful fishing. Later reports verified the fact that for a day off Martha's Vineyard he had been seen with rod and reel. Then a curtain of secrecy fell over the President's movements—how he transferred to the cruiser *Augusta*, how in Placentia Bay, Newfoundland, the British battleship *Prince of Wales* dropped anchor, and how next day, on the *Potomac*, Roosevelt and Prime Minister Winston Churchill met for lunch. Many discussions followed. On Sunday, August 10, Roosevelt joined Churchill on the *Prince of Wales* and they sang hymns deeply loved by the people they represented: "O God, Our Help in Ages Past," "Onward Christian Soldiers," and "Eternal Father, Strong to Save."

In time the world would read the Atlantic Charter written by the two statesmen during their conferences in Placentia Bay. Basically this charter reaffirmed the "four essential human freedoms" that President Roosevelt already had enumerated in a message to Congress—freedom of speech, freedom of religion, freedom from want, freedom from fear. Roosevelt and Churchill stated that neither nation sought any type of "aggrandizement," that they respected "the right of all people to choose the form of government under which they will live," and that by bringing full economic cooperation between countries they hoped "to see established a peace which will afford to all nations the means of dwelling in safety." The two men followed a historic pattern, a common heritage born in the meadow at Runnymede where the Magna Carta had been signed, and later reaffirmed in a room in Philadelphia where the pen of Thomas Jefferson had scratched out the Declaration of Independence.

In 1940, another secret meeting had been held in Berlin, but the world did not learn at once that Hitler and Japan's Saburo Kurusu had agreed to an anti-American alliance. In the summer of 1941, Americans secured bases in Greenland and Iceland, and vessels of the United States Navy were ordered to sink German U-boats on sight. Smiling jovially that November, Saburo Kurusu arrived in Washington. He was described as a "peace envoy."

Americans were still talking in those days of how after twenty-one years the Brooklyn Dodgers finally had won a pennant only to drop four games out of five to the New York Yankees. College and high school football drew avid crowds on Saturdays, and radio broadcasts were building a rabid following for professional football. In fact, many Americans were spending a lazy Sunday afternoon at home, listening to the broadcast of a pro game, when on December 7, 1941, an excited voice broke in to announce:

"Bulletin—Japanese bombers have struck Pearl Harbor!"

In many homes there was a rush for the atlas, or an old geography text. Pearl Harbor—that was in Hawaii! Our ships were being bombed! All over America, people sat down, feeling a bit numb, a bit hollow. Then their anger began to burn.

For one hour and fifty minutes that fateful Sunday, Japanese bombers, operating from a secret task force, swarmed over the island of Oahu. In the United States Navy's billion-dollar base at Pearl Harbor were eight battleships, twenty-eight destroyers, and five submarines. Early radar-screen warnings of approaching aircraft were ignored; planes on the army's nearby Hickam Field remained grounded when out of the clouds overhanging Oahu, the Japanese bombers came roaring in

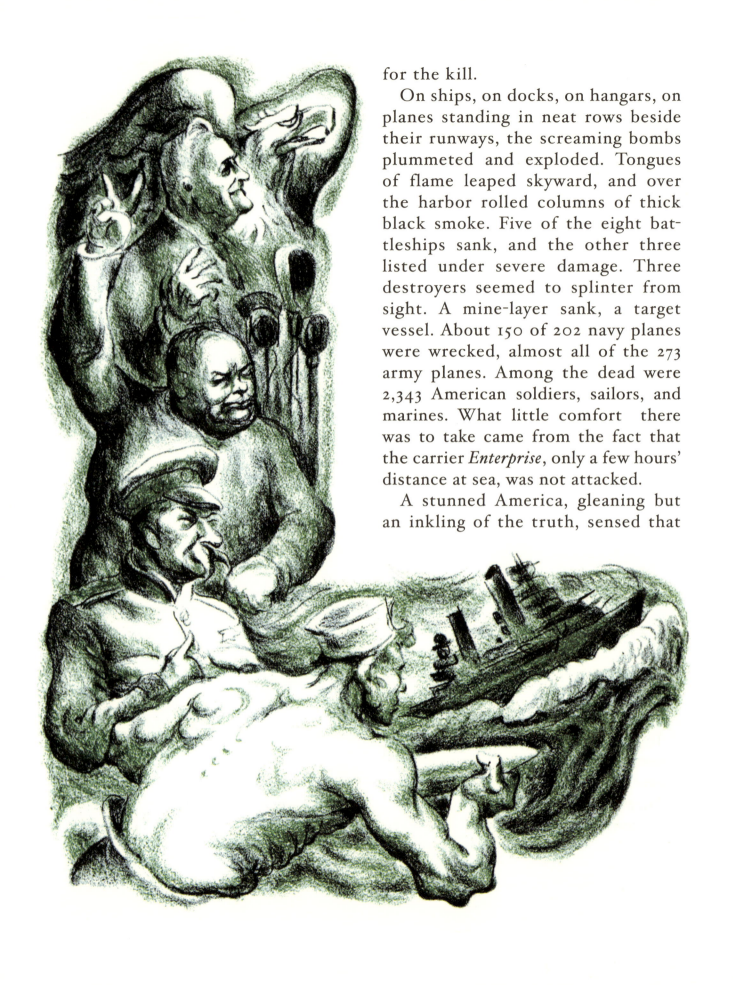

for the kill.

On ships, on docks, on hangars, on planes standing in neat rows beside their runways, the screaming bombs plummeted and exploded. Tongues of flame leaped skyward, and over the harbor rolled columns of thick black smoke. Five of the eight battleships sank, and the other three listed under severe damage. Three destroyers seemed to splinter from sight. A mine-layer sank, a target vessel. About 150 of 202 navy planes were wrecked, almost all of the 273 army planes. Among the dead were 2,343 American soldiers, sailors, and marines. What little comfort there was to take came from the fact that the carrier *Enterprise*, only a few hours' distance at sea, was not attacked.

A stunned America, gleaning but an inkling of the truth, sensed that through the "sneak attack"—on this day, the President said, that would live in infamy—our Pacific Fleet had been seriously, and perhaps disastrously, damaged. When next day the President asked Congress for a declaration of war against Japan, the country was united in a grim spirit of vengeance. Three days later, Germany and Italy declared war against the United States.

So, for the second time in twenty-four years, we entered a world war. Perhaps underneath we still felt that we fought to make the world safe for democracy, but outwardly we went to war tight-lipped, expecting a long, hard struggle and not knowing what the end might be. We were engaged, President Roosevelt said, in "a war of survival."

49 · Operation Overlord

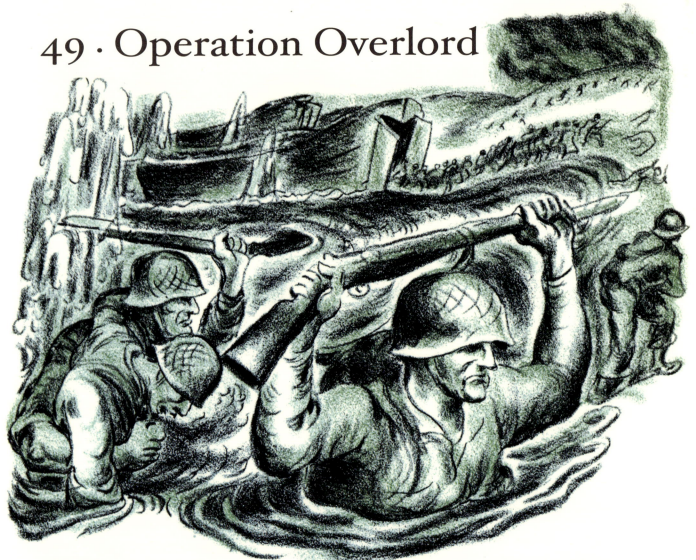

We Land on Normandy Beach, 1944

THE MEDICAL board at West Point wasn't sure whether to approve the commission. The candidate had wrenched his knee playing football. Later, jumping from a horse, he had aggravated the injury.

"Gentlemen," the examiners said, "we must be realistic. Possibly the best this officer ever can give us is limited service."

Fingers crossed, the medical board took a chance. Ike Eisenhower received his commission.

The smiling, affable Ike was twenty-five when in 1915 he graduated from West Point, and his "advanced years" alone had made him an army man. Too late, Ike had applied for an appointment to the Naval Academy. He had passed the age limit of twenty.

Now that Ike was an army man, however, he was an army man in dead earnest. Three years after West

Point, already a lieutenant colonel, he commanded 6,000 men of the Tank Corps at Camp Colt in Gettysburg, Pennsylvania. In the service, Ike early was tabbed as a mechanized army zealot. All he wanted to talk was tank warfare, air power. Still he advanced steadily in reputation and in responsibility, serving at army posts in New Jersey, Georgia, and Maryland, as executive director of Camp Gaillard in the Panama Canal Zone, as an assistant executive in the Office of the Assistant Secretary of War, and then becoming an aide to the chief of staff, General Douglas MacArthur.

The two men who would hold the final responsibility for American military operations in World War II always worked well as teammates. In the early 1930s MacArthur hammered at Congress for a bigger, better-mechanized army; Ike, the silent champion, compiled thousands of pages of facts in support of MacArthur's arguments. Understandably, when in 1935 MacArthur left for the Philippines to build stronger defenses there, Ike went also. During the next five years, Ike organized the Philippine Air Force, established the Philippine Military Academy, designed secret airfields, developed training planes. It was a typical Eisenhower act that in order to make others air-minded he decided to learn to fly. So, at the age of forty-seven, he qualified for his pilot's license.

As chief of staff of the Third Army, Ike was stationed at San Antonio, Texas, when five days after Pearl Harbor he was summoned to Washington. Ike had a new job, a big job. The war-plans division was the army's thinking cap. Its new chief was Eisenhower. In June, 1942, Ike left for London, one month after his old friend, MacArthur, had left the Philippines, grimly promising that he would one day return.

The hour in American history was bleak. The fall of Bataan had given Japan 10,000 American and 45,000 Filipino prisoners. The grim "death march" from Bataan had followed, and in two months 2,200 Americans and 27,000 Filipinos died. Some starved, some contracted fatal diseases, some were willfully murdered. On the seas, no word but terrifying could describe the rate at which German U-boats were sinking British and American vessels. The way ahead looked long and hard and bloody.

America rolled up its sleeves and went to work. Housewives and soda jerks learned welding. In World War I to build a transport or cargo ship had required 150 days; in World War II ships were finished in four and a half days. In shipyards, in factories, in steel mills, in mines, and on farms, America toiled around the clock.

In London, Ike worked almost same hours. The Germans boasted that their Afrika Korps under the brilliant Marshal Erwin Rommel was unbeat-

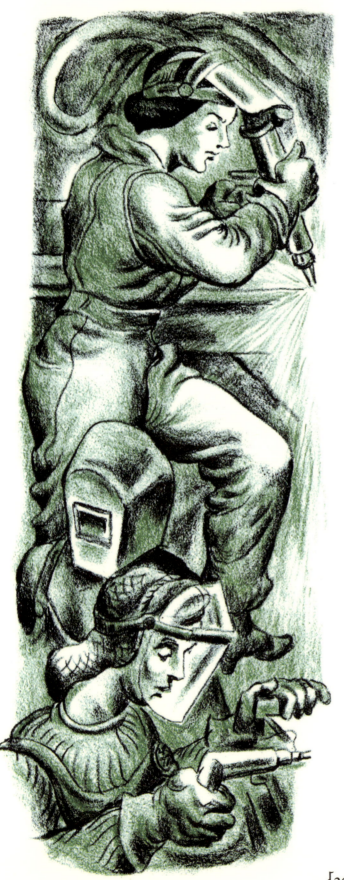

able. Ike just grinned and scratched the ear of Telek, the Scottie his staff had given him for a birthday present. The code names he gave to the plans on which he worked suggested the kind of blow he wanted to strike at the Axis. "Sledgehammer," "Torch," "Roundup,". . . there was American fight in those names.

For the invasion of North Africa, Ike said he would need 850 ships. The figure was new in military thinking, but by November, 1942, Ike had them and was ready to move. Within a year Rommel had been swept out of Africa, Sicily invaded, Italy forced out of the war!

Christmas Eve, 1943, found Ike in Algiers. Someone who had received a can of corn from home had popped it, strung the stuff on strings and decorated a headquarters Christmas tree. Ike had a remembrance for each member of his staff—an old Roman coin. Then an Italian radio broadcast told Ike that he had been picked for a job without precedent in history. He was now the supreme commander of "Operation Overlord." Decoded, those words meant the invasion of France.

War often is fought against time. Weeks, days, even hours can become vital. On Christmas Eve, 1943, Ike knew that Hitler's vaunted "secret weapon" was far from an idle threat. Allied agents in Madrid had reported the Germans building, at nine sites, launching platforms for rocket-propelled glider bombs—the so-called "Buzz-bomb." Only through Operation Overlord could such attacks be stopped. No one was more eager than Ike to be started.

First Operation Overlord was set for a "favorable period of the May moon," then changed to a "favorable period" in June. A factor beyond human control was involved—the lunar cycle gave each month just six days when tidal conditions on the coast of Normandy would permit an invasion. The army wanted to hit those beaches in the pre-dawn darkness. The navy and air force said no—their bombers needed the first daylight to soften up beach defenses. A compromise gave the bombers until thirty minutes after dawn, then the army was coming in. Ike listened to the disputants, made the decisions, passed on to the next of the colossal problems that comprised Operation Overlord.

By mid-March, as estimates of the materials needed or available became fully understood, the magnitude of the invasion began almost to stagger the imaginations of the experts. In round figures, the number of ships involved, of all types, approximated 2,000; of troops to be engaged, 140,000; of airlift for airborne troops and transport, 1,300 planes and 2,000 gliders; of bombers and fighter planes, somewhere in the hundreds. Allied policy permitted a few German spies to operate under

surveillance in England (when D-Day approached, the spies would be bottled up, even where the touchy question of Irish neutrality was involved). Meanwhile, by keeping check on the spies, the Allies knew that the secret of Operation Overlord hadn't leaked.

The date at last was set—June 5, 1944. Ike remained his natural self. He liked to stop and talk to individual GPs. The old habit of inspecting everything for himself stuck with him, even when it meant running up to Scotland to review a regiment of Polish troops. As the rhododendron flowered, he occasionally could be found sketching. He played a tough game of checkers. So the king refused to let Churchill go over on one of the invasion boats? Ike chuckled.

On June 4 the weather broke badly—rain over the channel, high

waves, squalls along the Normandy beaches. Allied hearts sank. Those six days when the tide would be absolutely right included June 5, 6, and 7, then a two-week interval must occur before the next three. True, June 8 or 9 could be risked—but it was a risk, with thirty minutes more of daylight each morning before the tide was right. How long could you keep 140,000 men sitting incognito in an invasion fleet?

Ike made the hard decision—D-Day was moved to June 6. Allied nerves remained on edge, waiting through that extra day. Low patches of bad weather spread from Canada to Europe. Where was the high pressure area to clear the skies? Even if the dirty weather lifted, how about those waves in the channel? If troops arrived too seasick to fight, then what did you do? Suppose the force couldn't move on the 7th, or until the next lunar cycle? The Army newspaper, Stars and Stripes, carried a story of how Detroit had defeated the Yankees in fourteen innings. But who could get a kick out of anything, thinking about the lousy weather?

Go or stay? Ike alone must decide. Weather reports, though cautious, gave hope. Then at midnight everyone knew. Operation Overlord was underway!

A general can only carry an invasion up to the point where the boats approach the beaches. Then the second louies, the GI's take over. They have to clear out the underwater obstacles, wade through the surf, get the tanks rolling ahead of the foot troops. A kid with a rip cord drops out of a plane, strikes for a gun commanding the landing beach, and taking it makes him more important at that moment than a five-star general. Waiting in England, Ike in the end could cling to only one faith—the fighting quality of GI Joe!

The guns of the Allied battleships awakened the Normandy coast that morning of June 6. The planes came over on schedule, dropping their bombs, dotting the shore with jets of orange flame. And GI Joe came out of the barges, gun overhead—a resolute, khaki-clad figure wading through the morning haze and hitting the beach spread-eagled. Ike had not misplaced his faith in GI Joe.

Within five days, the Allies held eighty miles of the coast of Normandy and had landed sixteen divisions. In time came the capture of St. Lô, the break through, the liberation of Paris—then on into Germany and on May 2, 1945, the surrender of Berlin. Dwight D. Eisenhower—GI Joe's respected Ike—received the news in Rheims. The characteristic Ike grin lighted his face. Reaching down, he scratched Telek's ear.

50 · The Lone Plane

*Birth of the
Atomic Age*, 1945

GENERAL DOUGLAS MACARTHUR had kept his word. Beginning in the summer of 1942, he had traveled the long road back—through Guadalcanal, Tarawa, the Marshall Islands, the Marianas, New Guinea —clearing Pacific jungles of the Japanese invaders. When in May, 1945, Berlin surrendered, the Philippines again lived under the protection of the Stars and Stripes, and American forces, island-jumping to Iwo Jima and Okinawa, poised for direct attack upon the Japanese mainland.

Now it was summer. American bombers, roaring at will over the great cities of Japan, had left many of them burned-out ruins. The Third Fleet, under Admiral Halsey, cruised unthreatened along the coast of Asia. Submarines held Japanese shipping in a trap. July brought an ultimatum from the Allies. Japan could not win. To follow her political leaders and continue the war could only amount to a fantastic act of national suicide. Japan ignored the warning.

Then the date was August 6, 1945. Under sunny skies, the 343,000 inhabitants of the Japanese city of Hiroshima went about their normal occupations. Thus far they had been lucky. No bomber squadron yet had struck Hiroshima, raining fiery terror and destruction upon its homes, its stores, its factories.

At midday the air-raid siren sounded. In the crowded streets of Hiroshima people stopped, looked skyward, fought off the numb queasiness of stomach that such moments always produced. But there was no rattle of antiaircraft guns. Then, far overhead, a lone plane could be seen through the peaceful clouds. A sense of sweet relief flooded the inhabitants of Hiroshima. At worst, the plane might be on a reconnaissance flight and the bombers might come later, flying in their tight, deadly formations. No one worried over a single plane. The citizens of Hiroshima returned to their normal tasks.

The American crew in the B-29 sat tensely as the plane found a hole in the clouds and came in over the city. Now every pair of hands reached for arc-welder's glasses. Straps were pulled tight. The plane leveled off.

From the belly of the B-29 a black object dropped. The crew thought of the object falling, falling, growing smaller, smaller. Could what they had been told possibly be a reality? Could this one bomb have the explosive force of 20,000 tons of TNT? Could the story be true that when the first atom bomb had been tested on the desert in New Mexico, the steel tower on which the bomb had hung had disappeared in vapor and ten miles away men had been knocked down from the rush of air created by the explosion?

The B-29 swung to get out of range. The plane's mighty engines roared. Through the dark mask of the arc welder's glasses broke a light so intense that the cabin seemed aflame. Over the sky hung a bluish-green light—unreal in its quality, frightening. Then the blast wave struck. The B-29 rocked as though cannon fire raked it from nose to tail. The blasts came quickly then— one, two, three, four. . . .

With glasses removed, one of the crew said, "*Look!*"

In the sky coming through a white ring of smoke, rose a great ball of fire. Beneath it was a pillar of fire, purplish in color, that in seconds

had climbed 10,000 feet, in more seconds had reached 20,000, and still went upward—to 40,000, to 50,000, to 60,000 or whatever its ceiling was somewhere in the unseeable stratosphere. It grew, took shape like a mushroom, then sprouted a second mushroom below.

Looking back, two hundred miles from Hiroshima, the crew of the B-29 could still see those shapes.

In time, the smoke, the dust, the fire disappeared above Hiroshima. The Japanese dead amounted to 78,150; the missing, 13,933; the burned and injured, 37,425; the homeless and sick, 176,987—many of whom later died. Four square miles of buildings had been devastated. In the average American city, six hundred blocks would have been destroyed.

Thus in agony, in destruction, in war, a cycle of civilization ended, another began. When Japan still refused to surrender, a second atom bomb was dropped a few days later on the city of Nagasaki. Japan capitulated.

The complicated, highly technical story of the atom bomb actually began on an August day in 1939 in Princeton, New Jersey. There Albert Einstein, discoverer of the theory of relativity, a scientist renowned throughout the world, wrote a letter to President Roosevelt. In part, Einstein wrote:

"In the course of the past four months it has been made probable ... that it may be possible to set up a nuclear chain reaction in a large mass of uranium, by which vast amounts of power and large quantities of new radium-like elements would be generated. Now it appears almost certain that this could be achieved in the immediate future.

"This new phenomenon would also lead to the construction of bombs, and it is conceivable—though much less certain—that extremely powerful bombs of a new type may thus be constructed. A single bomb of this type, carried by boat and exploded in a port, might very well destroy the whole port together with some of the surrounding territory...."

In a concluding paragraph, Einstein informed the President that Germany had confiscated the uranium mines of Czechoslovakia and that in Berlin scientists were working on the same principles. The President acted promptly and the Office of Scientific Research and Development was created. What followed in succeeding months, as the most brilliant scientific minds in America worked in secret on building an atom bomb, was expressed on the day the Atomic Age was born at Hiroshima. That day Harry S. Truman, who succeeded Roosevelt as our thirty-third President (1945-1952), said: "We have spent two billion dollars on the greatest scientific gamble in history—and won."

In those weeks when the end of World War II approached, uppermost in the minds of statesmen was the need for some effective organization to negotiate disputes between nations and eliminate the senseless wastes of life and property that war produced. After World War I, the League of Nations had been created for a similar purpose, but the unwillingness of the United States to be a member of that body had crippled its power. Now America took the lead in trying to learn from the bitter lessons of the past and at San Francisco during June, 1945, the United Nations was

formed. Addressing the delegates at the time the Charter of the United Nations was adopted, President Truman said: "What a great day this can be in history!"

No one doubted that the years ahead would pose tremendous problems. Later, with the experimental explosion of the hydrogen bomb, man's ability to kill became even more staggering to contemplate. The basic challenge of the 20th century was squarely before us:

"We must cultivate the science of human relations—the ability of all peoples, of all kinds, to live together and work together in the same world, at peace."

Such were the last words written by Franklin Delano Roosevelt before, on April 12, 1945, a cerebral hemorrhage ended his life. His signature, creating the Office of Scientific Research and Development, made him the first statesman of the Atomic Age. His last recorded thoughts were of the people who would inherit that age.

So came America to the middle years of the 20th century. War never had been made more fearful or peace more beautiful. A great new source of power had been created. Men had not yet fully conceived what unimagined riches could flow from this source of energy. But to men of good will the future is bright with hope.

Postscript

The modern Viking, who soars to adventure among the clouds, finds that looking down on America from an airplane is an exhilarating experience. We live in a land of many marvels, and, from the air, much of it can be seen in a single day.

A fascinating adventure that awaits the air traveler is the sight of a city at night. The surrounding country often is so black that one must guess where the rivers, the forests, the swamps, the farms are located. Then, all at once, this darkness is transferred into a setting of rich velvet, upon which glistens the jewel—the lights of an approaching city! No matter how ugly by day this metropolis may have seemed, from the air at night it is beautiful. As the city draws closer, as the lamps of highways and streets form twinkling patterns, as moving bits of light indicate the position of the little bugs that automobiles now are, as thousands of houses shed their tiny glimmers upon a hillside or along a river valley, the feeling of what our country represents grows in the heart of the observer. America is people and homes.

By daylight the vista is no less thrilling. Much of America is farmland—varied patches of color, where fields of corn run into fields of rye and wheat, or drowsy meadows, or the neat furrows of the truck farm. Below, too, are the gentle valleys that drain this land, and looking down even the mighty Mississippi, "flowing unvexed to the sea," seems no more than a winding thread of silver and gold. Houses are far apart here, yet everywhere are the roads and railway tracks, the airports with their trim runways and fluttering wind socks, the millions of miles of telephone and telegraph wires, climbing the mountains and jumping the rivers, so that no part of our country really needs to be isolated. So America is also food and communication.

By day, the cities tell another story. From many miles away the air traveler sees the smoke and glow of the great blast furnaces around Pittsburgh or Birmingham or Gary, Indiana. Approaching Chicago across Lake Michigan, one sees the freighters and tankers moving like toy boats, and then, flying above the tall buildings, one looks for the stockyards and enormous grain elevators fed by the cattle ranches and farms of half a continent. On either coast, and New York or San Francisco are fine examples, harbors and bays dance with vessels from every port of the globe. So America is a country of industry and commerce.

Yet the picture is not complete. Among the greatest fascinations of air travel in America are the towns, the villages, the crossroad hamlets that spring up at regular intervals along every highway and every route of railroad track. Each shares with the others many characteristics—the church steeple, the school, the local baseball park. But the almost unending number of churches and schools one sees as one flies over our country linger longest in memory. America is a country of faith and freedom, children and enlightenment.

All these vistas, and countless others that can be seen, are parts of a song, a poem. Not only do they share the common history, but they also possess a single meaning. America's peace—a full, abundant peace is the fruit that freedom and tolerance can produce. Lincoln once said: "We must meanly lose, or nobly save, the last best hope of earth!"

The modern Viking, soaring through the clouds above America, sees everywhere signs of the greatness of God. It is indeed the one truth in which we all believe. It is indeed our richest heritage.

E. S. M.

Index

A

Abenakis, 69
Abilene, 224-6
Acushnet, 166
Adams, Andy, 226-8
Adams, John, 91
Adams, Samuel, 74, 78, 88, 91, 111
Adams Express Company, 161
Afrika Korps, 300
Alabama, 203, 246-7
Alamo Mission, 145-51
Alamo River, 144
Albany, 209
Alcock, John, 287
Alder Creek Valley, 174
Alexandria, La., 214
Allegheny Mountains, 56, 133, 230
Allegheny River, 68, 258
Allen, Ethan, 88
Allies: in World War I, 279, 280; in World War II, 301 ff.
A. L. Shotwell, 158
American Fork, 180
American League, 267-8, 270
American Revolution, 79-107, 114, 132, 141, 159, 258
Anderson, Robert, 203-4
André, John, 104
Antietam Creek (battle), 208-9
Antillia, 25-6, 28
Apaches, 134 ff., 139, 144
Apperson brothers, 254
Appomattox, Lee's surrender at, 218-9
Argonne Forest (battle), 282
Arikaras, 119, 121
Arizona, 28, 133, 186, 187, 231
Arkansas, 123, 203
Arkansas River, 48
Arlington, 207
Armistice, World War I, 282
Army of the Potomac, 209
Arnold, Benedict, 104
Arrendondo, Joaquín, 145-6
Articles of Confederation, 110
Atlanta, 212, 215
Atlantic Charter, 294-5
atom bomb, 305-7
Augusta, 294
Augusta, Ga., 230, 252
Augusta, Maine, 252
Austin, Moses, 146
Austin, Stephen, 146
Austin, Tex., 226
automobile, history of, 252-7
aviation, history of, 287-91

B

bad men, 225
Baird, James L., 286
Balboa, Vasco Núñez de, 26
Baltimore, besiegement of, 125-6
Baltimore and Ohio Railroad, 229-30
Bangor, 252
Barataria Bay, 124, 126-7
Barbary pirates, 17
baseball, history of, 266-70
Bass, Sam, 225
Bataan Death March, 299
Baxter Springs, 226
Bear River, 133
Beauregard, Pierre G. T., 203-4
Bell, John, 202
Belleau Wood (battle), 281
Benteen, Frederick W., 242-3
Berlin, surrender of, 303
Best Friend of Charleston, 230
Bible, 64, 92, 116, 144, 201
Big Harpe, 225
Bighorn River, 241
Bill of Rights, 111-2
Billy the Kid (William H. Bonney), 225
Bixby, Horace, 156-7
Black Hawk War, 190
Black Hills, 231, 240-1
Bonham, James Butler, 146
Boone, Daniel, 132-3
Boonesboro, 133
Boston, 61, 73-8, 104, 268-9
Boston Commons, 267
Boston Harbor, 77, 79
Boston Latin School, 140-1
Boston Massacre, 74
Boston Tea Party, 73-8, 109
Boudinot, Elias, 114
Bowie, Jim, 146, 149
Braddock, Edward, 56, 66, 68-70
Bradford, William, 43-4
Brandywine River, 93
Branly, Edouard, 284
Brazos River, 149
Breckinridge, John C, 202
Breed's Hill (battle), 84-7, 104
Brown, Arthur, 287
Brown, Harry Box, 161
Brown, John, 202
Brown University, 141
Brownsville, 185
Buffalo Bill. See Cody, William.
Bull Run (battle), 205, 208, 240
Bunker Hill. See Breed's Hill.
Bunyan, John, 62
Burgoyne, John, 93
Burke, Edmund, 80
Burlington, 61, 63
Burras, Ann, 40
Butten, William, 44

C

Cabeza de Vaca, Álvar Núñez, 27-8, 144
Cabot, John, 33
Cabot, Sebastian, 33
Cabrillo, Juan Rodríguez, 178
Caesar, Julius, 104-5
Caesar's Gallic Wars, 104
Cairo, Ill., 157
Calhoun, John C, 125
California, 49, 132, 138-9, 171 7, 178-9, 182-3, 186-7, 231, 267, 286, 288
California, Gulf of, 152
California Republic, 179
California Trail, 198
Canafataugas, 57
Canary Islands, 19
Cape Breton Island, 14, 56
Cape Cod, 44, 167, 288
Carnegie, Andrew, 258

Carroll, Charles, 229
Carson, Kit, 139, 179
Carson City, 198
Cartier, Jacques, 32
Cartwright, Alexander J., 267
cattle trails, 226
Caughnewagas, 59, 69
Central Pacific Railroad, 230-1
Central Powers, World War I, 279
Cerro Gordo (battle), 186
Cervera Topete, Pascual, 261-4
Chad's Ferry (battle), 93
Chancellorsville (battle), 209
Chapultepec (battle), 186
Charbonneau, Pomp, 123
Charbonneau, Toussaint, 122
Charles River, 75, 81, 83, 85
Charleston, 203-4, 214, 230
Charlestown, burning of, 86
Château-Thierry (battle), 281-2
Chattanooga (battle), 215
Chequamegon Bay, 46
Chesapeake Bay, 93, 105, 110, 126
Cheyenne, Wyo., 224
Cheyennes, 121, 240 ff.
Chicago, 254, 288, 292; massacre, 125; fire, 235-9
Chicago River, 236
Chicago *Tribune*, 237
Chickahominy River, 36-7
China trade, 132
Chisholm Trail, 226, 229
Churchill, Winston, 294-5, 302
Churubusco (battle), 186
Cincinnati, 153-5, 159
Civil War. 159, 200-219, 221, 226, 230, 258, 266
Claiborne, William, 124, 153
Clark, George Rogers, 98-102, 103, 118, 140
Clark, William, 118-23, 164
Clay, Henry, 125
Clemens, Samuel Langhome, 7-8, 152-9, 198
Cleveland, 254, 267
Clinton, Henry, 84, 87, 106
Coahuiltecans, 144
Cody, William Frederick, 199
Coffin, Levi, 164
College of New Jersey (Princeton), 141
Colorado, 182, 186, 230

Colorado River, 133, 226
Columbia, S.C., 211-7
Columbia Law School, 292
Columbia University, 141
Columbus, Christopher, 17-24, 46
Columbus, Ohio, 209
Comanche (horse), 243
Comanches, 134, 144, 148
Committee on Correspondence, 74
Commodore Rollingpin's Almanac, 157
Compromise of 1850, 187
Comstock Lode, 182
Concord (battle), 83, 103
Confederate States of America, 151, 184, 203
Connecticut, 294
Constitution, U.S., 109-12
Continental Congress, 79-80, 83, 88-9, 110
Cook, James, 132
Coolidge, Calvin, 286
Cooper Union, 194
Copley, John S., 87
Cornwallis, Charles, 93, 104-5
Coronado, Francisco Vásquez de, 144
Cos, Martin Perfecto de, 146
Cowpens (battle), 105
cow towns, 224-5
Creek Confederacy, 28
Crockett, David, 146-9
Crown Point, capture of, 70-1, 88
Crows, 121
Cruzatte, Pierre, 120
Cuba, 28, 258-9, 261
Cugnot, Nicholas Joseph, 253
Custer, George A., 240-4

D

Dakota Territory, 230, 240-1
Dare, Virginia, 33-4
Dartmouth College, 141
Davis, Jefferson, 184, 203
Davis, John W., 286
Dayton, 290-1
D-Day, 301
Declaration of Independence, 89-92, 93, 103, 110, 112, 229, 295
Defoe, Daniel, 47, 62
De Forest, Lee, 285
Delaware River, 93, 116
Delawares, 57-60

Deliverance, 40
de Soto, Hernando, 28-32, 45, 47, 49
de Triana, Rodrigo, 22
Detroit, 125, 254-5
Dewey, George, 259-60
Dinneen, Big Bill, 268-70
Discovery, 35
Dodge, Grenville M., 231
"Dogood, Mrs. Silence," 62
Donner, George, 174
Donner, Jacob, 174
Donner Lake, 174, 177
Dougherty, Patrick Henry, 268-9
Douglas, Stephen A., 192-4, 202
Doyle, Larry, 270
Drake, Francis, 178
Drang nach Osten, 278
Duke of Wellington, 126
Dunkerque (battle), 294
Duryea, Charles, 254
Duryea, J. Franklin, 254
Dyche Museum, 243

E

Eclipse, 158
Edgartown, 165
Edison, Thomas A., 271-7
education, 140-3
Einstein, Albert, 307
Eisenhower, Dwight D., 298-303
El Caney (battle), 261
Elizabeth Islands, 34
Elliott, Milt, 175-7
Emancipation Proclamation, 208-9, 247
Embargo Act of 1807, 125
Embarrass River, 99
Eric the Red, 11-3, 15
Ericson, Leif, 11-6, 24
Eternal Light, 274
Eutaw Springs (battle), 105
"Evangeline," 70
Everett, Edward, 210
exploration: Norsemen, 11-6; Columbus, 19-24; Spaniards seek Seven Cities, 25-8; de Soto, 30; English, 33-4; Jacques Cartier, 32; Marquette and Joliet, 46-9; Lewis and Clark, 118-23; fur trapping in Southwest, 130-9; the Spanish in Texas, 144-5; the Spanish in California, 178

[314]

F

Fairfax, Lord, 68
Fairfield, John, 161
fall line, 252
Far West, 241
Federalist Papers, The, 112
Ferdinand (of Spain), 18, 24
Fessenden, Reginald A., 284-5
Field, Cyrus, 258
Finley, John, 133
Five Forks (battle), 218
Flatheads, 135
Fleming, James A., 285
Florida, 26-8, 125, 203
football, history of, 220-3
Ford, Henry, 254-7, 258, 276-7
Ford, Mrs. Henry, 255
Forlorn Hope, the, 175, 177
Fort Churchill, 199
Fort Duquesne, 57-8, 66, 68-71, 132
Fort Kearney, 199
Fort Laramie, 240
Fort Loudon, 56
Fort McHenry, 125-6
Fort Necessity, 68
Fort Niagara, 66, 70-1
Fort Riley, 243
Fort Ross, 178
Fort Sumter, 203-4, 211
Fort Wayne, 267
four freedoms, Roosevelt's, 295
Fox River, 47
Franklin, Benjamin, 61-6, 68, 89, 91, 93-4, 96, 103, 110, 141; *Autobiography*, 66
Franklin, James, 62-3, 141
Franklin, Josiah, 61-2
Frederick the Great, 96
Fredericksburg (battle), 209
Frémont, John C., 139, 173, 179, 184
French and Indian War, 56, 66, 68-72, 96, 132
Fulton, Robert, 153
Fulton's Folly, 129
fur trapping, 130-9

G

Gage, Thomas, 80-2
Galveston, 144
Galveston Island, 129
Gates, Thomas, 40
George II (of England), 69
George III (of England), 74
Georgia, 79, 203, 212, 215, 230, 252, 293, 299
Germantown (battle), 93, 97
Gettysburg, 299; battle of, 209, 211
Gettysburg Address, 210, 264
Ghent, Treaty of, 128
Gibbon, John, 241-2
Gila River, 133
Gilbert, Humphrey, 33
Godspeed, 35
gold: in the Black Hills, 240; in California, 179-81; in Colorado, 182; in the Yukon, 182
gold mining, 181-2
Goliad, 149
Gosnold, Bartholomew, 34-6
"Grandmother's Story of Bunker Hill," 85-7
Grand Trunk Railway, 272-3
Grant, Ulysses S., 184-5, 208-9, 212, 214-5
Grasshopper Plague, 234
Great Salt Desert, 133
Great Salt Lake, 198
Green Bay, 47
Green Mountain Boys, 88
Green River, 133
Greene, Nathanael, 104-5
Greenfield, 276
Greenland, 14-5, 295
Groton School, 292
Guadalcanal (battle), 304
Guadalupe Hidalgo, Treaty of, 186
Guam, 264
Guilford Court House (battle), 105
Gutierrez, Pedro, 21
Gwin, William H., 198

H

Haig, Douglas, 281
Hakluyt, Richard, 34
Half Moon, 113
Halsey, William, 305
Hamburg, Ga., 230
Hamilton, Alexander, 110, 112
Hampton Institute, 247, 250
Hannibal, Mo., 153, 156
Hardin County, 188
Harding, Warren G., 286, 293
Harvard College, 141, 292
Havana, 28
Hawaii, 264, 295
Hawkeye State, 158
Haynes, Elwood, 254
Hays City, 226
Helm, Boone, 225
Henry VII (of England), 33
Henry, Patrick, 80, 98, 111
Heriulfson, Biarni, 11-3
Hertz, Heinrich, 284
Hessians, 93
Hewes, George, 73-8
Hickam Field, bombing of, 295
Hickok, James Butler (Wild Bill), 225-6
Hidalgo y Costillo, Father Miguel, 145-6
Hiroshima, 305-7
Hitler, Adolf, 292, 295, 300-301
Holmes, Oliver Wendell, 85
Hoover, Herbert, 276
Houston, Sam, 149-51
Howe, William, 84, 87, 93
Howland, John, 44
Hudson, Hendrik, 46, 113
Hudson River, 93, 105, 153
Huguenots, 44
Humboldt River, 133, 136
Hurons, 69
Hutchinson, Thomas, 74-5
Hyde Park, 292-3

I

Iceland, 14-5, 166, 295
Idaho, 122
Illinois, 140, 157, 162, 174, 181, 187, 190-4, 267
Indian wars: before the Revolution, 55-6, 69-70; in Dakota Territory, 240-5
Indiana, 102, 140-1, 189-90, 194, 230, 254, 267
Indianapolis, 209
Indians: as Columbus found them, 24; worshipers of Cabeza de Vaca, 27-8; awed by de Soto, 28-30; and Jamestown, 36-40; loved by Marquette, 45-6, 48-9; how they lived in 1700, 50-4; the Delawares capture James Smith, 57-60; in the West, 133-6, 139; in Texas, 144, 148. *See also* names of individual tribes.
Iowa, 194, 198. 231

Isabella (of Spain), 18, 24
Iwo Jima (battle), 304

J

Jackson, Andrew, 127-9, 258
Jackson, Thomas (Stonewall), 184, 205
James I (of England), 34, 41
James II (of England), 91
James Brothers, 225
James River, 36
Jamestown, 34-40, 50, 160
Jamestown Island, 35
Japan, 292, 295
Jay, John, 112
Jefferson, Thomas, 89-92, 112, 117-20, 123, 295
Jenkins, C. Francis, 286
Jesuits, 45
J. M. White, 157
John II (of Portugal), 18
Joliet, Louis, 46-9, 152
Jones, John Paul, 103
Junction City, 226

K

Kansas, 194, 224, 230, 277
Kansas, University of, 243
Kansas City, Mo., 267
Kansas Pacific Railroad, 224
Kansas River, 120
Kaskaskia, Ill., 98-9
Kaskaskia Indians, 49
KDKA, in Pittsburgh, 285-6
Keith, William, 64
Kennebec River, 34
Kentucky, 117, 125, 127, 162, 164, 188, 191, 202
Kentucky rifle, 127-8
Kentucky River, 133
Key, Francis Scott, 126
King George's War, 56
King Philip's War, 55-6
King William's War, 56
King's College (Columbia), 141
King's Mountain (battle), 104
Kiowas, 134
Kitty Hawk, 290-1
Kokomo, 254
Kurusu, Saburo, 295
Kurz, Rudolph Friederich, 137

L

Lafayette, Marquis de, 105, 280
Lafitte, Jean, 124, 127
Lafitte, Pierre, 127
Lake Michigan, 47, 238-9
Lake Superior, 46
Langley, Samuel P., 290
Langmuir, Irving, 285
Lansing, 254
Laramie Plains, 231
LaSalle, Robert, 152
Lawson, John, 50-4
Laydon, John, 40
Laydon, Virginia, 40
League of Armed Neutrality, 104
League of Nations, 307
LeConte, Emma Florence, 211-7
Lee, Henry, 88-9
Lee, Robert E., 184, 207, 209, 211-2, 216-9
Leggett, William, 223
Lewis, Meriwether, 118-23, 164
Lexington (battle), 82-3, 103
liberty, American concept of:
Jamestown as cradle of civil rights, 34-5, 40; freedom to worship God, 41-2, 44; opposition to taxation without representation, 74, 79-80; Declaration of Independence, 88-92; Bill of Rights, 111-2; opposition to slavery in South, 159-60, 191, 193; Emancipation Proclamation, 208-9; education for African Americans, 246-51; as cause of Spanish-American War, 258-9, 265; as cause of World War I, 277, 280, 282; Atlantic Charter and Four Freedoms, 294-5
Liberty Bell, 92-3
Liberty Loan, 280
Library of Congress, 89, 140
Lincoln, Abraham, 140-1, 159, 183, 187, 188-94, 199, 202-4, 207-10, 264, 292, 312
Lincoln, Benjamin, 107, 109
Lincoln, Mary Todd, 191
Lincoln, Nancy Hanks, 189
Lincoln, Sarah, 190
Lincoln, Sarah Bush Johnston, 190
Lincoln, Thomas, 189-90
Lincoln-Douglas debates, 192-4
Lindbergh, Charles A., Jr., 287-91
Lindbergh, Charles A., Sr., 288

Little Bighorn River, 241-2, 245
Little Harpe, 225
Little Rock, 146
Little Wabash River, 99
Locke, John, 112
Lodge, Henry Cabot, 259
London Company, 34
Longfellow, Henry Wadsworth, 70, 81
Long Island, British occupation of, 93, 116
Lost Colony of Roanoke, 34
Louisiana, 123, 145, 153, 201, 203
Louisiana Military College, 214
Louisiana Purchase, 117-8, 164
Louisburg (battle), 71

M

McAdoo, William, 286
MacArthur, Douglas, 299, 304
McClellan, George B., 184, 208
McGuffey, William Holmes, 142
McKinley, William, 259, 265
Mackinac Island, 46
Macon, 252
Madison, James, 110-2, 125
Magee, Augustus, 145-6
Magellan, Ferdinand, 26
Magna Carta, 111-2, 295
Maine, 125, 252, 294
Maine, 259, 264
Mandans, 119
Manhattan Island, British occupation of, 93
Manila, 265
Manila Bay (battle), 259-60
Marconi, Guglielmo, 284
Marianas (battle), 304
Marion, Francis, 105
Markland, 14
Marne River (battle), 281
Marquesas Islands, 166
Marquette, Father Jacques, 45-9, 152
Marshall, J. F. B., 250
Marshall, John, 179
Marshall Islands (battle), 304
Martha's Vineyard, 34, 167, 294
Maryland, 50, 110, 112, 162, 208, 299
Mason, John, 164
Massachusetts, 44, 50, 56, 108, 111-2, 140, 254, 267
Mather, Cotton, 62
Maxwell, James Clark, 284

[316]

Mayans, 50
Mayflower, 43-4
Mayflower Compact, 44
Meade, George G., 184, 209
Medina River, 145
Melville, Herman, 166-70
Menlo Park, 273, 276
Meteor, 230
Mexican War, 183-7, 191, 258
Mexico, Gulf of, 26, 28, 117, 153
Mexico City, besiegement of, 186
Michael, J., 222-3
Michigan, 254, 271, 276, 293
Middle Shawnee Trail, 226
"Midnight Ride of Paul Revere, The," 82-3
Milan, Ohio, 271
Miles City, 224-5
Milton, Mass., 75
Mingos, 69
Minnesota, 157, 230, 288
Minnetarees, 119
Mississippi, 157, 164, 201, 203
Mississippi River, 28, 30, 32, 47-9, 98, 102-3, 117, 124, 152-9, 215
Missouri, 32, 120, 123, 138, 153, 162, 184
Missouri Compromise, 191
Missouri River, 118-20, 130-1, 234
Moby Dick, 167-70
Model T, 257
"Mohawks," 73-9
Mohicans, 59
Mojaves, 136
Monongahela River, 68, 153-4, 258
Monroe, James, 117
Montana, 135, 224, 241
Montcalm, Louis, 71-2, 96
Monterey, Calif., 178, 180
Monterey, Mex. (battle), 185-6
Monticello, 89
Montopolis, 226
Morgan, Dan, 105
Morris, Gouverneur, 110
Morristown, 93
Moscoso, Luys, 30, 32
Mount Vernon, 69, 72, 83, 88, 95, 107, 110, 114
Mountain Men, 131-9
Muskingum River, 59
Mussolini, Benito, 292
Mystic (battle), 55

N

Nagasaki, bombing of, 307
Nantucket, 34, 165
Napoleon, 117, 125, 159
Narragansett Bay, 56
Natchez, 157
Natchez, 158, 159
National Baseball Association, 267
National League, 267-8
Naval Academy, United States, 298
Nazi Germany, 292, 294-5
Nebraska, 133, 198-9, 224, 230
Nebraska Bill, 191-3
Nevada, 133, 182, 186, 198, 231
New Amsterdam, 113
New Bedford, 132, 165-6
New Brunswick, 221
New England Courant, 62-3
New Guinea (battle), 304
New Hampshire, 56, 112
New Helvetia, 179
New Jersey, 93, 114, 221, 273, 277, 299, 307
New London, 294
New Mexico, 28, 138, 144, 183, 186, 187
New Orleans, 117, 124; battle of, 126-8, 156-8, 159, 190, 258
New Orleans, 153-157
New Salem, 190-1
New York, 88, 93, 110, 114, 286, 289, 292-3
New York City, 106, 113, 153, 194, 230, 288
Newfoundland, 14, 26, 33, 72, 287-9, 294
Newport, Christopher, 35-6
Nina, 22
Nipkow, Paul, 286
Nolin Creek, 188
Nootka Sound, 132
Normandy Beach, invasion of, 302-3
Norsemen, 11-6
North, Lord, 80
North Carolina, 33, 104-5, 112, 133, 203, 290
North Dakota, 118
Nova Scotia, 14, 56, 70, 288
Nueces River, 183-4

O

Oahu, 295
Ogallala, 224
Ohio, 117, 194, 214, 254, 267, 271, 286, 290
Ohio Line, 162-4
Ohio River, 56, 68
Ohio Territory, 60
Okinawa (battle), 304
Oklahoma, 27
Old Shawnee Trail, 226, 229
Olds, Ransom E., 254
O'Leary's Cow, Mrs., 236
Olivares, Father, 144-5, 148
Omaha, 230
On American Conciliation, 80
"Operation Overlord," 300-303
Oregon, 123
Orteig, Raymond, 288
Osages, 134
Overland Mail, 198, 225-6

P

Pakenham, Edward, 126, 128
Palo Alto (battle), 185
Panama, 26
Panama, Isthmus of, 180, 231, 264
Panama Canal, 264, 277
Panama Canal Zone, 299
Panhandle Trail, 226, 229
Paris: liberation of, 303; Treaty of, 264
Patapsco River, 125
Patience, 40
Pattie, James Ohio, 136-7
Paul Jones, 156
Pawnees, 134
Pearl Harbor, bombing of, 295-7
Pecos River, 226
Pecos Trail, 226, 229
Pemberton, John C, 184
Peninsular Campaign, 208
Penn, William, 50
Pennsylvania, 69, 112, 127, 162, 209, 299
Pennsylvania, University of, 65-6, 141
Pennsylvania Gazette, The, 64
Pequot War, 55
Pershing, John J., 280
Peru, conquest of, 26, 28
Petersburg (battle), 218

[317]

Philadelphia, 61, 63, 65, 79, 83, 88, 92-4, 104, 110, 161, 259- 60, 264-5, 295
Philippine Islands, 299, 304
Phillippe, Deacon, 268-70
Pierce. Franklin, 184
Pike, Nicholas, 141
Pilgrims, 43-4, 144
Pinckney, Charles C., 110
Pinta, 21-2
Pitcairn, John, 81
Pitt, Leonard, 75-7
Pitt, William, 71, 80
Pittsburgh, 153, 270
Pizarro, Francisco, 28
Placentia Bay, 294-5
Plains of Abraham, 72
Platte River, 120, 198
Plymouth, 44, 144
Plymouth Company, 34
Pocahontas, 39-40
Polk, James Knox, 183-4, 191
Pony Express, 195-9
Poor Richard's Almanack, 64
Pope, John, 208
Popoff, Professor, 284
Port Huron, 271
Portland, 252
Potomac, 294
Potomac River, 110, 290
Pottawattamies, 69
Powhatan, 38-40
Prince of Wales, 294
Princeton, 307
Princeton University, 141, 221-3, 277
Pring, Martin, 34
Promontory Point, 231-2
Provincetown, 44
public school, first, 140
Puerto Rico, 264
Putnam, Israel, 84-6

Q

Quakers, 44, 63, 66, 104, 160, 164
Quebec, 46, 71-2, 96
Queen's College (Rutgers), 141
Quitman, John A., 164

R

radio, 283-6
railroads, 229-32
Raleigh, Sir Walter, 32-4

Ratcliffe, John, 35
Read, Deborah, 63, 65
Red Flag Laws, 254
Red River, 226
Reed, James F., 174
Reed, Mrs. James F., 174-7
Reed, Virginia, 174-7
Refugio, 149
Reno, Marcus A., 242-3
Republican Army of the North, 145
Resaca de la Palma (battle), 185
Revere, Paul, 80-2
Rhode Island, 50, 104-5, 110, 112
Rhode Island College (Brown), 141
Richmond, 36, 89, 161, 205, 215, 217-8
Ringo, John, 225
Rio Grande River, 138, 183-4
Roanoke Island, 32-4
R.E. Lee, 157, 158, 159
Rock Island, 239
Rock Island & Pacific Railroad, 239
Rocky Mountain Rendezvous, 133
Rocky Mountains, 119, 121, 123, 139, 231, 234
Rommel, Erwin, 300
Roosevelt, Franklin Delano, 292-5, 297, 307-9
Roosevelt, Nicholas, 153-4
Roosevelt, Theodore, 259, 261
Rosebud Creek, 241
Rough Riders, 260-1
Roughing It, 198
Ruffin, Edmund, 204
Rugby School, 221
Runnymede, 111, 295
Russell, Majors and Waddell, 198
Rutgers University, 141, 221-3
Ruth, George Herman (Babe), 270
Rutledge, Ann, 190

S

Sacagawea, 121-3
Sacramento, 179, 196, 198, 230
St. Anthony of Padua, 144
St. John's Newfoundland, 289
St. Joseph, Mo., 196
St. Lawrence River, 32
St. Lô, capture of, 303
St. Louis, 120, 133, 153, 158, 288
Saint Mihiel (battle), 282
St. Paul, Minn., 158
St. Pierre and Miquelon, 72

Salem, 132, 165
Saltillo (battle), 186
Sampson, W. T., 262
San Antonio, 144, 299
San Diego, 288
San Diego Bay, 178
San Francisco, 177, 180, 307
San Jacinto River, 150
San Joaquin Valley, 138
San Juan Hill (battle), 261
San Juan River, 133
San Salvador, 24
Sanchez, Rodrigo, 21
Santa Anna, Antonio López de, 145-51
Santa Fe Trail, 133-4
Santiago Harbor (battle), 261-4
Saratoga (battle), 103
Saunders, Richard, 64
Savannah, 212-3
Schuylkill River, 94, 96-7
Scientific Research and Development, Office of, 307, 309
Scott, Dred, 191, 193
Scott, Winfield, 184-6
Second Treatise on Government, 112
Separatists, 41, 44
Seven Cities, 25-6, 28
Sevier River, 133
Shades of Death, 69
Shadwell, 89
Sharpsburg (battle), 208-9
Shays, Daniel, 108-10
Shays' Rebellion, 108-111
Sheridan, Philip, 218
Sherman, Minnie, 214
Sherman, William T., 184, 212-7
Shoshones, 122, 123, 136
Sidney, Nebr., 224
Sierra Mountains, 172-177, 198
silver, discovery of, 182
Sims, William S., 280
Sioux, 46, 121, 240 ff.
slavery: history of, 159-60; as cause of War with Mexico, 184; Southern attitude, 200-202
Slidell, John, 183
Smith, Alfred E., 286
Smith, James, 55-60
Smith, Jedediah S., 133, 179
Smith, John, 35-40
Smithsonian Institution, 290

Snake Indians, 122, 136
Sonoma (battle), 179
South Carolina, 104-5, 110, 125, 203, 211-7, 230
South Carolina Railroad, 230
South Pass, 198
Spanish Armada, 33
Spanish Inquisition, 111
Spanish-American War, 258-65
Speedwell, 43
Spirit of St. Louis, 287-90
Springfield, Ill., 174, 190-1
Springfield, Mass., 109, 254
Staked Plain, 226
Stamp Act, 91
Stars and Stripes, 302
"Star-Spangled Banner," 126
Staten Island, British occupation of, 93
Staunton, Vir., 277
steamboating, 152-9
Steuben, Baron von, 96-7, 102, 104
Stowe, Harriet Beecher, 191
Susan Constant, 35
Sutter, John A., 179

T

Tarawa (battle), 304
Taylor, Zachary, 184-6, 208
television, 286
Tennessee, 117, 127, 133, 146, 202-3
Terán de los Rios, Don Domingo, 144
Terry, Alfred H., 241
Texas, 27-8, 49, 144-51, 164, 183, 185, 203, 226, 299
Thirteenth Amendment, 209
Thomas, Evan, 230
Thorvald, 16
Ticonderoga, capture of, 88
Tisbury, 167
Tonkawas, 144
transatlantic telegraph, 258
transcontinental railroad, 230-2
Travis, William Barret, 146-9
Trenton (battle), 93
Trevithick, Richard, 253-4
Truckee Lake, 174
Truman, Harry S., 307-8
Tubman, Harriet, 161, 164
Tucker, Reasen P., 177
Tuskegee Institute, 249-51

Twain, Mark. *See* Clemens, S.L.
Tyrker the German, 12-6

U

U-boats, 280-1, 295, 299
Uncle Tom's Cabin, 191, 202
Underground Railroad, 160-4, 202
Union Pacific Railroad, 230-1
United Nations, 307
Up From Slavery, 247
Upper Mamel River, 100-101
Utah, 133, 186, 198, 231

V

Valley Forge, 93-7, 103, 116
Vermont, 88, 110, 112, 294
Verrazano, Giovanni da, 113
Vicksburg (battle), 209, 211, 214-5
Victoria (battle), 186
Vigoras, Arnold, 57
Vincennes, march to, 98-102, 140
Vineland, 16
Virgin Islands, 18
Virgin River, 133
Virginia, 69, 80, 88-9, 93, 98, 102, 105, 111-2, 117-8, 133, 161-2, 201, 203-4, 205, 207, 209, 212, 217, 247, 277
Virginia, University of, 89
Virginia City, 198

W

Wabash River, 98-9, 103, 140
Wagner, Honus, 268
Walker, Joseph R., 132, 138
Wampanoags, 56
War Between the States. *See* Civil War
War of 1812, 125-9
Warm Springs, 293
Warren, Joseph, 81
Washington, Booker T., 246-51
Washington, George, 56, 68-72, 83, 88-9, 93-7, 104-7, 109-12, 114-6, 117, 140, 167
Washington, D.C., burning of, 125, 207-8
Washington, Tex., 149
Watling Island, 23
Webster, Daniel, 312
Webster, Noah, 141
West Orange, 273

West Point Military Academy, 104, 214, 298-9
West Shawnee Trail, 226
Weyler y Nicolau, Valeriano, 259
Weymouth, George, 34
whaling, 165-71
White, Horace, 237
Whitney, Eli, 129, 159
Wichita, 226
Wild Rice Indians, 47-8
Wilderness Road, 133
Wilhelm, Kaiser, 281
William and Mary College, 89, 141
Williams, Baylis, 174
Williams, Roger, 50
Wilson, Thomas Woodrow, 277, 279-80, 293
Winton, Alexander, 254
Wisconsin, 267
Wisconsin, University of, 288
Wisconsin River, 47
Wisconsin Territory, 191, 194
Wolfe, James, 71-2
Wood, Leonard, 261
World Series, 266, 268-70
World War I, 277-82, 299, 307
World War II, 292-307
Wounded Knee Creek, Battle of, 245
Wright, Katherine, 291
Wright, Orville, 290-1
Wright, Wilbur, 290-1
WWJ, in Detroit, 285
Wythe, George, 89
Wyoming, 133, 186, 198, 224, 240

Y

Yale College, 141
"Yankee Doodle," 80, 82
Yazoo River, 28
Yellowstone River, 120, 241
Yorktown (battle), 105-7, 116
Yosemite, 132
Young, Joaquin, 138
Younger Brothers, 225
Yucatan, 129
Yukon, 182

About the Author

EARL SCHENCK MIERS was an American historian (1910-1972), who wrote over 100 books, mostly about the Civil War. In the words of another notable historian–Paul Angle, Miers was one "who stressed the essential drama of events and brought the human beings of the past back to life." Despite struggling with cerebral palsy from birth, which made even holding a pen or pencil nearly impossible, Miers began writing as a youth, by carrying a typewriter to school each day. He attended Rutgers University where he studied journalism and founded the Rutger's University Press. Some of his more popular children's works include the *We Were There* series published by Grosset & Dunlap.

About the Artist

JAMES DAUGHERTY, as an illustrator and author (1889-1974), was passionate about the American story and believed it ought to be told through vigorous illustration and spirited text. He is best known for his folksy all-American retelling of the fable of Androcles, in *Andy and the Lion*, which earned the author/illustrator the Caldecott Honor Medal in 1938. In Carl Sandburg's *Abe Lincoln Grows Up*, a perfect marriage blended Sandburg's lyrical prose with Daugherty's tender yet powerful sketches of Abe as he grows from a boy to a young man. In *The Magna Charta*, Daugherty tells the often humorous, yet inspiring story of one of Western civilization's most significant milestones in the progress of civil liberty–the signing of the Magna Charta by King John at Runnymede in 1215. *Of Courage Undaunted* brings Daugherty's manly illustrations to full flower in the adventure of Lewis and Clark's remarkable exploration of the Louisiana Purchase. *Poor Richard* captures the essential nature of Benjamin Franklin with energetic and dramatic three-color lithographs that reveal the witty and ever-genial printer, inventor, statesman, diplomat, and brilliant Founder. Beautiful Feet Books is honored to publish a number of Daugherty's works for a new generation of young Americans.